Everyday Use

Rhetoric at Work in Reading and Writing

AP* Edition

Hephzibah Roskelly

University of North Carolina at Greensboro

David A. Jolliffe

DePaul University

PEARSON

Longman

New York   San Francisco   Boston
London   Toronto   Sydney   Tokyo   Singapore   Madrid
Mexico City   Munich   Paris   Cape Town   Hong Kong   Montreal

For James Kinneavy and Joseph Comprone
rhetoricians, teachers, mentors

Vice President and Publisher: Eben W. Ludlow
Development Editor: Francine Weinberg
Executive Marketing Manager: Megan Galvin-Fak
Production Manager: Douglas Bell
Project Coordination, Text Design, and Electronic Page Makeup: WestWords, Inc.
Cover Designer/Manager: Wendy Ann Fredericks
Cover Illustrations: (left to right) Copyright © Stock Connection Distribution/Alamy;
    Copyright © Polaris/Photos12; Copyright © MPTV.net; Copyright © Royalty-Free/CORBIS;
    AP Wide World Photo.
Photo Research: WestWords, Inc.
Manufacturing Buyer: Roy L. Pickering, Jr.
Printer and Binder: R. R. Donnelley & Sons, Crawfordsville
Cover Printer: Coral Graphic Services

For permission to use copyrighted material, grateful acknowledgment is made to the copyright holders on pp. 247–249, which are hereby made part of this copyright page.

Library of Congress Cataloging-in-Publication Data

Roskelly, Hephzibah.
    Everyday use : rhetoric at work in reading and writing / Hephzibah Roskelly, David A. Jolliffe.—
Advanced Placement teacher's annotated ed.
        p. cm.
    Includes bibliographical references and index.
        ISBN 0-321-09325-9 (pbk.)—ISBN 0-321-09384-4 (case)—ISBN 0-321-24359-5 (case)
1. English language—Rhetoric—Study and teaching. 2. Report writing—Study and teaching. 3. English language—Rhetoric. 4. Report writing. I. Jolliffe, David A. II. Title.

    PE1404.R668 2005
    808'.042'071—dc22

                                                                                        2004021081

Please visit our website at http://www.ablongman.com

ISBN 0-321-09325-9 (College Edition)
ISBN 0-321-09384-4 (Advanced Placement Edition)
ISBN 0-321-24359-5 (Advanced Placement Teacher's Annotated Edition)

7 8 9 10—DOC—07 06

*Advanced Placement Program and AP are registered trademarks of The College Board, which was not involved in the production of, and does not endorse, this book.

Brief Contents

Detailed Contents

Preface

High school English courses meet a number of goals for you as a student. They teach you to be a careful and critical reader, interacting with a great variety of texts—fiction, poetry, drama, and all kinds of nonfiction—and to construct meanings for those texts actively, not to decode them passively, not to try to find some single meaning. Your English course helps you conceive good, compelling ideas to write about, to develop those ideas fully and effectively and in appropriately correct English. In your course, you study both the structures of language—whole texts, paragraphs, sentences, words, punctuation, mechanical conventions—and ways writers and readers use these structures in making meaning. Rhetoric, the art of crafting effective texts, is deeply a part of all these goals. Writing, whether "literary" or "ordinary," is purposeful—that is, rhetorical—and so is reading. The central goal in high school courses (and elementary and college courses too, for that matter) is to help you read texts to see how their purpose gets communicated to you and to write texts that accomplish the purposes you wish to communicate.

Everyday Use: Rhetoric at Work in Reading and Writing is designed specifically for use in Advanced Placement* English courses that try to achieve these goals. In six chapters and a series of interchapters, this book provides a foundation for reading insightfully and writing effectively and strives to teach students how to produce their own texts that are rich, purposeful, and effectively crafted. These goals align with those of Advanced Placement English students, who seek to demonstrate their ability to *read* and *write* at a level of proficiency that will enable them to earn college credit for English. *Everyday Use* builds your skills as a reader and writer, a maker of meaning. Here's a brief summary of how each chapter works toward that end.

Chapter 1 raises the seemingly simple, yet ultimately complex, question, "What is rhetoric?" In responding to this question, the chapter addresses three common misperceptions, which often prevent students from becoming effective readers and writers. The first is that rhetoric is something public figures—politicians, academics—display but not something useful for you as a student. The second is that rhetoric suggests inauthentic language, overly embellished and disguising a lack of substance or a covert, unethical intention. The third misperception is that rhetoric comprises only visible features of style and organization. To counter these views, the chapter generates a dynamic definition of

---

*Advanced Placement Program and AP are registered trademarks of The College Board, which was not involved in the production of, and does not endorse, this book.

rhetoric as the ability to discover what writers might do in a situation to lead readers to respond in particular ways and to use those discoveries—techniques for generating ideas and arguments, methods of organization, strategies of sentence structure and diction—confidently. The chapter explains that rhetoric includes activities (reading, writing, speaking, listening, and discussing) that all people—students, teachers, and politicians alike—participate in every day. Comprehending what rhetoric is and how it works is vital to understanding that written texts influence thought and action, in school and in life outside school, as well as how that influence works.

Chapter 2 introduces you to the tradition of rhetoric, its concepts and terms. It's a tradition with roots in antiquity but with great applications in our own time. In this chapter, activities are designed to teach and help you practice the five major canons of rhetoric—invention, arrangement, style, memory, and delivery. The canons are really processes that writers engage in as they work, and the discussion of these processes will stimulate your best writing in and out of school.

Chapter 3 focuses on the relationship between reading and writing. It reviews writing as a process and shows how much richer the process becomes when you see your writing process as a rhetorical one as well. Then it offers case studies of student writers who work to put into practice many of the concepts and principles considered in the first two chapters.

Chapter 4 turns its attention to a subject rarely examined in discussion of rhetoric but central to all the ways you use language—reading. This chapter explains how readers read rhetorically and how they analyze the "landscape" of a text, the rhetorical moves a writer makes to communicate intentions to readers. The activities in this chapter help you understand that reading itself is a kind of writing; you must actively construct what you read, not passively wait to have some one-and-only meaning provided to you.

Chapter 5 builds on the earlier chapters by showing the organic connection between reading and writing. The chapter demonstrates how reading rhetorically helps you become a more skilled, aware writer, and how writing with a conscious sense of your rhetorical strategies can lead you to become a more observant and perceptive reader.

Chapter 6 helps you apply many of the principles of rhetoric, which have been developed in the previous chapters, to reading literature—particularly, short stories, novels, and plays—and writing about it. Working with activities in this chapter, you see literature not as rarefied or difficult or far removed from real-world concerns but as writing that represents real people's responses to a world of real problems, desires, and delights.

Each chapter in the book is followed by an interchapter, which invites you to get to know three texts well, drawing on the variety of perspectives and ideas that each chapter discusses. The three works are "Civil Disobedience," the famous essay by Henry David Thoreau; "It's a Woman's World," a wonderful and challenging poem by the contemporary Irish poet Eavan Boland; and "Everyday Use," the marvelous short story (whose title we gratefully borrowed for the title of this book) by Alice Walker. These three works appear in their entirety in the "Readings" section, pages 209–234. We hope that by reading Thoreau, Boland, and Walker intensely, you will learn to see all the texts you read and write, in school and beyond it, as acts of rhetoric.

For users who wish to connect the content in *Everyday Use* with Advanced Placement* English Language and Composition courses, the chart below illustrates how the book accommodates the objectives outlined for the course in the course description on The College Board Web site.

Correlation of *Everyday Use: Rhetoric at Work in Reading and Writing* with the Advanced Placement* Course Description for English Language and Composition, 2003–2004

Course Description for AP English Language and Composition calls for students to:	Coverage in *Everyday Use: Rhetoric at Work in Reading and Writing* (with some example pages)
engage in informal and formal writing contexts.	The text advises writers to examine the context before they begin writing so that they know how informal or formal the piece should be (page 56).
keep a journal.	Journal writing is mentioned as an activity for both writers and readers. • Journal writing is explained as a way to generate material for writing at a later date (page 51). • A model from a student's journal leads into an activity that asks students to produce reading journals (page 105).
write collaboratively.	A case study illustrates the advantages of discussing a writing project with others and working on it with them (page 106).
read pieces from many subject areas and many periods.	Besides the Thoreau, Boland, and Walker pieces, readings include a sports-magazine editorial (page 8), op-ed pieces about race relations (page 111), an introduction to chaos theory (page 124), and a reflection on family life in the Middle East (page 141). Readings range from a speech by Shakespeare (page 170), through 18th-, 19th-, and 20th-century writing (pages 156, 10, 158), to prose written in the last few years (pages 14, 22, 26).
develop a more mature prose style, one marked by • varied sentence structures. • organization and coherence based on repetition, transitions, and emphasis. • balance between generalizations and specifics. • control of tone and voice.	The first three bulleted items get major focus on pages 60, 72, and 67. The fourth item is a topic that comes up throughout the textbook—for example, on page 102.

---

*Advanced Placement Program and AP are registered trademarks of The College Board, which was not involved in the production of, and does not endorse, this book.

The next chart illustrates how this textbook responds to the advice of AP teachers who have written essays for the AP Web site about teaching AP students.

Correlation of *Everyday Use: Rhetoric at Work in Reading and Writing* with Suggestions from AP* Teachers

AP teachers published on <http://apcentral.collegeboard.com> encourage students to:	Coverage in *Everyday Use: Rhetoric at Work in Reading and Writing* (with some example pages)
read not only broadly but also deeply.	As noted earlier in this preface, the six interchapters (the first of which begins on page 29) give six separate opportunities to read and reflect on a Thoreau essay, a Boland poem, and a Walker short story. Returning to a selection to examine it from different perspectives shows the possibilities of in-depth reading. The book also explains the difference between reading for pleasure and reading for information (page 126).
make nonfiction the heart of the course but incorporate poetry, fiction, and drama as well.	In addition to a wealth of nonfiction, models in the textbook come from drama by Stoppard (pages 190, 206) and Ibsen (page 196), poetry by Dove (page 204) and Browning (page 203), and fiction by Dickens (pages 132, 183), Morrison (page 137), Proulx (page 185), Twain (pages 10, 199), Kingston (page 199), Hawkes (page 201), and others.
master terms and strategies to call on when analyzing or responding to texts.	Rhetorical terms and strategies are defined and illustrated in the textbook proper. In addition, a glossary of more than 200 rhetorical terms and strategies appears at the back of the textbook (page 235). Activities call on students to read rhetorical analyses and to write their own.
practice recognizing and using large-scale organizing strategies such as comparison/contrast as well as sentence-level techniques such as figurative language.	Chapter 2 gives practice in using the five canons, including arrangement, and covers the standard parts of various genres. Chapter 2 also covers style—the choices a writer makes in words, phrases, and sentences.
practice multiple-choice questions about the rhetoric of passages.	In addition to the model passage and multiple-choice questions in Chapter 5 from a recent AP English Language and Composition exam, the teacher will have other multiple-choice questions to give students more close-reading practice on passages in the book.
practice essay prompts calling for • textual analysis of a passage. • a position that supports, qualifies, or disputes an author's point in a passage.	In addition to the essay prompts that appear in Activities throughout the chapters and interchapters, the teacher will have other essay prompts to give students more practice with timed writing.

*Advanced Placement Program and AP are registered trademarks of The College Board, which was not involved in the production of, and does not endorse, this book.

Acknowledgments

We are grateful to the following outstanding teachers from all over the country. We've worked with many of them over the past fifteen years at Advanced Placement readings, and many of them reviewed the manuscript of *Everyday Use* and offered us valuable advice and invaluable encouragement. We've learned much about teaching and about rhetoric from them all.

Elizabeth Ackley, Wilmington College, Ohio
Timothy C. Averill, Manchester Essex Regional High School, Massachusetts
Rebecca Funderburk Brown, North Carolina School of the Arts
Cathy A. D'Agostino, New Trier Township High School, Illinois
Mary Kirkpatrick, West Brook High School, Texas
Marianne Kjos, Miami-Dade County Public Schools, Florida
David Leshan, Germantown Academy, Pennsylvania
Debra McIntire, Yukon High School, Oklahoma
Bernard A. Phelan, Homewood-Flossmoor High School, Illinois
Robert W. Reimer, Grosse Pointe North High School, Michigan
Margaret Rostkowski, Ogden High School, Utah
Susan P. Sanchez, Mark Keppel High School, California
Alice Twombly, Teaneck High School, New Jersey

We'd like to thank Fran Weinberg, our creative and patient editor; Matt McNees and Michelle Hubbard for their fine work on the Teachers' Annotated Edition; and Eben Ludlow for his encouragement, vision, and sense of humor.

Our loving thanks go to Gwynne Gertz, Michael Roskelly, and Natchez, Claire, Charlie, Levi, and Daisy for their loyal support.

H.R.
D.A.J.

Everyday Use
Rhetoric in Our Lives

1

"Write about dogs!"

> Late night on Route 66, somewhere in Arizona.
>
> Nick checks the speedometer, slows. He looks over at Kate quickly, then focuses on the road. He clears his throat.
>
> Kate stares out her window. The corner of her mouth twitches.
>
> NICK: So, do you think there are many cops on the road?
>
> KATE: This time of night?
>
> NICK (SPEEDING UP):   Well . . . guess not.
>
> Kate reaches for the radio buttons. He reaches at the same time. Their fingers touch.
>
> NICK AND KATE (AT ONCE):   Sorry.
>
> NICK: I mean . . . for the radio.
>
> KATE: Me too.
>
> Kate looks out the window again. She begins to hum with the radio. Nick looks over at her again, longer this time. He begins to hum too. She turns to him now. He slows the car.
>
> NICK: So, do you still want to go to the Grand Canyon?

What do you think is going on in this movie **scene?** If you were to explain it, your analysis might go something like this: These two people have had an argument. He wants the fight to be over, but he doesn't want to be the first to apologize. She wants it to be over too, but she doesn't want to give in. They're looking for a way to say they're sorry without saying it. They're going to be back together before they get to the Grand Canyon. The writer of the script has used gestures, actions, and sounds, as well as words, to convey the message that these two people want to make up, and the reader of the scene gets the message, probably without any difficulty.

How this communication between the writer and the reader happens is the subject of this book. Readers and writers can understand one another so well because every day they use **rhetoric,** which might be defined initially as the art that humans use to process all the messages we send and receive. Messages are all around us—in books and magazines, in our conversation, in the news, in music and art, and in the movies we watch. When we produce messages, rhetoric helps us get ideas, emotions, and opinions across to others. When we receive messages, rhetoric helps us understand the ideas, emotions, and opinions of those around us.

The writer of the movie scene above uses what he knows from experience, **reading,** or observation to write the descriptions of how each **character** moves and acts. The reader also uses experience, reading, or observation to understand the characters' actions and to understand what the writer is suggesting. As the writer writes and the reader reads, they negotiate through the **rhetorical**

choices they have made, and they begin to anticipate, making decisions about what's happening and what will happen next.

Reader and writer decide these things, moreover, based on how they perceive the scene and how they understand the scene in context. If the movie is billed as a horror film, the last line of the scene might take on a sinister implication. If the main characters are played by comedians, readers wait for a punchline.

We all use rhetoric every day, whether we use it deliberately or not, and we all respond to rhetoric every day, whether we're conscious of it or not. Since the world around us carries messages that get received or lost or translated or transformed, to understand rhetoric is to understand the world better and to participate in it more fully.

Rescuing Rhetoric from Its Bad Reputation: Definitions and Examples

It's sometimes difficult to overlook the unsavory (and undeserved) reputation that the term *rhetoric* has. Many people are most familiar with the word only in its negative sense, describing something that has style but no substance: "His speech was mere rhetoric." Or, even worse, rhetoric sometimes characterizes a speaker's lack of sincerity or deliberate falseness in order to coerce an **audience** to follow a wrongheaded or evil course of action. To be an effective rhetorician, in this ill-considered definition, means to hoodwink the audience, to get them to believe that what is false is actually true, and to manipulate facts or emotions to serve the speakers' unscrupulous ends. In this sense, someone might claim that Hitler was a "good" rhetorician because he could, through his language and skillful manipulation of events, encourage people to believe the worse cause was the better one.

When someone uses rhetoric in this way, he or she is making a negative **assumption** about the ethics of the person who's speaking. To call a **speaker** "full of rhetoric" is to suggest that he or she doesn't have much to say or is using false and misleading language. Indeed, for many historical reasons, people also tend to think that rhetoric is the opposite of clear communication, exists in contrast to reality, and acts as a roadblock to making progress on important issues. Consider, for **example,** the following sentence from a newspaper article about parental involvement in schools.

> After all of these years and all of this rhetoric, the infrastructure to help families know what to do to support this partnership that everybody talks about is still not there.
>
> —Washington Post, *January 16, 2001*

The writer of this sentence obviously thinks that, at best, the discussions of parental involvement in the media, in school boards, and in parent-teacher associations—what the writer refers to as "all of this rhetoric"—have not helped such involvement to take place. At worst, the writer apparently believes, "all of this rhetoric" has impeded progress toward parental involvement in schools.

These definitions about the misleading, cloudy, potentially evil nature of rhetoric are, quite frankly, wrong. They are legacies of several moments in history when some influential philosophers misunderstood rhetoric.

A better definition of rhetoric, one that explains how and why communication works, presumes that a speaker or writer (or **rhetor (reh-tor)**, to use an ancient Greek term that encompasses both speakers and writers, *a term we will use throughout this book when we are referring to someone who may be a writer, speaker, reader, or listener*) is searching for methods to persuade hearers or readers *because* he or she has something valuable to say, something that arises from his or her position as an honest, inquiring, ethical person. The rhetor must be a "good person speaking well," to use a phrase coined by the classical Roman rhetorician Quintilian.

Here, then, is a useful definition of rhetoric. Rhetoric refers to two things:

- The art of analyzing all the language choices that writer, speaker, reader, or listener might make in a given situation so that the text becomes meaningful, purposeful, and effective
- The specific features of texts, written or spoken, that cause them to be meaningful, purposeful, and effective for readers or listeners in a given situation

Activity

What follows is a situation that might be quite common where you go to school. Read the scenario carefully. Then, in a group, discuss the choices involving language that Randall Leigh makes in order to be persuasive. Evaluate the specific features of his requests to his classmates.

Randall Leigh is a bright but rather forgetful person, and because of the latter, he is a compulsive calendar keeper. Nearly every day, he gets up, looks at his day planner, figures out what he needs to do when, and then heads out, either to school or to his part-time job at Computers 4 U, where he works 20 hours a week. Randall lives close enough to school so that he can walk to his classes, but he has to rely on the city bus system to get to work since he does not own a car.

One day, Randall slips up. He neglects to check his day planner until after he gets to school. He thinks he is not scheduled to work that afternoon, but, alas, he is wrong. He is due at work exactly 30 minutes after his last class—just enough time to get there on the city bus. But here is the problem: Randall has come to school flat broke—he doesn't even have the $1.50 bus fare it costs to get to work. He is pretty sure he can borrow the money from someone at work that will enable him to get home, but getting to work is another matter.

He decides he needs to appeal to his classmates for the $1.50 bus fare. Seeing his buddy Brandon approach in the hallway, Randall tries his first maneuver.

"Hey, Brandon, you have to help me out," he says. "I just realized that I have to be at work this afternoon, and I'm completely broke. I can't call in sick, man—you've been there, you know how important I am to the store. I have to answer all the customers' technical questions that the manager can't answer, and that's most of them. So, is there any way you can stand me $1.50 for bus fare?"

"Sorry, dude," Brandon replies, "I'm really short myself, and I have to take Louanne out for a burger after school today and patch some things up between us. Wish I could help out, but I just can't."

"Sheesh," Randall thinks to himself, "I lose out to Brandon's temperamental girl-friend." But then Randall sees the object of his own affections, Kim, walking his way.

"Hey, Kim, how's my best friend in the whole world doing today?"

"What do you want, Randall?"

"Now, what makes you think I want anything? It's always just such a joy to see you, that's all. You light up my life, and all that—you bring me bliss, love, compan-ionship. Why, just to be seen with you makes me the envy of most of the guys in the school."

"Uh, huh."

"But since you mention it," Randall goes on, "there would be something you can do that would make me very, very happy. You see, like the fool I am, I came to school today without any money, and I have to get to work right after class today. I don't suppose you could spare a buck fifty for bus fare, do you?"

"Oh, Randall, all that buttering up for just bus fare?" Just then, a gaggle of Kim's friends ambles by, and she joins them. "Ta ta, Randy," she says. "Good luck getting to work!"

Randall is beside himself—how is he going to get the bus fare? He spies Nate walking his way. He doesn't know Nate very well—they were partners in a bio lab once, and they got along pretty well. Randall decides to try a long shot.

"Hi there, Nate—long time no see."

"Oh, hi, Randall. What's up?"

"Nate, I'm in a really tight spot. You know me to be an honest, dependable guy, don't you? Remember when we worked on the lab report together? I held up my end of the project, didn't I?"

"Of course, you did," Nate says. "You were the best lab partner I've ever had."

"Well," Randall proceeds, "since you know you can trust me, and you know I'm good to my word, how about lending me $1.50, just till I see you again? See, I have to get to work right after class today, and I absentmindedly left home without any money for bus fare, and, well, if there's anybody you can count on to pay you back, you know I'm the guy."

"Hmmm, let me check to see if I can help you out," Nate replies. "I might have an extra $1.50 that I can front you."

What Does "Being Skilled at Rhetoric" Mean?

Once you accept the broader, more inclusive definition of rhetoric, you begin to understand that becoming skilled at rhetoric is a valuable part of your educa-tion, one that you will work on throughout your school years and beyond. Consider the following:

- Being skilled at rhetoric means being able to make good speeches and write good papers, but it also means having the ability to read other people's compositions and listen to their spoken words with a discerning eye and a critical ear.

- Being skilled at rhetoric means reading not only to understand the main and supporting points of what someone writes but also to analyze the decisions the rhetor makes as he or she works to accomplish a purpose for a specific audience.

- Being skilled at rhetoric means being able to *plan and write* compositions, not just write them.

- Being skilled at rhetoric means being able to examine a situation—in school, in your community, in society as a whole—and determine what has already been said and written, what remains unresolved, and what you might say or write to continue the conversation or persuade readers to take action.

What all these statements add up to is that a person skilled at rhetoric needs to develop a very full menu of reading and writing techniques, strategies, and skills, and needs to be judicious in how he or she uses them. There is so much you can do when you write a paper to make it effective for readers. For example, you might open your paper with a surprising question or quotation. You might challenge your readers' assumptions about a topic. You might write a long, complicated sentence followed by a short, abrupt one. You might rely on complex, carefully selected vocabulary that will show your reader you have an in-depth knowledge of the subject you're writing about. Being skilled at rhetoric does not mean that you have to *use* everything you know in every composition you write. It means that you are able to take an inventory of what you *might* do to make a paper impressive and select the options that work most effectively with your readers.

Developing Skill with Rhetoric: The Rhetorical Triangle

The best way to begin developing skill with rhetoric is to envision the basic rhetorical activity—creating a text that you hope will be meaningful, purposeful, and effective for a reader, or reading a text so that it becomes meaningful, purposeful, and effective for you—as a triangle. The **rhetorical triangle** has its roots in the work of Aristotle, a fourth-century B.C.E. Greek philosopher who wrote extensively about rhetoric. The rhetorical triangle (or **Aristotelian triad,** as some people call it) suggests that a person creating or analyzing a text must consider three elements:

- The subject and the kinds of **evidence** used to develop it
- The audience—their knowledge, ideas, attitudes, and beliefs

■ The character of the rhetor—in particular, how the rhetor might use his or her personal character effectively in the text

Here is a diagram of the basic rhetorical triangle.

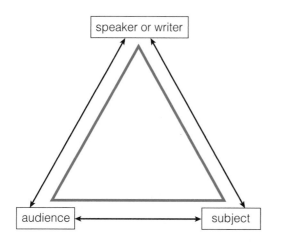

Rhetorical Triangle

Notice that the triangle has arrows from one point to another and that the arrows go both ways. These arrows show the dynamic nature of the rhetorical **act.** The rhetor understands something about his or her audience—who they are, what they know—and that understanding makes the rhetor highlight certain elements of his or her own character and personality and downplay others. The rhetor creates a **persona**—literally a "mask" but figuratively the character he or she wants the audience to perceive himself or herself as—based in part on who he or she presumes the audience to be and in part on what he or she knows and believes about the subject of the text: that is, on what bits of evidence or proof he or she finds most compelling and persuasive. Members of the audience, in turn, hold some beliefs, based on knowledge and past experience, about the rhetor and about the subject, and they tap into these beliefs as they listen or read. Moreover, members of the audience also use their ability to reason—to put together evidence logically—and they are persuaded by the strength of the evidence presented about the subject.

Throughout the remainder of this chapter, we will use the diagram of the rhetorical triangle, initially in its basic form and later in a slightly modified form, to introduce six keys to developing skill with rhetoric. The first three keys—understanding persona, understanding appeals to an audience, and understanding subjects—emerge from the basic triangle. The last three keys—understanding context, understanding intention, and understanding genre—grow out of the triangle in its modified form.

Activity

Reread the scenario about Randall Leigh and the bus fare in the previous activity (pages 4–5). Then, in a group, discuss the following questions:

- What kind of persona did Randall try to present to each of his three audiences—Brandon, Kim, and Nate?
- What assumptions do you think Randall made about each of the three audiences—Brandon, Kim, and Nate—that led him to make decisions about how to present his case?
- What kinds of plea, evidence, or proof did Randall employ with each of the audiences to try to persuade Brandon, Kim, and Nate to lend him the bus fare?
- What do you think Brandon, Kim, and Nate knew about Randall—his personality, his job, and so on—that led them to react the way they did to his entreaties?

Key #1: Understanding Persona

A rhetor who understands persona is able to do two things. First, he or she can speak or write so that the audience perceives him or her as a distinct character, usually one who is educated, considerate, trustworthy, and well intentioned. Second, he or she can make **inferences** and judgments about the character and personality of another writer or speaker, analyzing how that writer appeals to the audience, invites the audience to interact with current or historical events, and wants the audience to act after they have finished reading or listening to the text.

Listen to this **voice** from an editorial in the *Sports Illustrated* of August 5, 2002:

> Subjects we're tired of hearing about, because nothing-is-ever-going-to-change-anyhow:
>
> 1. Does the Second Amendment mean just the militia?
> 2. Did Shakespeare really write Shakespeare?
> 3. Yes, but what about the Grassy Knoll?
> 4. Is Oprah going to marry Stedman?
> 5. Should Pete Rose go into the Hall of Fame?

What can you tell so far about the position the writer is developing? How do you know it? Have you ever asked yourself any of the questions the writer poses? They vary in seriousness, but the writer has linked them together because they're all seemingly unresolvable. The writer seems to be humorous and a little mocking, as though there's no point in writing about any of the questions he's posed. Here's the next word:

Still.

So the writer, Frank Deford, is going to write about something that he already believes to be useless. "Still," he just can't help it. He's going to write. About Pete Rose, which you've probably guessed because the piece appears in *Sports Illustrated.* You've also guessed it for a rhetorical reason—it appears last in the group of questions. The next paragraph suggests reasons that Rose belongs in baseball's Hall of Fame.

> It is Hall of Fame induction time again (Ozzie Smith went in on Sunday), so we ought to at least mention the lunacy of baseball's freezing Charlie Hustle out of Casa Immortality. First of all, it is irrational to deny the man who made the most hits in history a place in Ye Olde Shrine. Second, it is stupid. Third, it is not working: the only person the ban benefits is Pete himself.

What strikes you here? Deford sets the situation for his piece—"It is Hall of Fame induction time again"—to suggest that Rose's failure to be inducted should at least be mentioned. Deford appears reasonable, listing three reasons that Rose should be admitted. What about Deford's **tone,** his **attitude** toward the subject he's writing about? Given that one of the three reasons is "It is stupid," we might see Deford continuing the tone of light mockery that his questions at the beginning suggest. The **diction** of the paragraph—"Charlie Hustle" (a nickname for Rose?), "Casa Immortality," "Ye Olde Shrine"—is informal and at the same time specialized. Baseball fans would know whether Rose was called Charlie Hustle or not, and they'd know who Ozzie Smith was.

As you might predict from the last sentence of Deford's paragraph, the writer goes on to develop his case about how Rose has benefited from being the "Official Pariah of Baseball," selling his **image** and his case in products, on talk shows, and on Main Street in Cooperstown, New York, the home of the Hall of Fame itself. Deford develops his case with anecdotes about baseball fans, with the history of baseball commissioners' unfair exclusion of other figures like Shoeless Joe Jackson in the early twentieth century, and finally with this admission:

> Of course Pete Rose is guilty of betting on baseball. He's as guilty as, well, Paul Hornung, who bet on NFL games while playing in the NFL but is properly plaqued in Canton. He's as guilty as all sorts of putative baseball immortals who stoke up on steroids. But Rose was guilty only when he was a manager. Even if he bet on baseball, even if he disobeyed the infield fly rule or shot Cock Robin, there is not a scintilla of evidence that he did anything untoward when he was playing the game. Even if you fervently believe that Manager Rose soiled the National Pastime, how unfair, how Un-American, is it that the glories of his youth should be censored by the sins of male menopause? That's just not right.

Comparing Rose with other rule violators in sports who have nonetheless been honored for their accomplishments, Deford makes his logical point: there is no **logic** in denying Rose. The last paragraph slams baseball by noting that in the matter of Pete Rose, "Baseball has long had a trust exemption." The surface logic and the light tone are both obvious as you read. You might have to read it again to hear the **irony** and underlying displeasure, even anger, at those who are responsible for making decisions about the national pastime. This is a writer who loves baseball and who believes unjust punishments sully the game.

Writers usually want the persona they develop and the voice they use to be genuine, to reflect who they really are. Occasionally, however, writers use the mask of another voice for comic **effect** or to underscore the seriousness of a position they believe in. You might be familiar with Jonathan Swift's famous essay "A Modest Proposal" (1729), in which he mock-seriously suggests that a good solution to the economic woes of Ireland would be to begin eating Ireland's children. His tone sounds reasonable, in contrast to the outrageousness of his proposal. Readers are led to understand the tragic plight of the Irish by reading the details of suffering and deprivation in the supposedly dispassionate voice of the speaker. As readers, we do more than sympathize. We are moved to anger and to a desire to change the situation we read about.

Writers thus use their voices—indeed, they create and sustain a tone with those voices—to affect readers' understanding and belief. Using the term *persona*, Aristotle referred to the character that readers could discern from the writer's or speaker's use of words, arrangement of ideas, and choice of details. The persona was the mask that Greek actors wore when they performed, the exaggerated smile and frown masks of tragedy and comedy that you're familiar with as a **symbol** of theater. That word today is used to show the artfulness of the speaker's creation of voice, how deliberately the speaker should select words, tell a story, and repeat phrases in order to help listeners hear the voice that the speaker has decided will be most effective. Swift wore a mask of high good humor and reasonableness that served to underscore his appalling suggestions and reinforce the horror of poverty in Ireland. The mask you wear as a writer doesn't hide you from your readers—it meets them head on and interacts with them purposefully and effectively.

Activity

In his novel *The Adventures of Tom Sawyer*, Mark Twain creates a scene in which a student reads the following composition to the class. Read the composition carefully, and then in your group discuss how Twain wants us, his readers, to characterize the persona of the speaker. Be sure to point out specific parts of the composition that support your **claims.**

IS THIS, THEN, LIFE?

In the common walks of life, with what delightful emotions does the youthful mind look forward to some anticipated scene of festivity! Imagination is busy sketching rose-tinted pictures of joy. In fancy, the voluptuous votary of fashion sees herself amid the festive throng, "the observed of all observers." Her graceful form, arrayed in snowy robes, is whirling through the mazes of the joyous dance; her eye is brightest, her step is lightest in the gay assembly.

In such delicious fancies time quickly glides by, and the welcome hour arrives for her entrance into the elysian world, of which she has had such bright dreams. How fairylike does everything appear to her enchanted vision! Each new scene is more charming than the last. But after a while she finds that beneath this goodly exterior, all is vanity: the flattery which once charmed her soul now grates harshly upon her ear; the ballroom has lost its charms; and with wasted health and embittered heart she turns away with the conviction that earthly pleasures cannot satisfy the longings of the soul!

Key #2: Understanding Appeals to the Audience

A text becomes rhetorical only when an audience reads or hears it and responds to it. A key to developing skill with rhetoric, therefore, is understanding *how* a text appeals to an audience. Once again, Aristotle's ideas are influential. In ancient Athens, as Aristotle taught his students to discuss and create speeches about important issues, he developed a system that explained to his students how to locate the "available means of persuasion" as they developed their **personae** (the plural of persona), understood the needs and the knowledge and experience of their hearers, and researched and developed their topics. Rhetoric, he argued, could help students accomplish their aims as they spoke, primarily to persuade hearers to a course of action based on a common search for truth.

This persuasion happens, Aristotle taught, because a rhetor makes three kinds of closely related **appeals** to his or her audience through a spoken or written text.

- A rhetor appeals to **logos** by offering a clear, reasonable central idea (or set of ideas) and developing it with appropriate reasoning, examples, or details.

- A rhetor appeals to **ethos** by offering evidence that he or she is credible—that he or she knows important and relevant information about the topic at hand and is a good, believable person who has the readers' best interests in mind.

- A rhetor appeals to **pathos** by drawing on the emotions and interests of the audience so that they will be sympathetically inclined to accept and buy into his or her central ideas and arguments.

The rhetor does not necessarily make these appeals in separate sections of a text. A single sentence can appeal to logos, the audience's interest in a clear, cogent idea; ethos, the audience's belief in the credibility and good character of the writer; and pathos, the audience's emotions or interests in regard to the topic at hand. And a rhetor seldom uses one of the appeals to the exclusion of all others. Think about Deford's piece (pages 8–9). He uses logic, or reasonableness, to argue for Rose's induction into the Hall of Fame. But he connects his logical explanations to emotion as he comments on "the glories of his youth" and to ethics as he calls baseball authorities to task for their less than even-handed dealing with Rose's case: "That's just not right."

Aristotle believed that speakers and hearers really did want to know the truth or the best course of action. He said that rhetoric is useful because "things that are true and things that are just have a natural tendency to prevail over their opposite," which makes rhetors and audience members mutually responsible as they communicate their best thoughts about a subject. The "good person speaking well," as Quintilian put it, wants to persuade to the better course, not the worse one; Deford wants to convince his readers that inducting Pete Rose is only fair, the best course of action to take in a case that is complicated by other ethical considerations. Rhetoric works because speakers and writers and listeners and readers engage together in the process of making meaning and coming to understanding.

Key #3: Understanding Subject Matter and Its Treatment

To become a successful rhetor—that is, to be a "good person speaking well"— you must develop skill in treating the subject matter fairly, fully, and effectively in a text. Some people might contend that the treatment of subject matter goes beyond the realm of rhetorical skill—in other words, that generating material for a text and producing the text itself are separable activities. We disagree. It is vital for a successful rhetor to comprehend that *what* he or she decides to include in a composition is intimately connected to *why* he or she is speaking or writing, *whom* he or she is speaking or writing to, and *what kind* of text he or she is composing.

To develop skill with treating subjects, a rhetor needs to understand four essential concepts. First, he or she needs to recognize that any topic, proposition, question, or issue that might generate the subject of a text must offer at least two paths of interpretation, analysis, or argument—the subject must be an "open" one. A text can never be effective rhetorically if it covers a subject matter about which everybody already agrees. So, for example, if you were taking a class on the works of William Shakespeare and you wrote a paper claiming that Shakespeare was a famous late-sixteenth- and early-seventeenth-century English playwright, your audience might say, "Well, of course. We already know that." But if you wrote a paper claiming that William Shakespeare was a famous late-sixteenth- and early-seventeenth-century English playwright whose plays demonstrate remarkable insights into European history and politics, even though Shakespeare himself never traveled or studied in Europe, then members of your audience would probably perk up and say to themselves, "Hmmm, that's an interesting angle. Let's see what this writer can do to flesh out that claim."

Your audience's response to the fuller, more debatable topic illustrates the second concept about subject matter treatment that a budding rhetor needs to understand: A successful speaker or writer generates effective material by capitalizing on what his or her audience already knows, making them curious to know more about the topic, and then satisfying their curiosity by providing facts, ideas, and interpretations that build on what they already know. To continue our example from above: the audience for your paper about Shakespeare already know that he was a famous late-sixteenth- and early-seventeenth-century English playwright, and they may even know (as you do, once you've learned it in class) that there is some dispute about whether Shakespeare himself actually wrote the 34 plays that bear his name. Such an audience would find your topic compelling because it would speak to their curiosity about how a young man with only a grammar school education in a rural town in England could write such historically, politically, and socially rich plays. In your Shakespeare paper—indeed, in all effective compositions that you produce—your audience will look for believable material that supports a point that you are making about a topic that they either are curious about already or become curious about because your title and the opening of your composition have made them so.

And this desire for believable material in support of a general point illustrates the third and fourth concepts that a person developing skill with rhetoric needs to understand about subject matter treatment: the basic move of all effective rhetorical texts is claim-plus-support, and the central responsibility of a rhetor developing a subject is to generate ample, substantial material to support the points he or she wants to make. A budding rhetor can use the phrase *claim-plus-support* as shorthand to remind himself or herself of this fact: All successful texts, written or spoken, are made up of a series of points the rhetor wants to make. One of these points may be the main point of the text, sometimes called the **thesis statement.** To develop this main point, the rhetor generates a series of subsidiary, supporting points, and to flesh out these points, the rhetor comes up with facts, details, examples, illustrations, and reasons—all those things that cause a reader or listener to think, "Ah, I see *why* and *how* the point is being made." And this ability to create appropriate, effective points and supporting material must be active and robust. As we will explain in Chapter 2, the first of the ancient canons of rhetoric was **invention,** the craft of generating material to flesh out the topic of a text. A good rhetor will often produce *more* material—more general points and supporting material—than he or she actually needs in a text, just so he or she can *choose* the points and material that will be most effective with the audience.

Activity

Read the following editorial that was published February 1, 2001, by the nationally syndicated columnists Jack Anderson and Douglas Cohn. Then, in your group, discuss the following questions:

- Who might be the audience for this column?
- How do Anderson and Cohn appeal to this audience (or these audiences)?
- Select one audience that you think might pay attention to this column, and describe how the column addresses or alludes to what the members of this audience probably feel, think, believe, and know about the subject matter.
- What is the principal claim that Anderson and Cohn make? How do they support that claim? Can you detect one or more claims besides the principal one? If so, how is that claim (or are those claims) supported?
- If you were working as an assistant to Anderson and Cohn and had to generate *more* material for additional columns on this subject, what kinds of questions would you raise or issues would you address?

HOW ABOUT ONE STUDY AT A TIME?

Prompted by first lady Laura Bush, education is the front-burner issue for the Bush administration, but the arguments are centering around the wrong issues: vouchers and accountability.

The real issue is the structure of education. Vouchers are generally being discounted because they would divert badly needed funds from the public school system. Accountability is a problem only in the remedy; schools whose students do not meet the standards are to be penalized when they should be counseled and assisted.

The solution is to change the system. Socrates educated his students in very small numbers, one subject at a time. It was a good method—a method we could use today.

True, we cannot provide one instructor for every five to 10 students, but we can teach one subject at a time. It is well known that students do better in summer school than during the regular school year, and the reason is that they are immersed in one subject for a short period of time. They can focus, they can concentrate, they can explore, they can question—and they cannot be ignored.

The idea of trying to have students simultaneously learn six or seven subjects forces unwanted choices upon them, because they must choose how they will allocate their time. And there are educators who defend this system, claiming that time management is an important element of education. Baloney. Is it more important than learning the subjects?

The primary goal of education is to graduate students who have actually learned the subject matter. Why impose extraneous forces and decisions upon them? Why complicate their lives? Why increase rather than decrease the pressures?

Instead, imagine an educational system that mirrors summer school. The school year would be divided into six or seven units. Each unit, lasting five or six weeks, would be devoted to the study of a single subject. Students who hate mathematics, language, history or science would be able to devote all of their scholastic energies to those subjects, one at a time. And teachers, keenly aware that not all of their students love the particular subject as much as they do, would have enough time to provide individual attention to each of them.

Next comes the curriculum. There was a time in our history when Latin was mandatory. Today, the study of a foreign language is mandatory for most college-bound students. However, since virtually none of them can expect to graduate from high school or college fluent or even conversant in the language, the study of foreign languages should be elective.

Mathematics has a similar problem. A study of algebra, geometry and trigonometry is fine, but what possible purpose is served by forcing students in their last years of high school or first years of college to study calculus if they are not planning to major in math or science?

While some of these suggestions may be controversial, the objective of graduating students who have learned the subjects is not.

—United Feature Syndicate, *Jack Anderson and Douglas Cohn*

Modifying the Basic Rhetorical Triangle: Rhetoric Occurs in a Context

While the basic rhetorical triangle sets out the three initial keys to developing skill with rhetoric, the triangle needs to be modified so that it reflects three vital facts. First, rhetorical transactions always take place in a **context**—a convergence of time, place, people, events, and motivating forces—that influences how the rhetor understands, analyzes, and generates the persona, the appeals, and the subject matter material. Second, every rhetorical transaction is designed to achieve an **aim,** a **purpose,** or an **intention.** Third, when rhetors consider what aim they hope to accomplish in a particular context, they select an appropriate type of text, or **genre,** to achieve that purpose. These three facts thus lead to three additional keys to developing skill with rhetoric.

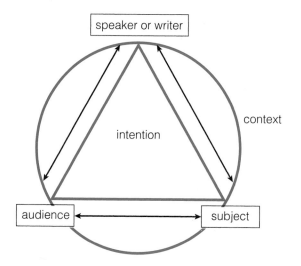

Revised Rhetorical Triangle

Key #4: Understanding Context

Just as the seventeenth-century poet John Donne argued in his famous Meditation 17, "No man is an island, entire of itself," so budding rhetors need to understand that no text they create or analyze is an island, separate unto itself. Every speech or written composition arises from a context: the convergence of the immediate situation calling forth the text, any pertinent historical background information about the topic, the persona and identity of the rhetor, and the knowledge and beliefs of the audience. The context of a speech or written composition strongly shapes how rhetors argue their positions or explore their ideas. An effective speaker or writer knows how to allude to the context in his or her work; a careful reader understands how context affects a text he or she is analyzing.

Consider an example involving writing. Let's say that a writer is writing about gun control in the wake of the Columbine High School shooting tragedy, the terrible event of April 20, 1999. The writer would probably be remiss not to acknowledge Columbine, since it would have been so much in the news and in the public consciousness. The climate of fear and sadness about the Columbine events is part of the context the writer needs to address whatever his or her position on gun control issues. Rhetors can refer to topical events—that is, time-bound moments like the Columbine shooting, the O. J. Simpson trial, the voting problem in Florida in the 2000 presidential election, the Teapot Dome scandal, the McCarthy hearings, the Watergate break-in, or the Chicago Seven—as they consider how to approach subjects, how to provide evidence, and how to connect with audiences. One problem with using current events, of course, is that their currency fades quickly. Some of the events mentioned above, for example, may seem far in the past to readers. (The Teapot Dome scandal was a corporate double-dealing scandal during the administration of Warren Harding in the 1920s, the McCarthy hearings were a congressional inquiry prompted by fears of communism in the 1950s, the Watergate break-in happened in 1974 and led to the resignation of President Richard Nixon, and the Chicago Seven was a group of antiwar activists tried in court for their protests during the Democratic National Convention in 1968.) Still, even though they lose force quickly, topical events serve an important purpose of locating time and space for an audience and in explaining and exploring the contexts that lead rhetors to conclusions.

Rhetors also use wider cultural contexts as they make decisions about their texts. A writer on gun control issues might allude to the American West and the frontier in order to connect the American present to the American past, a past that many readers have seen mythologized over and over again in movies and books. That cultural context is part of what writers consider when they write about issues, such as gun control, that reflect on something about the way the culture views itself. Do Americans see themselves as cowboys? And if they do, what associations do they bring to that word? Free, independent, powerful, dangerous? If a rhetor considers the cultural images that the word *cowboy* evokes, he or she might see how the words alone begin to help him or her understand how and why Americans have difficulty reconciling the problem of guns in this country. Knowing the cultural context thus will help a rhetor generate evidence and create an effective persona.

Context, then, can be immediate or distant, bound by current events or ongoing events. You might stop to think about how you would work with context if you were writing about gun control. Is there an event that has happened in your school or your community that would provide strong evidence and help connect with your readers if you used it? Is there some local history that might contribute to your argument? In Greensboro, North Carolina, many residents remember a school shooting in 1993, when a 16-year-old boy who had been suspended from school for smoking went home, got his father's gun from a locked cabinet, and returned to wound the assistant principal and then turn the gun on himself. His death provoked a lot of discussion about both school safety and gun control. Many places in the country have a long tradition of hunting and a history of parents teaching children responsible gun ownership and safety that a writer could use to draw other conclusions about safety and gun control.

In summary, an effective rhetor knows how to refer to context to help the audience understand the position he or she takes and to connect positively with the text's argument.

Key #5: Understanding Intention

A fifth element that a rhetor must understand is intention, also called aim or purpose. A rhetor's intention is what he or she wants to *happen* as a result of the text, what he or she wants the audience to *believe* or *do* after hearing or reading the text. In some rhetorical situations, the rhetor knows his or her intention right from the start; in other situations, the intention becomes clear as the text evolves.

Consider the first option. You may begin with an intention, saying to yourself: "I want to write an essay to persuade people to use public transportation." Often when you begin with an aim, you already have strong feelings and opinions about the issue, maybe because you've read a lot about it already or because you have personal experiences that have convinced you of the rightness of your position. Your task in this case is to find enough evidence and to present it fairly enough to justify the aim you begin with.

In other situations, you begin with a topic you're interested in but don't yet carry strong opinions about: "I want to write about using public transportation." Or you're assigned that topic by a teacher: "Write about the advantages and disadvantages of public transportation." When you begin with a topic, you discover your aim as you write. Part of the mark of a successful writing process and a successful writing product is the ability to take a topic and discover an aim through the exploration of ideas and evidence.

As a reader, you discover intention in the process of reading much as a writer discovers intention in the process of writing. In one text, the writer may announce a purpose—in this case, a persuasive one—at the beginning of an essay: "We need to take the bus to work. And here's why." In that case, you the reader understand immediately what the writer has in mind, and you make a decision quickly about what your disposition is with regard to that aim. You the reader might think about what you know and believe about pollution, buses, and city problems. (Notice how you are drawing on context as you interpret?) And you will think about how the writer sounds, and whether you like the voice that states its aim so quickly and assertively.

In another text, the writer might begin with a story and wait to announce the aim, or use the story to imply the aim. The writer might marshal facts and figures to prove the case and end the essay with a sentence that generalizes about the purpose. You the reader comprehend the reason for the story or the use of figures as you begin to understand the aim. And you decide whether or not the evidence or the stories have been effective to convey the aim. You analyze the rhetoric of the piece, in other words, to decide on its success.

Activity

Choose an issue or subject that relates to some event at your school. Draw your own illustration of it. Keep in mind the triangle. Share your drawings with your group, and see if your "readers" understand the context, your aim, and your persona.

Key #6: Understanding Genre

A sixth key to developing skill with rhetoric also emerges from the modified rhetorical triangle. Because every act of writing and reading is embedded in a context, and because every writer writes to accomplish an aim and every reader reads to discover that intention, every rhetor chooses to produce a certain *type* of text—a genre that is appropriate to accomplish his or her intention in the particular context. A rhetor needs to understand that there are many types of texts, many genres, to produce and analyze as a student and a citizen.

Let's look at a scenario that might make this context-intention-genre connection clearer. Suppose that your advisor tells you that a local service organization, the Retired Senior Volunteer Program (RSVP), is inviting students to apply for a partial scholarship in psychology or social work, two fields you're considering as majors. Immediately, you understand part of the context—you have a motivation to write a letter of application, and you have an incentive to produce a text. You do a bit of research on the program, and you discover that RSVP places a strong emphasis on what it calls "intergenerational volunteer" work—projects that involve both senior citizens and younger citizens in community improvement. This is right down your alley; just last year, in fact, you and your grandmother volunteered to work together at a drop-in food pantry sponsored by a church in your neighborhood. Voilà, you understand a little more about the context—you know something about one of the areas stressed by RSVP. Since you know that RSVP has money to support college students and because you think you might need some financial assistance for college, you also have an intention: You need to persuade the scholarship committee at the local RSVP chapter that you are an extremely deserving candidate for their scholarship. So, in this context with this intention, what type of composition do you write? Do you write a poem that shows your creativity with words and images? No. Do you write a scientific laboratory report about some aspect of aging and psychology? No. You write a courteous, convincing letter, detailing your credentials as a student, your interest in the fields the organization wants to support, and your experiences with your grandmother that show how much you have already learned from intergenerational research and how much you think you can continue to learn. Context plus intention lead to genre.

Students who are just beginning to develop their rhetorical skills some-times have difficulty thinking "outside the box" about genre. Many students have been taught that every paper they write for their courses needs to be the same type: It needs to have an opening paragraph that "hooks" the reader and ends with a **thesis** statement; then it needs to have three "body" paragraphs, each of which begins with a topic sentence and develops some aspect of the thesis statement; and then it needs to conclude with a paragraph that restates the thesis. This type of writing, commonly called the five-paragraph essay, is taught in many American high schools. (Curiously, almost no other system of secondary education in the world puts so much emphasis on this particular genre.) There is absolutely nothing wrong with knowing how to write a five-paragraph essay. It is a genre that students ought to master early in their school years because it is especially useful when students have to write a timed, impromptu essay for a test. But it is not the only genre students should learn to produce. A rhetor needs to look at the particular context that's calling forth the writing, consider his or her intention in this context, and then ask, "Is the five-paragraph essay *appropriate* for this context and this intention?" It may be the case that some assignments would be better served with a paper that ranged beyond five paragraphs; that offered a more provisional, tentative thesis that the writer would want to qualify or rethink part of the way through the paper; and so on. In summary, students should understand that as valuable as the five-paragraph essay is, it remains a relatively "closed" genre, one that suggests that a writer has drawn all of his or her conclusions and put them "in the can," rather than thinking deeply about the topic at hand and reflecting that complex thinking in a more complicated genre.

Think of all the genres you could write by tapping into this connection between context and intention. For example, let's say that you, a part-time worker yourself, have just read two or three really interesting magazine articles about the effects on students of holding a part-time job. Given that so many students you know work while they are in school, you know that the context is a rich one, and you would like to write something that would combine the insights you gained from the articles with your own thoughts about the benefits and drawbacks of part-time employment. Given this context and this intention, you decide to write a feature article that might be published in your school newspaper. Or, to consider another example, let's say that you, along with other people who live in your neighborhood, are concerned about the potential traffic congestion (and danger) that might come about if a large hardware store opens near a very busy intersection, as has been proposed. The city development commission has announced a public hearing on the proposed construction. So you and your neighbors might go to the intersection, conduct a study of the current rate of traffic, speculate based on your best estimates about how traffic will increase if the hardware store opens, and then write a documented, scientific study, complete with an introduction, methods of investigation, findings, and implications, and present it with a cover letter opposing the construction of the store to the development commission. Both of these examples illustrate the kind of thinking a skillful rhetor does about genre. He or she asks, "What is the context calling forth a piece of writing? Who needs to know what I intend to write about? Therefore, what is the *best,* most *appropriate* genre to produce?"

Rhetoric in Everyday Life: *Your* Life, *Your* Community

Just because you are using this book in a course, don't think that the study of rhetoric is something that applies only to school projects. While it is important to apply the six keys to developing skill with rhetoric to school projects that require you to read, write, speak, and think clearly and effectively, it's equally important to consider how these rhetorical abilities help you prosper in your life beyond the school walls.

The following text and three activities are designed to see how being a skillful rhetor can help you become an active, contributing citizen and a conscientious consumer of the many texts that you must analyze.

Rhetoric and Citizenship

What does it mean to be a good citizen? One way to answer this complicated question is to use a metaphor: Citizenship is a two-way street, and being skilled at rhetoric gives you the ability to travel in both directions successfully. Here's what we mean.

When you are a citizen, you belong to a series of governing units that you expect certain things from. In turn, they expect certain things of you. Let's say, for example, that you are a citizen of the United States, the state of Illinois, and the city of Downers Grove. (As you might have guessed, this describes the citizenship of one of the authors of this book!) Among other things, you expect the United States to provide a strong and stable set of armed forces—the Army, Navy, Air Force, Marines, and Coast Guard—that can protect the country from attacks by individuals or groups who oppose our nation. In turn, the U.S. government expects 18-year-old men (but, for now, not women—more on this issue below) to register with the Selective Service System and in times of national crisis to be willing, within the limits of their conscience, to be drafted into the armed forces. Among other things, you expect the state of Illinois to establish and enforce regulations by which the public schools operate. In turn, the state of Illinois expects elementary and high school students to study a pre-scribed set of subjects in secondary school in order to receive a high school diploma. (Do you recall the activity, earlier in this chapter, that asked you to examine Jack Anderson and Douglas Cohn's argument for "one-subject-at-a-time" schooling?) You also expect Downers Grove to maintain large, open, wooded areas as parks where residents can relax and enjoy nature. In turn, Downers Grove expects you to respect the cleanliness and safety of the parks by not littering, not chopping down trees, not allowing pets to run wild in them, and so on.

Good citizens generally know a lot about these expectations—how they expect their country, state, and city or town to behave toward them, and how they are expected to behave in return. And, whether they know it or not, these good citizens use their skill at rhetoric to understand what their citizenship pro-vides for them and expects of them. Many of the rights and responsibilities of citizenship are not set in stone. They are conveyed to us—sometimes directly from the governing bodies, sometimes indirectly through schools and the media—as propositions or proposals, and we, as good citizens, have to examine them critically and decide whether and how we want to assent to them. This process requires that we read documents and listen to speeches and conversa-tions about citizenship issues very carefully, working hard to understand the argument being put forward and the language used to embody the argument—in other words, to comprehend the rhetoric of good citizenship.

Let's consider an example of how being skilled at rhetoric can help you be a well-informed citizen. While women serve in all the armed forces of the United States, they have neither been required to register for the Selective Service Sys-tem nor been drafted. The federal government came close to drafting women in World War II because there was a shortage of military nurses, but a surge of volunteerism made the draft of women unnecessary. Three decades later, the draft of men was deemed unnecessary as well. As the Vietnam War ended, so did the drafting of young men in 1973, and from 1975 to 1980 18-year-old males were not required to register with the Selective Service. But when the Soviet Union invaded Afghanistan in 1980, there was concern about America's ability to deploy its armed forces quickly, and President Jimmy Carter asked Congress to reinstate the law requiring young men to register for the draft. Congress complied but only after debating the question of whether young women should also be required to register and, in times of crisis, be drafted. Since it was the policy of the Department of Defense not to involve women soldiers in combat, Congress decided not to require 18-year-old women to register. This decision, however, was challenged. A district court in Pennsylvania, respond-ing to a lawsuit brought by several young men, ruled that the exclusion of women from the draft violated a clause in the Fifth Amendment to the U.S. Constitution, which states that no citizen may "be deprived of his life, liberty, or property without due process of law." The case, *Rostker v. Goldberg,* was later appealed to the U.S. Supreme Court, which ruled that the exclusion of women was not unconstitutional. The question of whether 18-year-old women should be required to register for the draft has resurfaced regularly since then. Bodies ranging from the U.S. Senate to a Presidential Commission on the Assignment of Women in the Armed Forces to the General Accounting Office have debated the question, with decisions being reached in 1992, 1994, and 1998 not to require women to register and not to subject them to the draft.

Activity

The issue came to the fore again in early 2003, just as the United States and its coalition partners were planning to take military action against Iraq. Read the following editorial, which appeared in the *Daily Illini,* the student newspaper at the University of Illinois at Urbana-Champaign, on June 20, 2003. Then do two things: First, in your group, analyze how the anonymous author of this editorial creates a persona, appeals to the audience, and addresses the subject matter. Second, write your own response to the editorial. Pay attention to how you incorporate the context, determine an aim, and decide on the appropriate genre that will embody your response.

INCLUDING WOMEN IN THE DRAFT

Uncle Sam wants you. Be an army of one. Commercials, posters and pamphlets bearing these slogans—and others like them—encourage many to enlist in the military. But even more people are available to the armed forces.

In addition to all the men and women who enlist on their own, men must register for the draft. Men ages 18 to 25 are eligible to be drafted into the military during times of war. Only men.

The idea of conscription is distasteful to many, but the draft is an unfortunate necessity. While many people do become more patriotic in times of war, not all feel obligated to enlist. Running out of manpower at a crucial point in a war would be disastrous.

Critics of mandatory enlistment say it's wrong to force anyone to register for the draft. But when it comes down to the wire, the draft pool is a needed resource. Fighting wars without soldiers is impossible.

Historically, only men have had to register for the draft. But society is different now, and equality is a closer goal.

Women are able to enlist in the military voluntarily, and female soldiers are considered an asset. If women are able to enlist by choice, it should also be made mandatory for them to register to be drafted. It's unfair that only men are forced into combat. America is one nation, with one society. It's unfair that one sex can be forced to fight the battles of both.

Women in other countries are drafted into the military. Every Israeli citizen must serve in the Israeli army. Other countries have considered or implemented conscription for women already, and the United States should follow suit.

Opponents of women being in the military might argue that women may have to leave a family behind or become pregnant while on active duty. But health concerns that would distract from duty would need to be addressed and details would need to be hammered out for maternity leave.

Others argue that women shouldn't have to register because they won't be able to physically handle a combat situation.

This is a moot point because the military provides training and decides where each person will be placed, including less physical jobs. It's unlikely that a women who lacked the physical skills for combat would be placed in that situation. Nor would a man.

The military wants to win wars, and it would be detrimental to place people in positions they are not qualified for or lack an affinity for. But with a bigger pool of help to choose from, the military could only better itself.

Rhetoric and Community

When you are skilled at rhetoric, you are not only in a position to make good decisions about national political questions, such as whether all 18-year-olds should be required to register for the draft. When you are skilled at rhetoric, you are also in a better position to understand and respond to important issues and concerns in your local community.

Consider the following scenario, for example. In Downers Grove, a wooded suburb about 20 miles west of Chicago, drivers used to see interesting signs over and over as they traveled south on Belmont Avenue, a busy road. Planted in several front yards were large white placards, with a simple message in bold, black, all-capital letters: NO MEANS NO. The average motorist driving past these signs might not have known exactly what they meant, but passersby certainly perked up and paid attention to them. Why?

Here's the story behind the signs: Along the western edge of Belmont Avenue was a substantial parcel of undeveloped park land, owned by the city. A proposal was made that the Downers Grove Park District build a large, state-of-the-art water theme park on this site. Proponents of this plan said the theme park would draw both visitors and new residents to Downers Grove, provide an excellent venue for family recreation, and generate considerable income for the city. The opponents—including the homeowners who put the signs in their yards—conceded this last point: The theme park would indeed generate revenue. But the opponents believed that the theme park would also attract to Belmont Avenue hordes of people who didn't care about keeping the area clean and safe. The opponents envisioned regular traffic jams on the street in front of their homes. They worried that the theme park would become a site for loitering and potential vandalism.

Sensing that they would need community support, city officials who hoped to see the water theme park succeed put the question to a vote. In a referendum, voters were asked whether they supported the construction of the park on Belmont. They overwhelmingly voted no. But much to the voters' surprise, city officials appeared at the next council meeting after the election and, claiming the election was not a *binding* referendum, announced their intention to go ahead with the water theme park development. That's when the signs went up in people's yards: NO MEANS NO.

Why are these signs so effective? There are no fancy words—just three monosyllables making up one simple sentence. The graphics are not all that impressive: plain black capital letters on a white background. Yet the signs caught people's attention and motivated them to find out the story behind them. Why? At the level of literal meaning, the sentence was a **tautology,** a direct (and perhaps needless) repetition of an idea. But on a deeper level, the message was very strong. NO MEANS NO sounded like a strong, forceful parent disciplining an unruly child who was trying to get away with something forbidden. NO MEANS NO had a air of finality to it, suggesting that this was really the final word on the issue. And the appearance of so many signs in people's yards, all of which said NO MEANS NO, suggested that people in this neighborhood were unified, bonded, together.

Of course, not all the signs and public displays one might see in a community are as negative as NO MEANS NO. Throughout Downers Grove, for example, there are signs on posts that say *Downtown Downers Grove: Catch the Spirit,* a message that suggests the residents can find plenty to do in the small downtown area. Outside many of the schools, one sees signs that proclaim *Excellence in Education.* And not all of the rhetoric that defines and binds together a community can be found inscribed on signs in yards and on lampposts. Communities—like Downers Grove and, perhaps, the city, town, or village where you live—call upon their residents to identify with the municipality, to support and take part in events it sponsors through signs, brochures, newsletters, and town meetings. All of these materials together constitute the rhetoric of the community, the statements that the community makes about itself and that it wants its residents to believe and support.

Activity

With one or two classmates take a walk or drive through the community where you live. First of all, notice any signs and banners that are posted. How do these signs and banners suggest the community wants to portray itself? What points are they trying to convey? How effectively do the language and the graphics on the signs and banners contribute to conveying the message? Second, find a brochure or newsletter that is published by the town, city, or county where you live. Ask the same questions about it.

When you've finished examining signs, banners, and a brochure or newsletter (or perhaps two or three of them), discuss the community's rhetoric. Here are some questions you can ask:

- Do the artifacts you find—the signs, banners, brochures, or newsletters—create a persona? If so, how would you describe and characterize it?

- How do the artifacts appeal to you as an audience?
- What aspects of the "subject matter" of the city, town, village, or community do the artifacts emphasize? How do they do so?
- Are you able to see an overall aim or intention in the artifacts? If so, what is it?

Rhetoric and Conscientious Consumption

One message should be clear by now: Being skilled at rhetoric is one of the most important abilities you can develop in your quest to lead an active, successful life. If you can read materials with a discerning eye; if you can scope out a situation and understand what is at issue in spoken and written documents and discussions; and if you can speak and write clearly, fluently, and correctly, then you are going to be in a much stronger position to succeed in whatever intellectual task you tackle. Think about this: you are surrounded by, and often immersed in, language—from the books, magazines, and newspapers you read to the conversations you have, the television you watch, the radio and CDs you listen to, and the Internet you surf. A great deal of this language is trying, either openly or subliminally, to get you to do something: Vote for this candidate, buy that product, support this cause, oppose that movement. How do you know what to do, which advice to heed, which path to follow? To a certain extent, of course, you can follow a "gut instinct" in these matters. But certainly you don't want to rely solely on what your emotions tell you to do when an important decision faces you. You want to be able to survey the situation at hand—read, listen, consult, and think. You want to be able to consider the benefits and drawbacks of all the possible courses of action. You want to decide wisely. You want, in other words, to use your rhetorical skills.

As an example of how using your rhetorical skills helps you lead an active life, consider a project familiar to a great many students—selecting colleges and universities to apply to, and getting accepted by an appropriate school. This process may start very early in life for some students, especially if parents, teachers, or friends offer advice about choosing a good college. The process begins in earnest, however, in the sophomore or junior year, when students begin receiving solicitation letters. Colleges and universities throughout the United States want to attract the very best students, so many institutions acquire lists of students' names and addresses from educational testing organizations, marketing firms, student organizations, and alumni groups, and mail letters to high school students urging them to consider applying. Each of these letters aims to portray the college or university in a favorable light—the people at each institution, after all, want you to apply. You need a discerning, rhetorically skillful mind to read these letters carefully and decide whether you actually should apply. You need to notice what kinds of information and appeals to you are played up in such letters. You need to notice what is *not* said in such letters, as well as what is said, and you need to ask yourself *why* you think the writers of these letter chose to foreground, include, and omit certain material. Certainly, every college and university in the United States has attributes that will appeal to some students, but a rhetorically skillful reader will apply to those institutions that really speak to his or her interests and needs.

Activity

The following are passages from two college solicitation letters. Let's examine both of them as rhetorically skillful readers.

> What do the inventor of the Doritos snack chip, the director of the classic movie *The Sound of Music,* and the founder of the Save the Children Foundation have in common? They're all graduates of a small college that's been providing extraordinary educational and career opportunities for more than 160 years—Franklin College.
>
> Arch West, Robert Wise, Dr. John Voris and thousands of other Franklin grads will tell you that the choice of a college has a lifelong impact. That's why they continue to be active in events and activities at their college long after graduation. And that's why you should strongly consider Franklin as you look at your college choice.
>
> You already know that colleges like Franklin provide a unique educational atmosphere that includes small classes, a faculty that loves teaching, a warm and friendly campus, and outstanding opportunities to participate in athletics and extra-curricular activities. But you'll find so much more at Franklin:
>
> - A small-town atmosphere with convenient access to metropolitan Indianapolis and excellent shopping, cultural, and entertainment options.
> - Nationally recognized internship, leadership, and professional development programs that provide graduates with outstanding career options.
> - A top-quality education at an affordable price—Franklin has been consistently recognized as a "best buy."
>
> —*Franklin College, Franklin, Indiana*

> Think about what *you* want from your college experience. Then explore the remarkable opportunities available to you at Arizona State University. Discover why increasing numbers of academically talented students from around the world are choosing ASU.
>
> - 95 undergraduate majors, many of which are recognized as the finest in the nation.
> - Outstanding career and graduate study opportunities for ASU graduates.
> - A beautiful campus combining desert and tropical landscape in the Valley of the Sun.
> - Outstanding students. ASU's fall 1999 freshman class boasted a high school grade point average of 3.36 and included 132 National Merit Scholars, 12th best among all universities in the USA.
> - *The Student Guide to America's Best College Buys* has recognized ASU's combination of academic quality and affordable price as one of the 100 best buys in the USA.
>
> —*Arizona State University, Tempe, Arizona*

Analyze, and then compare and contrast, the rhetoric of these two letters. Ask yourself (or discuss with members of your group) the following questions:

- How would you characterize the persona created by each of the letters?
- How would you describe the way each letter appeals to its audience?

As you address each of these questions, be sure to point to specific passages in the two letters that support your answers.

Interchapter

After each chapter, you will find an interchapter, which summarizes the preceding material and raises questions about three pieces of writing. Those pieces of writing, which appear in their entirety toward the end of the book, are

- the 1849 essay "Civil Disobedience" by Henry David Thoreau (pages 209–225).
- the 1982 poem "It's a Woman's World" by Eavan Boland (pages 226–227).
- the 1973 short story "Everyday Use" by Alice Walker (pages 228–234).

We've borrowed the title of Alice Walker's short story for the title of this book, you'll note.

By asking you to apply to the three works the concepts about rhetoric raised in the preceding chapter, each interchapter expects you to look at the essay, the poem, and the story from a different angle; together, the interchapters will cause you to become intimately familiar with what the authors had to say and how they said it. If you are using this book in a writing or literature class, your teacher may ask you to read other pieces besides these, but Thoreau's essay, Boland's poem, and Walker's short story will give us a common set of works to explore together and to which you will respond as a rhetor—a person skilled at critical reading and purposeful and effective writing and speaking.

We hope that you'll read these pieces of literature several times as you proceed through the interchapters. It's always a good idea to read each one fairly quickly to get a sense of the whole piece and then begin to read in a more focused way as you engage in the activities and respond to the questions we present in the interchapter.

Overview of the Major Points in Chapter 1

- Rhetoric is not some complex art that only scholars and specialists know how to use. Rhetoric is a technique and a set of practices—which *you* can acquire, experiment with, and master—to find all the available means of shaping people's thinking, changing their minds, or influencing their actions in a situation that calls for you to speak or write.

- *Rhetoric* also refers to the actual features of a written or spoken text— its central ideas; its organization, emphases, and focus; and its syntax, diction, and imagery—that lead listeners or readers to pay attention to it and to take up the writer's or speaker's purpose.

- A **rhetorical situation,** one that calls for speaking or writing, contains six elements you can analyze, either in isolation or in relation to one another: the writer or speaker; the reader or listener (sometimes referred to as the audience); the subject matter, or content; the aim, or intention, of the document created; the context (the time, the place, and the community or forum) in which the written document or spoken text is operating; and the genre (the type of composition, its structure, and its organization).

- You can analyze each of these elements by looking at specific features of texts and asking yourself these questions:

  1. What kind of person does the writer or speaker seem to be?
  2. Who is the audience for this text—in other words, whom does the speaker or writer seem to be addressing?
  3. What seems to be the relationship between the speaker or writer and the audience?
  4. What is the central idea that this text develops?
  5. How is the text developed—through examples? descriptions? stories?
  6. How is the text organized? How are its parts arranged? How are the parts connected? How does this arrangement of parts help the development of the text?
  7. What is the context for the text? In what community, or forum, is this text operating?
  8. How does the context influence the writer or speaker or the relationship of the writer or speaker with the audience?

Activities and Discussion Questions for Chapter 1   Use these questions and comments as guides for your own discussion and writing about these works.

Henry David Thoreau, "On the Duty of Civil Disobedience" (published 1849)

The text appears on pages 209–225. In a discussion with a group of your classmates, or in a well-developed, well-organized essay, address one or more of the following questions.

1. Based on your reading of "Civil Disobedience," what kind of person does Henry David Thoreau seem to be? How would you characterize his state of mind and emotion as he composed "Civil Disobedience"?

Cite specific examples from "Civil Disobedience" to support your claims about Thoreau's voice and persona.

2. What does Thoreau do in "Civil Disobedience" to urge his readers to believe in him as a trustworthy, credible person? Point out specific passages where you felt Thoreau was (or was not) particularly believable.

3. One device a writer can use to get a point across is **metaphor,** a comparison of two dissimilar objects or ideas that does not use the words *like* or *as.* Thoreau uses metaphor extensively in "Civil Disobedience." Notice, for example, what he compares *machinery* to, or how he uses *gaming* metaphorically. Select one or two metaphors and explain, citing specific examples from the text, how they help Thoreau's central idea become more vivid for his readers.

4. How do you think Thoreau wanted his readers to react to "Civil Disobedience"? What did he want them to feel? think? believe? do? How do you know? Again, point to specific places in the essay that help you determine Thoreau's purpose.

Eavan Boland, "It's a Woman's World" (published 1982)

The text appears on pages 226–227. Discuss the following ideas in your small group, or choose one and write a well-developed essay of your own. Remember that poetry depends so much on sound for its message that you should listen to someone read "It's a Woman's World" aloud or read it aloud yourself.

1. Create a character description for the speaker in the poem. What might she look like? What kind of work does she do? What are some words in the poem that suggest how she feels about women and their roles? What clue does the title give you about her attitude?

2. Consider the speaker's ethos. How does she make herself believable? Find specific places in the poem where you hear the speaker establishing her own right to speak. Notice especially how she uses pronouns. Why is it important that she uses first-person plural?

3. One striking feature of this poem is the way that the speaker uses details. Pick a few of the details she uses and comment on how they contribute to the meaning of the poem and to the attitude of the speaker toward her subject. Pay attention to the way she uses verbs and the way she makes verbs out of nouns—for example, in "milestone our lives"— as she creates these details.

4. Repetition is an especially useful strategy for poets, since it aids both in stressing meaning and in creating rhythm. Find places where repetition helps reinforce the speaker's purpose or create effect.

5. Explore how the speaker makes connections to her readers. What does she want readers to feel at the end of the poem? Are there particular words in the text that suggest how she wants readers to react?

Alice Walker, "Everyday Use" (published 1973)

The text appears on pages 228–234. In a discussion with a group of your class-mates, or in a well-organized essay, address one or more of the following questions.

1. "Everyday Use" was written in the 1970s, a time when civil-rights issues had begun to focus on matters of ethnic pride and heritage. How does knowing that context help you to comment on the **conflict** this story presents as well as on its message?

2. Which character do you feel the most sympathy for? Explain why, using lines from the story to illustrate your position.

3. Although there are no white people who are obvious characters in the story, racial difference and racism are subtly made part of the story's context. How do you see that racial context in the story, and how does it contribute to the meaning?

4. As you think about the writer's intention, consider why this story begins with the dedication "for your grandmama."

Using the Five Traditional Canons of Rhetoric

"My heartfelt thanks to Kitty Lundell for writing my speeches, and to Keith Donegan for delivering them."

One clear message in the first chapter is that rhetoric is something you do every day. When you decide to read something challenging—one of your lessons for school, an editorial column in a magazine you subscribe to, or an informative site on the Internet—you don't say to yourself, "Okay, now I have to be a rhetorician." You simply say, "Okay, now I'm going to read," and then you *use* skills and strategies to guide and assist your reading. Similarly, when you begin to write something—a paper for one of your classes, a letter applying for an award, or an e-mail to a friend—you don't say, "Now, I must be a rhetorician." You simply write (knowing what a complex process that is!), and you employ the skills and strategies that have worked for you in the past.

The goal of this chapter is to raise your awareness of *how* you do these things. In this chapter, we explain a set of traditional rhetorical concepts and examine strategies for using those concepts as you read and write. These concepts include what classical rhetoricians called the **canons**—invention, arrangement, style, memory, and delivery—all the elements involved in written or spoken communication. As you learn about each of the five canons, you will understand how valuable they are for shaping your thoughts as a rhetorically sensitive reader and for guiding your actions as a rhetorically effective writer. You will also see how helpful they are as **heuristic** devices, points of reference that you can return to regularly and systematically as you analyze what you read with a rhetorician's eye and as you plan writing that will be rhetorically effective.

Like the angles on the rhetorical triangle, the canons are useful perspectives from which to see rhetoric at work in everyday life. We'll review quickly two concepts that come from Chapter 1 to show how they're related to the canons: context and appeals.

Rhetoric at Work: Context and the Three Appeals

Chapter 1 explains two truths about every piece of writing. First, a piece of writing always exists in context. A situation prompts the writer to write about a certain subject, members of an audience read the piece, and a purpose determines how the writer approaches both the situation and the audience. Second, a piece of writing works in three closely related ways to convey information to readers, to influence their thinking, and perhaps even to change their actions.

- Writing appeals to readers by making a clear, coherent statement of ideas and a central argument. Teachers of rhetoric refer to this appeal as logos, a Greek term that is best translated into English as "embodied thought."
- Writing appeals to readers by offering evidence that the writer is a trustworthy, well-educated, believable person who has done his or her homework and has the best interests of the readers in mind. Teachers of

rhetoric refer to this appeal as ethos, which translates roughly as "good-willed credibility."

- And writing appeals to readers by relating to, and sometimes even speaking directly to, their emotions and interests. Teachers of rhetoric refer to this appeal as pathos, which translates roughly as "feeling." The English cognate words *sympathy* and *empathy* are directly related to this appeal. A good writer wants his or her readers to empathize with—or, literally, to feel—his or her ideas and arguments.

While there is some value in examining how a piece of writing accomplishes each of these appeals separately, it's important to remember that the appeals are closely related. In other words, when you are analyzing the rhetorical effectiveness of a piece of writing, you need to examine how its statement and development of central ideas and larger claims both establish the credibility of its writer and tap into the emotions and interests of the reader. When you are planning your own writing, you need to analyze the same intertwined appeals in your own work.

Each of the five canons of rhetoric described below suggests strategies you can use to make a text appeal to your readers.

- Invention strategies help you to generate material that is clear, forceful, convincing, and emotionally appealing.
- Techniques of **arrangement, style,** and **delivery** help you to put your material in structures, patterns, and formats that will be understandable to your readers and help them to see you as a credible, sympathetic, even impressive person.
- Methods of tapping into your readers' **memories** and cultural associations will assist your efforts to clarify your ideas and arguments for readers and will help them to see you as a person who is on their side, who is one of them.

Activity

Picture the following magazine ad. The advertisement is for *Stone Soup: The Magazine for Young Writers and Artists*. The ad lists two quotations: "The *New Yorker* of the 8 to 13 set," from *Ms.* magazine, and "Blessings on the adult advisers of this enterprise," from the *New Yorker*. The copy then reads: "Christmas, Hanukkah, birthdays—*Stone Soup* is a gift that brings hours of enjoyment, not just on the day it is received but throughout the year. *Stone Soup*'s stories, poems, and illustrations are all by children. It's the perfect gift for creative 8- to 13-year-olds."

In a small group, discuss the central argument of this ad and decide its primary appeal—to logos, pathos, or ethos. Rewrite the ad with another primary appeal.

Invention

Most people think of invention as the act of creating something new—a new product, process, device, or formula. This is not exactly the meaning of invention that rhetoricians use. The term *invention* in rhetoric comes from the Latin verb *invenire,* meaning "to find." Inventing as a rhetorician is like conducting an inventory. Stores have to close every now and then to take an inventory— they need to *find* what products they have on their shelves and analyze their stock so that they can plan sales better. Similarly, rhetorically skilled readers need to take inventories, finding and analyzing what a writer did to state and develop the main ideas in a work. Rhetorically skilled writers, likewise, take inventories of what they have in their storehouses of experiences, ideas, reading background, and observations that they can effectively pull together in a composition. Invention, then, is the art of finding and developing material.

Just as some writers like to make a definite plan before they begin a writing project and others simply begin writing and see what emerges, some people find it helpful to invent using a clearly defined strategy, while others like to invent more spontaneously. We'll call the clearly defined invention strategies *systematic* and the more open and spontaneous ones *intuitive.* In this chapter, we'll describe the systematic strategies in some detail and then show you intuitive strategies at work in scenarios in Chapter 3.

Systematic Invention Strategy I: The Journalist's Questions

Perhaps the most widely known systematic invention strategy is the journalist's questions. When journalists write news stories, they ask six questions:

- Who was involved?
- What took place?
- When did it happen?
- Where did it happen?
- Why did it happen?
- How did it happen?

A skilled journalist can write a lead that answers all six of those questions, and then write the remainder of the news story simply by unpacking, or describing point by point, the details about each of those six points.

The journalist's questions are a useful device for comprehending clearly what you read. Consider, for example, the section of "Civil Disobedience" in which Thoreau discusses spending a night in jail. Using the journalist's questions as a guide, the reader can say that Thoreau was arrested and put in jail for one night sometime prior to 1849 when he composed "Civil Disobedience."

The jail was in Concord, Massachusetts. Thoreau was jailed for refusing to pay his poll tax. The arrest apparently happened without resistance from Thoreau himself. That's the simple who-what-when-where-why-and-how of the case.

This bare outline, of course, does little to explore the rich substance of Thoreau's piece. Let's work through the journalist's questions a second time and see what taking a thorough inventory with the six questions reveals about how Thoreau appeals to his audience and achieves his purpose.

- **Who was involved?** Certainly Thoreau himself, but what about the other jailed person we learn about, Thoreau's cellmate, the person whom the jailer introduced as "a first-rate fellow and a clever man"? Why do you suppose Thoreau describes him in such detail? Here is a man who is allegedly a criminal, yet he gets several months of free room and board in a neatly decorated cell and goes out every day to work at harvesting hay. Do you think Thoreau is making any comment about the American system of justice and incarceration with such a description?

- **What took place?** Clearly, on one level, the event was just a night in jail for Thoreau. But take a closer look at the paragraph that begins, "It was like traveling into a far country, such as I had never expected to behold, to lie there for one night." Thoreau clearly did more than simply sleep in the cell. What ideas do you think Thoreau is trying to suggest by seeing his "native place in the light of the Middle Ages"?

- **When did it happen?** The timing is vital, and you need to know a bit more background information to understand fully this passage from "Civil Disobedience." In 1848, the United States was involved in a war with Mexico, a war that many intellectuals, including Thoreau, thought was unwarranted and unethical. Knowing this, how do you think Thoreau capitalizes on the times he's living in?

- **Where did it happen?** The location is very important, but its significance emerges only when you know that Concord, Massachusetts, where Thoreau was jailed, was not simply some small New England town. Concord was a site of one of the major battles in the American War for Independence, fought some 70 years before Thoreau wrote "Civil Disobedience," and was during his lifetime a center for intellectual ferment in the young United States.

- **Why did it happen?** The arrest happened because Thoreau failed to pay his poll tax, but that fact as well warrants more examination. A poll tax was a tax levied against all citizens of voting age to support the activities of the government. Since Thoreau disagreed with the government's actions, particularly its waging war against Mexico, he refused to pay the required tax.

- **How did it happen?** Thoreau was arrested with little fanfare, but the quiet uneventfulness of Thoreau's arrest underscores a major point he makes in "Civil Disobedience." If a person is morally justified in objecting to the laws under which he or she lives, that person has a right—Thoreau might even say a duty—to refuse to obey those laws. But the refusal must be civil—no big protests, no violence, just refusal.

A conscientious and comprehensive application of the journalist's questions, as you can see, produces an ample inventory of the ideas introduced and developed in a text.

Activity

Consider the following lead paragraph: "For his efforts in promoting stability in the Middle East, former President Jimmy Carter yesterday was awarded the 2002 Nobel Peace Prize." Given this lead, what details is this news story obligated to unpack for readers?

Activity

Just as the journalist's questions can be used systematically to take an inventory of what a writer does to achieve a purpose, so you can use them when you are planning to write. Think about a paper you are working on right now or will begin soon, and use the journalist's questions to come up with as much material as possible. You may have relatively little to say about some of the questions and a lot to say about others, and you may not eventually *use* everything you generate, but writers almost always have more material than actually gets into final drafts.

- In the situation you are writing about, who was involved? Who was the central person? What people were around this person in the situation, interacting with him or her? How were the central person and the other person(s) in the situation connected or related?

- What took place? What were the obvious main actions and events? What are some other actions and events that might be related to the main ones?

- When did it happen? Why was the timing important? Was there a feeling of crisis or immediacy in the situation? If so, what caused it? If not, did its absence make any difference in the situation?

- Where did it happen? Why was the location important? What persons, actions, and events surrounded the main one you are writing about?

- Why did it happen? What were the main obvious causes? Were more subtle, difficult-to-detect causes present?

- How did it happen? What means were used to achieve a result in the situation?

Systematic Invention Strategy II: Kenneth Burke's Pentad

In his influential book *A Grammar of Motives,* the twentieth-century critic and philosopher Kenneth Burke sets out a systematic invention strategy called the **dramatistic pentad,** which on the surface looks like the journalist's questions. (*Pentad* is a Greek word meaning "group of five.") But there is a difference between the two strategies, and this difference makes the **pentad** a good device for analyzing the substance of a text you read and for taking an inventory of what you might write.

Burke proposes the five points of the pentad as things a person could say not only about a written text but also, more broadly, about any purposeful or intentional act that communicates meaning. Here are the five points:

- **Act:** What happened?
- **Scene:** When and where did it happen?
- **Agent:** Who did it?
- **Agency:** How was it done?
- **Purpose:** Why was it done?

Instead of the who-what-when-where-why-and-how of the journalist's questions, Burke's pentad offers a what-when-where-who-how-and-why series. It also offers a way to see these questions as potentially related to one another, with some relationships potentially more significant than others. Because it provides a way to understand relationships, it is particularly useful as a strategy for analyzing human behavior, in real life or in literature.

Burke's pentad becomes most useful for both analysis of a situation and invention of one as you consider those elements in relationships, which Burke called **ratios.** Burke makes clear that constructing these ratios can be playful. There are no "right" or "wrong" answers about them. Instead, they may be what he calls **casuistries,** little mental games a rhetorical analyst or writer can play to examine a particular communicative act or to plan a piece of writing.

Here's an example of a casuisty, the mental exercise of creating ratios from a situation by using the elements of the pentad.

George Washington chopped down the cherry tree.

Scene-act: The act follows from the circumstances.

In the eighteenth century, boys chopped down trees.

Agent-act: The act follows from the character of the person.

George was a practical action-oriented fellow even as a child.

Agency-act: The act follows from the available means.

The axe was sharper than George thought and sliced through the trunk.

Purpose-act: Something needs to be done to accomplish the act.

> *George was given the axe so that he could learn to chop.*

Act-act: The act follows from other acts.

> *George had chopped down many other trees before without notice.*

You can see how creating ratios from situations allows you to consider possible motives or reasons for behavior. Consciously or unconsciously, writers formulate ratios as they decide which elements of stories they will highlight and which they will omit or play down. You could create other statements, and other ratios, from the sentence "George Washington chopped down the cherry tree," and each would reveal something potentially interesting about the situation.

To see how the pentad can help you both analyze the substance of a text and take an inventory of what you might do in a successful one yourself, let's return to an issue introduced in Chapter 1, the proposal by the Downers Grove village council to build a water amusement park on Belmont Road in that suburb. As you recall, it was the village's persistence in planning this theme park that led residents to put signs in their yards that read, defiantly, NO MEANS NO. The protest came in response to the village's proposal. Here are some possibilities that might explain the situation:

> *Scene-act:* The residents put up the sign because a theme park is not appropriate in their neighborhood.
>
> *Agent-act:* Residents, feeling betrayed by their elected officials, demonstrated their frustration with the village council.
>
> *Agency-act:* The signs were unambiguous and demonstrated the solidarity of the residents in their protest.
>
> *Purpose-act:* Signs along the major street in the village would make officials and the media take notice.
>
> *Act-act:* Other businesses that had negatively affected the neighborhood had been allowed to encroach upon property.

Activity

Work with the five points of Burke's pentad and several ratios to analyze the following editorial, which was posted on "The Scrivener," a Web site that welcomes submissions from high school writers. First of all, consider the *act* as Mike Cameron's wearing the Pepsi shirt to school. What would you say about the other four points in the pentad? Which ratios would you emphasize in taking an inventory of what the author, Joel Caris, did in the piece? Then think of the act as Mike Cameron's suspension from Greenbrier High School, and answer the same questions. Finally, consider the act as the prize money awarded by the Coca-Cola Bottling Company.

A somewhat disturbing event occurred in Evans, Georgia. Greenbrier High School suspended a 19 year old student, Mike Cameron, for wearing a Pepsi shirt. The shirt did not have a marijuana leaf on it, did not promote alcohol or tobacco, and implied nothing sexual. It was simply a shirt with a Pepsi logo on it. Most schools do not consider wearing a Pepsi shirt a punishable offense. Greenbrier, however, did consider it a punishable offense—at least for one day.

It was Coke Day at the high school. Coca-Cola executives were visiting the school, which was competing for a $500 prize in a contest set up by the Coca-Cola Bottling Company of Augusta. Greenbrier High School was also competing nationally for a much more substantial prize of $10,000. The disturbing part of this story is not that a high school hoped to receive a little monetary assistance from a local company. The disturbing part is the implications that come with the awarding of corporate money to public schools and what that high school did in an effort to win the money.

Coke Day activities included the baking of Coke cakes in home economic classes. In science classes, experiments were conducted to determine the sugar content of Coke and the day's finale was a school picture of the high school students spelling out "Coke."

When Cameron and fellow classmate Dan Moxley decided to express their soft drink preference by proudly displaying Pepsi shirts during the school picture, they were both suspended for a day. Apparently, Greenbrier High School was quite upset at the boys' use of self-expression at such an inopportune time. Cameron was scolded by administration and told he might have cost the school $10,000.

What is frightening about this story is the school's reaction when faced with the possibility of free money. This was a public high school, supported by taxpayer money, blatantly pandering to a big corporation. So eager was Greenbrier to cash in on the contest that they condemned a teenager for professing a personal choice and forced their students to participate in classroom activities that resembled Coke commercials more than they did educational lessons.

Public schools should not be partaking in corporate sponsorship. By allowing such things to take place, we are hurting our education system—a system that has suffered too many blows as it is. Considering the funding crisis many schools are experiencing, it is understandable that they would be eager to come across a little extra cash. However, public schools can not be compromising their objectivity and true purpose—education—to appease corporations with deep pockets and a burst of generosity in the face of free advertising.

—*Joel Caris, "Corporate Sponsorship of Our Schools"*

Activity

Choose one of the following:

1. Use the five points of Burke's pentad and several ratios to take an inventory of what you might write in an editorial for your local or school newspaper about one of the following topics: homelessness in America, college scholarship funding, young voters' interest in politics, the cult of celebrity, or another situation of interest.

2. Use the five points of Burke's pentad and several ratios to decide how you might research one of these historical events: the Edict of Milan in 313, the defeat of the Spanish Armada in 1588, the Cherokee Trail of Tears Removal of 1838–1839, the Women's Rights Convention in 1849, the assassination of Dr. Martin Luther King Jr. in 1968, or a relevant event that you've studied in one of your courses.

Systematic Invention Strategy III: The Enthymeme

When you are taking inventory of how a writer has assembled material in order to make a point, or when you are planning your own writing, you need to keep in mind an important maxim about rhetoric. The maxim (paraphrased from Aristotle's *Rhetoric*) is this: People usually write about issues, problems, and subjects that admit to at least two possible viewpoints that are open to challenge or rethinking. In other words, nearly everything people write represents an **argument,** a carefully constructed and well-supported representation of the way writers see an issue, problem, or subject.

An editorial calling for more flexible attendance policies for students who work full-time would clearly be an argument. So would a petition seeking stronger governmental action against real-estate development near protected forest preserves. But you don't need a controversial, public issue in order to write an argument. Many, if not most, of the papers you might write for classes are arguments. A paper for European history about railroads in eighteenth-century England would not be simply an overview of the rail system; it would instead be a carefully reasoned, well-crafted argument about the influence of the railroads on, say, commerce, urbanization, or warfare. A paper for astronomy about the United States' lunar exploration missions in the 1960s and 1970s would probably not be simply a summary of all the flights to the moon; instead, it would be a well-planned, well-supported argument about the ultimate success of the Apollo program, or about future prospects for lunar colonization. A paper for English class calling for a comparative analysis of the styles of Ernest Hemingway and F. Scott Fitzgerald would not contain a bald listing of features of one and then the other author; instead, it would be a thoughtfully constructed, well-documented argument about the similarities and differences between the two writers' styles and about their contributions to creating influential American literature in the early twentieth century. Another way of putting all this is to say that when a writer decides on a topic, he or she has a reason to choose it. That reason—interest in rail systems, hope for space exploration, opinions about Fitzgerald—determines how and how much the writer will say to an audience.

Part of the invention of ideas involves the rhetorical concept of the **enthymeme** (pronounced **EN**-thuh-meem). When writers invent, they work through premises for the arguments they advance and write to guide readers in considering logical relationships among ideas as well as to accede to the beliefs that underlie them. This kind of logical reasoning from beliefs and statements Aristotle called the **syllogism** (**SIH**-luh-*jih*-zəm), and the enthymeme is itself a kind of syllogistic reasoning. The pattern of the syllogism is in three parts: **a major premise, a minor premise,** and a conclusion. The major premise is always some irrefutable **generalization** about the world, the minor premise is always some particular statement that falls under the general category, and the conclusion is always the statement that follows from the major premise and the minor premise. Here is a classic syllogism, taught in logic courses for centuries:

> *Major premise:* All humans are mortal. (irrefutable generalization)
>
> *Minor premise:* Socrates is a human. (particular instance of the generalization)
>
> *Conclusion:* Therefore, Socrates is mortal. (idea that logically follows)

And here is a syllogism about a more current topic.

> *Major premise:* All U.S. citizens who are single, under 65 years old, and earn more than $7,200 a year must file a federal income tax return.
>
> *Minor premise:* Jody McGillicutty is a single U.S. citizen under 65 who earned $7,300 last year.
>
> *Conclusion:* Therefore, Jody McGillicutty must file a federal income tax return.

Notice that the progression from premise to conclusion in the syllogism is airtight. You can't argue with the conclusion of a syllogism structured correctly—that is, when the major premise is an irrefutable general truth and when the minor premise is a particular instance of that general truth.

> *Major premise:* Women are wise.
>
> *Minor premise:* Kate is a woman.
>
> *Conclusion:* Therefore, Kate is wise.

But if the major premise is arguable—perhaps all women are not wise—the syllogism breaks down.

An enthymeme resembles a syllogism in the movement of its own logic, but it differs from a syllogism in two important ways. Instead of having an irrefutable general truth for a major premise, an enthymeme has as its starting point an assumption, a statement, or a proposition that the writer *presumes* the audience accepts and that the writer can build an argument upon. And, because the writer presumes, or wants to presume, that the audience believes and accepts the assumption that holds the major-premise slot, that part of the argument frequently goes unstated. In most arguments, the writer provides the other parts of the enthymeme and assumes that the audience is going to complete for itself the unspoken major premise.

> *Unstated premise:* [Women are wise.]
>
> *Minor premise:* Kate's a woman.
>
> *Conclusion:* Of course, she gave me good advice.

Consider an enthymeme that might sit at the center of the petition, briefly described above, that calls for stronger governmental action against excessive real-estate development near forest preserves. Let's say that the central argument in the petition is this: Because the construction of large housing developments that adjoin forest preserves upsets the ecosystem and drives wild animals out of their natural habitats, governments should limit the number and size of houses built in such developments. The enthymeme as presented here contains only a minor premise—that is, one or more observations about the situation at hand—and a conclusion.

> *Major premise:* [Unstated]
>
> *Minor premise:* The construction of large housing developments that adjoin forest preserves upsets the ecosystem and drives animals such as deer, raccoons, and skunks out of their natural habitats. (two particular observations about the situation at hand)
>
> *Conclusion:* Therefore, city, county, and state governments should limit the number and size of houses built in such developments.

What is the unspoken major premise here? What does the writer of this petition assume—or want to assume—that the audience already feels, thinks, believes, or knows about the situation at hand? It is this: As creatures of the earth, animals deserve a habitat, just as humans do.

A petition like this one would probably offer substantial documentation for its minor premise, providing statistics about the number of animals hit by automobiles in developing areas and about the possible spread of disease and destruction caused by animals being driven out of their natural habitats. The petition might also provide some details of a plan, hinted at in the enthymeme's conclusion, for governments to limit developments next to forest preserves. But the petition would never actually have to state its major premise explicitly. Would it be stronger and more effective if it did? Maybe the petition is stronger *because* the readers have to do the work of filling in the major premise themselves.

What happens when a writer makes an enthymeme that an audience might *not* accept? When you analyze an argument or plan one of your own, you should consider this possibility and look for it. As a case in point, let's look at the enthymeme we've just been working with, now presented in its fully stated form.

Major premise: Animals such as deer, raccoons, and skunks, as creatures of the earth, deserve a stable ecological habitat in which to live, as do humans.

Minor premise: The construction of large housing developments that adjoin forest preserves upsets the ecosystem and drives animals such as deer, raccoons, and skunks out of their natural habitats.

Conclusion: Therefore, city, county, and state governments should limit the number and size of houses built in such developments.

What if a reader responded to the argument by saying, "Animal rights are fine, but humans are more important than animals, and humans have a right to alter ecological habitats to suit their own needs"? If a reader responded this way to the argument, whether the major premise was explicitly stated or left tacit, then the writer would be up against an instance of what ancient rhetoricians called *petitio prinicipi,* or **begging of the question.** When readers respond in this way to an argument, the writer must attempt to change the audience's minds. What had been the unspoken major premise, the tacit starting point, of the central enthymeme becomes the conclusion of a new enthymeme. The writer thinks about what unspoken assumption this new enthymeme rests upon and considers a new major, unstated assumption. Here, for example, is how one might argue to change the minds of anyone who initially begged the question of the first enthymeme.

[Major premise:] [unstated: All creatures of the earth play a natural role in maintaining the ecological stability of an area.]

Minor premise: Animals such as deer, raccoons, and skunks contribute to the ecological stability of an area near rural property by feeding on vegetation and smaller animals.

Conclusion: Animals such as deer, raccoons, and skunks, as creatures of the earth, deserve a stable ecological habitat in which to live, as do humans.

Readers who begged the first question have objections answered by the writer's new enthymeme.

When writers chart out an enthymeme, they focus on just the skeleton—the structure, or the shape—of an argument. As the argument gets fleshed out in writing, writers would likely provide specific details to support the premises or the conclusion, and they might draw on stylistic and organizational resources to help make the case. These might include, of course, an appeal to the credibility and character of the writer (an appeal to ethos) or to the emotions and interest of the audience (an appeal to pathos) as well as to the audience's logical ability to reason through examples and proofs toward a conclusion (an appeal to logos).

Activities

1. In his book *High and Mighty,* Keith Bradsher labels the sports utility vehicle (SUV) "the world's most dangerous vehicle." He points out that the Ford Explorer gets 14 miles to a gallon of gas, less than half what the average new automobile in Japan gets. He notes that the Chevy Suburban emits 7.5 times more air pollution than the average automobile. He reports how in traffic accidents, "SUVs . . . slide over cars' bumpers and sturdy door sills, slamming into passenger compartments" of smaller vehicles. Describe Bradsher's argument as an enthymeme. Explain the unspoken assumption that forms the major premise.

2. Find a short piece of writing from class reading or from the newspaper. Create an enthymeme from the argument it makes.

Systematic Invention Strategy IV: The Topics

One of the most thorough devices for examining and analyzing the substance of something you read and for taking an inventory of what you yourself might write is the set of **topics** of invention drawn from Aristotle's works. It's easy for a modern student to be confused by the term *topics* because the people they know often use the term to mean the subject matter a writer might write about. But the topics as Aristotle described them refer not to the subjects of compositions but to the *places* a writer might go to discover methods for proof and strategies for presenting ideas. The word topos means "place," in fact, in Greek. The writer might find special places to reference—the public good for a paper on political issues, for example. But the most important use of the topics for invention is in the types of reasoning a writer might engage in to create an argument. As you'll see, each of the four basic topics and each of the common topics represent a place where writers can use particular patterns of reasoning to generate ideas and supporting material that audiences will probably accept as valid and legitimate.

The Basic Topics

According to Aristotle, there are four **basic topics** a writer can use to find material for writing on any subject. These four topics are such ordinary patterns of reasoning that Aristotle calls them the **konnoi topoi**—literally, the **"people's topics."** Here are the topics and examples of how they can be used to generate material for oral and written discussion.

- **Possible and impossible:** Using this topic for invention, you look for material that allows you to argue that if X is possible, then so is Y, or that if X is impossible, then so is Y.

EXAMPLE   Suppose you are writing a letter to your congressional representatives asking that they support increased funding for cancer research. Arguing the possible, you might say that since the scientific community came up with cures for typhoid fever, diphtheria, polio, and a range of other diseases, it's possible for them to find a cure for cancer provided there is sufficient funding for research. Or say you are writing about life-supporting conditions on planets other than Earth. Arguing the impossible, you might reason that since the polar ice caps on Earth can't support much life, it's certainly impossible for life as we know it to survive on planets largely covered by ice.

- **Past fact:** This topic allows you to consider ideas suggesting that, given all the known conditions, X probably happened in the past.

EXAMPLE   You are writing about Babe Ruth for a history of sports course, examining whether he really did "call the shot" on his famous home run at Wrigley Field. You read the inconclusive accounts of the event and, based on what you've read about Ruth's bold personality and showmanship, you argue that he did indeed point with his bat to the very place in the stands where he intended to hit the home run—just before he hit it right to that spot. Or suppose you are writing a paper about President Harry Truman's decision to order the atomic bombing of Hiroshima and Nagasaki at the end of World War II. You might argue, given all the historical facts and interpretations surrounding those events, that the United States was, as Truman maintained, simply trying to end the war more quickly than it could have without the bomb.

- **Future fact:** Using this topic, you can find ideas that allow you to argue that X will probably happen in the future.

EXAMPLE   You are writing a paper analyzing the proposals to build a Star Wars defense system—a system of satellites that would shoot down incoming missiles and protect the United States from attack. You argue that, given the history of defense systems built ostensibly for defensive purposes being used instead to attack other countries, in all probability any Star Wars system would be used offensively rather than defensively.

- **Greater and less:** This topic allows you to argue that since X happened, so will Greater-Than-X, or if Y happened, so will Less-Than-Y.

EXAMPLE   Imagine you are writing an analysis of whether increased standardized testing will lead to higher achievement in public schools. Arguing the greater, you could claim that if the state of Texas can show gains in student performance as a result of a rigorous program of testing in the schools, so can all the states if they simply follow the Texas model. Or suppose you are writing a paper for an education class about vertical teams, groups of teachers at different grade levels who try to sequence instruction so that one grade leads carefully to the next. Arguing the less, you could claim that if large corporations can improve their product by creating vertical teams across levels of management and labor, so can small schools.

The Common Topics

A second set of topics useful for taking an inventory of the substance of a text you might analyze or for generating material for your own compositions has its origin in Aristotle's philosophical treatise called, simply, the *Topics*. This second set, which includes the previously mentioned four basic topics as a single topic called *circumstances,* is referred to simply as the **common topics.** Again, let's look at them and examples of using them for taking an inventory of what you might write in a composition.

- **Definition:** Using this topic for invention, you generate material by defining key terms, providing for each term its genus, or the class of things it belongs to, and species, the features that distinguish the thing being defined from all other items in its class.

  EXAMPLE   Think about writing a paper arguing that students with learning disabilities ought to be exempted from taking standardized tests. You would need to demonstrate clearly what you mean by the term *learning disability* by describing as fully as possible what you mean generally by disability and then clarifying which disabilities specifically influence a person's learning.

- **Division:** Using this topic for invention, you divide some or all of your subject matter into parts.

  EXAMPLE   You are writing a paper on how to successfully perform a major role in a play. You might divide this whole topic initially into two parts: how to rehearse and how to perform. And then you might divide the rehearsal part into three additional sections: how to prepare for rehearsal, how to act during the rehearsal, and how to debrief yourself with your fellow cast members after each rehearsal.

- **Comparison and contrast:** Using this topic for invention, you generate similarities (comparisons) or differences (contrasts) about aspects of your subject matter.

  EXAMPLE   Imagine that you are writing a brochure about the best colleges for a person who is interested in community service. After consulting the catalogues and Web sites of a half dozen or so colleges with community service programs, you might show how the colleges are similar and different on these dimensions: relation of community service to students' majors, relation of community service to general education, range of community needs served by the programs, and proximity and accessibility of the community service programs to the college campus.

- **Relationships:** Using this topic for invention, you can generate material that shows different kinds of relationships between aspects of your subject matter.

  EXAMPLE   Suppose you are writing an analysis of whether increasing the number of lanes on a congested highway will actually eliminate most of the traffic jams. Arguing a **causal relationship,** or a cause-and-effect relationship, you could point out that increasing the number of lanes will actually make traffic worse because, with greater accessibility along the highway, more homes and businesses will be built, thus attracting even more cars. Or suppose you are writing a paper about the growth of women's sports in high schools and colleges. Arguing an **antecedent-consequence relationship,** you could make a case that when women's sports become as important to a school as men's, then women's teams will need the same kinds of institutional support in terms of locker rooms, travel arrangements, uniforms, cheerleaders, and so on. Or, to take another example, suppose that you are writing a paper about how slowly a bill providing funding for social programs moves through Congress. Arguing the relationship known as **contradictions,** or contraries, you could claim that since the complicated layers of governmental bureaucracy keep such programs in constant need of funding, a more streamlined procedure in Congress would keep a regular source of funds flowing to social programs.

- **Circumstances:** These topics include the (1) possible and the impossible, (2) past fact, and (3) future fact, all covered within the four basic topics outlined in Aristotle's *Rhetoric* and described above.

- **Testimony:** Using this topic of invention, you can generate material by investigating what authorities or people with extensive experience with your subject say about it. In addition, you can generate material by consulting any documents, laws, or precedents pertaining to your subject.

    EXAMPLE   Imagine, again, that you are writing a paper about the growth of women's sports in high schools and colleges. You could collect testimony by interviewing the athletic directors of several schools, and asking about their experiences with the growth of female participation in sports. You could read primary material from the federal government about Title IX of the Education Amendments of 1972, the law that helps to foster equal funding for men and women in all educational activities including sports, and secondary material—books, articles, and chapters about the sharp growth in women's participation in athletics.

Activity

Read the following editorial column, "The ABC's of Home Schooling," by Julia Morse. With the members of a small group, analyze how Morse uses the following topics to generate material for her column: (1) the greater, (2) the possible, (3) division, (4) cause-and-effect relationship, and (5) comparison. Once you have finished analyzing Morse's invention, make up a paragraph with your group on Morse's issue. Use at least one of the following topics: (1) definition, (2) future fact, and/or (3) testimony.

THE ABC'S OF HOME SCHOOLING
Julia Morse

As a blissfully unattached single devoid of responsibility for anything (except my rent) and anyone (save my bevy of blissfully unattached friends), I've always found nothing more frightening than the prospect of having kids of my own to feed and shelter. Recently, though, I've been dwelling on something far scarier: educating them—myself. With an estimated two million kids from all economic classes now schooled at home, this isn't just idle worrying on my part. And considering I will surely never make enough money to pay for private schools—and fancy myself always living in hip urban centers with shoddy public schools—somewhere down the line home schooling might actually prove the most attractive option. After all, I do write articles every week on how to fix the nation's schools. How hard would it be to actually do it?

My actual knowledge of home schooling was rather limited, mainly to those geeky kids who year after year win the national spelling bee with words I can't even pronounce. To find out more I spent last weekend at a home schooling exhibition at a Denver Holiday Inn, a 5000-strong confab of parents, children and education experts who got together to purchase curriculum, take seminars and talk shop. My first lesson: these people rise with the sun. When I arrived at 7:30 am on Saturday morning, a swarm of parents had already staked out the still-shuttered exhibition hall. When they finally opened the gates and I scanned the panoply of products now geared for home schoolers, I realized why they allowed the extra time. You name it, you could buy it: day-by-day lessons from kindergarten through high school, $600 state-of-the-art microscopes, fiddle lessons, membership in home schooling bowling and sewing leagues, natural oils meant to purify young minds. "Mom, look, they have owl pellets," one boy squealed over the crowd. I followed to find a biological supply booth ready to outfit those parents who'd delved into dissection. Also on sale: preserved sharks, sheep brains and frogs.

As much as I love formaldehyde, I was more drawn to the informational seminars. They promised to enlighten home school parents on, well, the very topics just about every parent everywhere obsesses over. What to do if your kid has ADD? How to discern your child's learning style and resolve conflicts? What kinds of foods help children concentrate—and keep them from bouncing off the walls? Unsurprisingly, the "Designing a College Preparatory High School Program" was bursting at the seams with parents. They probably made a beeline there from the vendor doing brisk business selling Princeton Review and Kaplan SAT prep software.

With support systems like this in place, home schooling certainly wasn't the lonely endeavor I'd imagined it—long days chained to the kitchen table with a couple of library books and low-tech science experiments of my own making. And after an exhausting day in Denver, I'm at least willing to admit home schooling to the realm of the possible—even the doable—provided I can ditch the lesson about the sheep's brain.

—Time.com, June 29, 2001

Intuitive Invention Strategies: A Preview

The systematic invention strategies are helpful for analyzing the strategies writers use and for planning your own writing. But in addition to the systematic strategies, writers can employ a number of more intuitive techniques to generate ideas, information, and perspectives. Chapter 3 presents case studies of writers using several of these strategies to plan their compositions. As a preview, here are thumbnail descriptions of these techniques.

- **Freewriting:** When you freewrite, you simply try to write, nonstop, for a set period of time—perhaps five to ten minutes—about whatever comes to mind when you think about your subject matter. Freewriting is sometimes difficult because it requires that you turn off your internal editor, that little voice inside your head that says what you *shouldn't write* because it might not be correct. Freewriting allows you to get as much writing accomplished as possible without concerning yourself with clarity, organization, or usage. The assumption is that you will shape, revise, amplify, and correct your prose as you proceed to work on a composition. Because writers often fear error overmuch at the beginning of a writing process, freewriting can allow good ideas and interesting perceptions to emerge and not get suppressed by the pressure to be right.

- **Keeping a journal:** Many writers keep a **journal** where they record their observations, their thoughts, and their responses to their reading. They may respond to prompts from their teachers or write self-generated questions and concerns. A person who writes in a journal for 20 minutes three times a week will generate a substantial amount of material that, like freewriting, can serve to encourage the flow of ideas. Journal writing can often become the basis for more formal writing.

- **Conversations:** Just talking, either with one friend or classmate or a group, can be a productive way to generate material for a composition. The better you know your conversational partners, the more you and they can ask probing questions, offer competing or complementary insights, and suggest new avenues that you should pursue in a writing project. Listening well and speaking up are ways to nurture what a writer knows and to suggest what a writer needs to know. Good talk may be your most effective strategy for invention.

Arrangement

Once a writer invents—comes up with topics, decides on a focus, plans an argumentative strategy, considers proof, and maybe writes a draft or a beginning of one—the writer begins to consider how and where to place ideas, facts, and examples to make them most effective. The second canon of rhetoric is arrangement. Just as the concepts underlying the first canon, invention, help you both to analyze the texts written by someone else and to plan your own compositions, so too can the principles of arrangement help you as both reader and writer.

The principles of arrangement help a writer plan to (1) order and structure the parts of a piece of writing and (2) support the different parts. Clearly, the principles of invention and arrangement work hand in hand. As a writer, your goal in invention is to discover ideas and to take inventory of everything you might say to make your position clear and compelling. Your goal in arrangement is to select the best and most appropriate ideas, examples, and propositions from that inventory and to decide how to order the parts of the composition most effectively to help you achieve your purpose.

Genres

An important principle that helps govern arrangement is genre, the type of composition writers produce. As you recall from Chapter 1, a writer decides which genre to produce based on the context at hand and the aim he or she wants to accomplish in that context. Genres usually have their own rules for arrangement. At the beginning of this book, we noted how a script writer would make decisions about the scene based on the kind of film the scene was a part of, its genre. To take another example, scholarship applications require different formats—openings, details, endings—than science reports, in which you'd include an abstract, an explanation of the research question, a description of methods and materials, a report on findings, a discussion of results, and a list of published works you referenced. And a sonnet you might write to a sweetheart would be arranged in fourteen lines of iambic pentameter, perhaps divided according to traditional Shakespearean form into quatrains, with a final two lines, or couplet. All these guidelines about how to write a sonnet, a lab report, or an application letter revolve around genre and conventions of arrangement.

Since most of the genres a writer must produce have their own rules of arrangement, it doesn't do you much good to look for one pattern of arrangement that works for all genres. To put it simply, there is no single pattern, no particular format, that will work in every writing situation. To be sure, though, almost every composition you write and every text you analyze have a beginning, a middle, and an end. In general terms, we can talk about the function of those sections.

- The beginning of a composition usually sets out the central question the paper will answer or the argument the paper will develop and hints at how the development will proceed.
- The middle of a paper usually offers points in support of the answer to the central question or the argument and substantiates or explores those points with examples, illustrations, details, and reasons.
- The end of a paper usually draws together the material developed in the middle and addresses the question "So what?" That is, the end tells readers what they might consider or act upon.

This basic pattern of beginning, middle, and end, in addition to making intuitive sense, also has historical roots in the literature of ancient rhetorical theory. Aristotle, for example, wrote in his *Rhetoric* that a composition needs to have only what some people might consider the middle section: a statement of the argument, including its central and supporting points, and a proof of those points. Introductions and conclusions, according to Aristotle, are optional and should be added in situations where the audience needs to have the argument introduced in the beginning and drawn together, or synthesized, at the end. Aristotle's teacher, Plato, on the other hand, wrote that a composition should be like a body—it needs to have a head, a torso, and feet.

As rhetorical theory developed in the 500-odd years following Aristotle's death in 322 B.C.E., teachers of rhetoric described in increasingly formal terms the principles of arrangement that then guided the construction of persuasive compositions. Most teachers of rhetoric in ancient Rome, for example, taught their students to produce a six-part speech, consisting of **exordium,** or introduction; narration; partition; confirmation; refutation; and peroration, or conclusion.

- In the **exordium,** literally the *web* that draws listeners into the speech, the speaker would introduce the subject at hand and include material that would make the audience both attentive and receptive to the argument.
- The **narration** would offer background material on the case at hand.
- The **partition** would divide the case and make clear which part or parts the speaker was going to address, which parts the speaker would not take up, and what order would be followed in the development.
- The **confirmation** would offer points to substantiate the argument and provide reasons, details, illustrations, and examples in support of those points.
- The **refutation** would consider possible objections to the argument or its supporting points and try to counter these objections.
- The **peroration** would draw together the entire argument and include material designed to compel the audience to think or act in a way consonant with the central argument.

The six-part oration was never intended to be a general format, a plan of arrangement for all arguments. It was a format for a specific genre—the courtroom declamation, in which an orator would speak on behalf of himself or a client he was called upon to represent. Now, the six-part oration is a strategic resource for readers to use in examining the many arrangement options in writing they read and for writers to use in planning moves of their own.

Functional Parts

What are these moves? What should you look for when you analyze arrangement? First of all, you can look at the entire text you are analyzing and try to divide it into some **functional parts,** remembering while you do so that not all texts are going to have all parts. Ask yourself these questions:

1. Is there some section that clearly lets the reader know what subject the composition is about and what the writer's purpose is? If so, where does this section begin and end? In this section, can you find an answer to the central question that the text has been written in response to, or can you find an indication of the text's central argument?

2. Is there a part that explains any background information that the reader needs to know in order to be able to understand the answer to

the central question or argument that the composition offers? If so, where does this section begin and end?

3. Is there some sentence or paragraph that focuses the readers' attention on some particular issue, aspect, or **theme** that the paper will examine in contrast to others that it might?

4. Is there some section that purposefully sets out material in support of the paper's answer to the central question or its argument? If so, where does this section begin and end?

5. Is there a part that examines possible objections to the answer, argument, or supporting material? If so, where does this section begin and end?

6. Is there a sentence or section where the writer specifically answers the "So what?" question? In other words, is there a section where the writer hints at what he or she hopes readers will think and do on the basis of what they have read in the text?

By answering these questions, you can get a sense, at least provisionally, of how the parts of the text work.

Activity

Return to the column by Joel Caris, "Corporate Sponsorship of Our Schools," on page 41. Ask the six questions above about the editorial, and discuss your answers with the members of a small group.

Questions About the Parts

Now you can turn your attention to analyzing the effectiveness of the way the writer works within the parts. If you can find a part that lets the reader know the subject of the composition and the writer's purpose, you might ask yourself questions like these:

- Are the subject and purpose directly stated or implied? How does the *degree* to which these elements are revealed or concealed strike you as a reader?

- Is some angle consciously foregrounded and other material downplayed? What is the effect of this foregrounding versus backgrounding in the opening section?

- Is there a statement that suggests to the reader the course that the remainder of the paper will take? How does the presence (or absence) of such a statement affect your reading?

If you can identify a part that explains any background information necessary for the reader to know in order to understand the paper's position, ask yourself the following questions:

- Is there a statement about the direction that this part of the paper will take—any terms or phrases at the beginning of paragraphs or passages that help you move through the material, or words like "first," "second," or "last"? What effect do these words have on you as a reader?
- Does the writer follow any discernable order in providing this background information? Is the order chronological (arranged by time)? spatial (arranged by location)? incremental (arranged by order of importance)? What effect does the ordering of the material have on you as a reader?
- Does the writer provide transitional words or phrases that connect the sentences or paragraphs of this part? Do these words or phrases suggest that the writer is *continuing* and *adding on* to the material already presented, relating a *result* to what came earlier, or *contrasting* what comes later with what appeared earlier?

If you can identify a sentence or paragraph that focuses the readers' attention on some particular issue, aspect, or theme that the paper examines, in contrast to others that it might, ask yourself questions like these:

- What does the writer do that *brings to the forefront* some material and consciously *puts in the background* other material? What is the effect of this foregrounding versus backgrounding in this section?
- Is there a sentence that suggests the course that the remainder of the paper will take? What effect does this mapping have on you as a reader?

If you can find a part that concentrates on support of the paper's central question or its argument, ask yourself these questions:

- Are there words or sentences that map out the direction a part of the paper will take—words like "first," "second," or "last," for example? What effect do these devices have on you as a reader?
- Do you detect any of the following methods of development in this section: relating anecdotes or longer stories, describing scenes and evoking sensory images, defining terms and concepts, dividing the whole into parts, classifying the parts according to some principle, or providing cause-and-effect reasoning? What effect on you as a reader do any of these methods of development have?

If you can identify a part that examines possible objections to the answer, argument, or supporting material, ask yourself questions like these:

- Is there language that suggests the writer wants to *counter* the objections? What is this language? What effect does it have on you as a reader?
- Does some language suggest that the writer wants to *concede* the objections? What is this language, and what is its effect on you?

Finally, if you can identify a part where the writer specifically addresses the question "So what?" ask yourself the following questions:

- Is there a direct charge to readers to think or act in a new way after reading the piece, or does the writer imply new ways of thinking and acting? How does the *degree* to which these elements are revealed (or perhaps concealed) persuade you?
- What does the writer do with the words, phrases, and sentences in this part to give the composition a *sound* of finality? What effect does this language have on you as a reader?

If you can generate good answers to these questions by referring to places in the text, you will have done a thorough analysis of its arrangement. In addition, you will have given yourself ideas to ponder when you follow conventions to arrange the genre that is appropriate for your own writing situation.

Activity

In a small group or by yourself, take a careful look at one of two kinds of texts, perhaps a paper you have recently written for one of your classes and a column on the op-ed page (that is, the page opposite the editorial page) of a major daily newspaper. Use the six groups of questions on pages 53–54 to identify the functional parts of the text. Then use the questions on pages 54–55 to analyze the effectiveness of the arrangement within each part.

Style

Simply put, style, the third canon of rhetoric, consists of the choices a writer makes regarding words, phrases, and sentences. To begin thinking about style, consider this hypothetical situation (or perhaps the situation is not completely hypothetical for you): Two people you know show up in class generally looking very different. One wears bright-colored clothes, with lots of flowing scarves and elaborate accessories—pins, bracelets, and necklaces. The other dresses completely in black—top, pants, socks, and shoes—and wears no accessories. Underneath, are both people alike, or does style reflect personality? Is style governed by occasion and appropriateness? Do you think these people make conscious choices about their style?

These questions provide a good entry point for thinking about style in writing. Each of the people described above has a style of dress, and every writer and piece of writing have a style. People choose styles to reflect themselves in their writing as well as in what they wear, and the style they choose expresses meaning. A particular clothing style or writing style can be appropriate in some situations and not in others. And, for all these reasons, stylistic choice in clothes and writing is, or can be, conscious. Conscious choice about stylistic decisions in writing can help writers reflect themselves, communicate meaning, and influence readers.

Style and Situation

If you are the kind of person who likes definite answers, style can be a baffling subject. Whether you are analyzing the style of a piece of writing or planning your own composition, the answer to nearly every question you might pose about whether particular words, sentences, or figures of speech is a *good* choice is almost always the same: "It depends."

"What does it depend on?" you might ask (or "Upon what does it depend?" if you want to vary your style!). It depends on the concept of *situational appropriateness.* Remember that all writing emerges from a situation—a convergence of a need to write, a writer, an audience, a subject matter, a purpose, a genre, and a time and place. The question of whether a particular word, sentence, or figure of speech is right is a question of whether it is right *for the particular writing situation.*

Consider, for example, the situation when you are required to write an analytical paper for a history class.

1. The need to write comes from the inquiry you are engaged in. The study of history involves many documents and incidents that are open to interpretation, and people write about history in order to close gaps in knowledge and to offer a possible reading of the past that makes good sense to other people interested in the same historical period.

2. You, the historian, are the writer. As a historian, you are expected to come across as a person who is genuinely interested in history, uses the terminology that historians use, employs their methods for interpreting texts and events, and generates the kind of reasoned, supported points in your writing that they admire.

3. You may think the audience for your paper is only your history teacher, but it's wise to think about the teacher as a member of a larger intellectual community of historians, who expect you to behave like one of them when you are writing a paper for their deliberation.

4. The subject matter is likely an aspect of the particular period of history you are studying—an economic, cultural, military, or social aspect—which might have some special terminology associated with it that you could be expected to use in your composition.

5. The purpose of your composition is to show you understand the history you write about enough to explain the particular piece of it you examine. Your goal is to present a clear, unified analysis of some historical material; to organize your analysis around a strong, salient thesis; and to support your thesis with a documented summary and with paraphrases, and quotations of material from primary and secondary historical texts.

6. The genre is the academic analytic paper, a composition that introduces the subject; states a thesis; provides ample points in support of the thesis; backs each point up with examples, reasons, illustrations, and details; and then offers a conclusion that reinforces the thesis for an audience of other historians.

7. The time and place for such a project are generally an academic term in a high school, college, or university, and all varieties of academic prose follow a rich array of stylistic choices.

Each of these individual elements in the writing situation, as well as the situation as a whole, can influence the choices you make involving words, sentences, and **figurative language.** Considering these situational elements carefully can help you decide, for example, whether to employ special terminology, to use first-person singular pronouns (*I, me, my, mine*) or to refer to the reader in the second person (*you, your, yours*), to use **contractions,** and to choose active or passive voice.

Style and Jargon

Many writing communities—academic disciplines, professional organizations, and so on—demonstrate an ambivalent attitude toward the use of specialized terminology. Admonitions such as "write for the general reader" or "avoid 20-dollar words" appear regularly in professional guides to effective writing. These cautionary statements are wise—to a certain extent. Good writers usually want to develop a style that the well-educated, diligent reader will find accessible. Moreover, writers who choose to use elaborate, complicated words *for no good reason in the writing situation* can often produce baffling, even comic effects. (A true story: One of the authors had a student who wrote the following sentence in a paper for a junior English course: "When my cat expired, I waxed lachrymose." When asked what she meant, the student said, "When my cat died, I started crying." The instructor urged her to use the simpler words.)

Such guiding statements as these, however, tend to oversimplify the actual word choice practices of communities of readers and writers. It's a plain fact that many communities have specialized vocabularies that readers expect to encounter in the community's documents and that writers new to the community are expected to know and use. Outsiders to the community often refer disparagingly to these sets of terms as **jargon,** but jargon is not necessarily bad. The use of specialized, complicated terms becomes a problem only when a writer (1) does not understand what the terms mean or (2) uses the terms in a composition that will have an audience beyond the community of readers and writers who know the terminology. The latter case becomes even more troubling when writers use jargon, either purposefully or subconsciously, to establish their insider status in a community, knowing that their readers are not part of it.

Are You and I Okay?

Young writers in nearly all intellectual communities often feel confused about whether they may use first-person and second-person pronouns and whether they may use contractions in their compositions. Once again, the answer depends on the situation. For most academic papers, like the analytical paper for history described above, the use of first-person pronouns is not appropriate because the focus in this kind of writing is on the subject rather than on the person writing about the subject. Further, in such papers, it is not appropriate for writers to refer directly to their readers as *you*. On the other hand, if the situation calls on writers to offer a personal response to a piece of literature or a historical event, then it would be inappropriate for someone to tackle this task *without* writing in the first person. Similarly, if the situation calls for an open letter on a controversial issue to congressional representatives working on legislation to address it, then it would be nearly impossible for the writer to produce a successful letter that did not refer to the representatives directly as *you*.

Style and Contractions

The use of contractions is also governed by the notion of appropriateness. In most formal, academic papers, and in business-oriented letters and reports, writers generally avoid contractions like *it's, can't, wouldn't,* and *doesn't.* In informal papers and personal letters, writers should feel free to use the same kinds of words, including contractions, they would speak to their audience if they encountered them face to face. To contract or not to contract depends on the writer's intention, in terms of relationship with the reader and with the subject matter at hand.

Style and the Passive Voice

Guides to effective writing in many fields often urge writers to "write in the active voice" and "avoid the passive voice." That's good advice but limited in its applicability. Remember the difference between sentences in the active voice and those in the passive voice. An active voice sentence follows this pattern:

> DOER → ACTION → RECEIVER
> The lab technician filtered the solution.

A passive voice sentence follows this pattern:

> RECEIVER → ACTION (BY DOER)
> The solution was filtered.
> The solution was filtered by the lab technician.

Notice three differences between the active and the passive. First, since the active voice emphasizes who did what, many readers think active sentences are stronger and more forceful. Second, since a passive-voice verb always consists of a helping verb and a main verb, sentences in the passive voice are often wordier than sentences in the active voice. Third, the doer of the action in a passive-voice sentence is expressed in a prepositional phrase following the verb, and passive-voice sentences are grammatically complete without this phrase—as "The solution was filtered" demonstrates. Therefore, some readers maintain that the passive voice is potentially irresponsible—that passive-voice sentences can conceal the doer of the action when the reader has a right to know who does what. Readers, teachers, and editors who make these claims are right. Active-voice sentences generally do sound stronger and more authoritative. Passive-voice sentences are often more difficult to process, and they do frequently conceal the doer of the action.

But a writer can rarely avoid using the passive voice altogether. It can't be done. (Notice the passive-voice sentence.) Once again, situational appropriateness needs to be your guide when you are analyzing or planning style. Passive-voice sentences occur frequently in scientific and technical writing, where writers are trying to emphasize not who did what but what was done. Writers also use the passive voice, consciously or subconsciously, to shift material around in a sentence. As any editor will explain, the most emphatic position in any sentence is usually at or near the end, and employing the passive voice is one of several ways a writer can emphasize a subject by moving it from beginning to end of the sentence.

Dimensions of the Study of Style: Sentences, Words, and Figures

Three broad categories of style help writers to analyze the style of a text and to make their own stylistic choices. Every choice we analyze or make in these categories potentially affects the meaning of a composition, the reader's perceptions of the credibility of the writer, and the willingness of the reader to accept the text's argument or exploration. These categories are

- **Sentences:** grammatical type, placement of details, variety
- **Words:** level of elaborateness and formality, difficulty, technicality
- **Figures:** schemes and tropes (terms defined below), figurative language

Sentences

Sentences can be classified in many ways, and it's helpful to consider the potential effect a particular type of sentence might have on a reader in a certain situation. One of the most basic ways of classifying sentences is according to the number and type of clauses in them.

- A **simple sentence** has a single independent clause.

  Abraham Lincoln struggled to save the Union.

Within its single clause, a simple sentence can have a **compound subject,** a compound verb, or both.

  Abraham Lincoln and Andrew Johnson struggled to save the Union.

  Abraham Lincoln struggled to save the Union and persevered.

  Abraham Lincoln and Andrew Johnson struggled to save the Union and persevered.

- A **compound sentence** has two clauses, each of which could exist as a simple sentence if you removed the conjunction connecting them.

  Abraham Lincoln struggled to save the Union, and Andrew Johnson assisted him.

  Abraham Lincoln and Andrew Johnson struggled to save the Union and persevered, but the leaders of the Confederacy insisted that the rights of the states were more important than the maintenance of the Union.

- A **complex sentence** has two clauses, one independent and at least one subordinate to the main clause.

  When the leaders of the Confederacy insisted that the rights of the states were more important than the maintenance of the Union, Abraham Lincoln and Andrew Johnson struggled to save the Union and persevered.

- A **compound-complex sentence** has the defining features of both a compound sentence and a complex sentence.

  When the leaders of the Confederacy insisted that the rights of the states were more important than the maintenance of the Union, Abraham Lincoln struggled to save the Union and persevered, and Andrew Johnson assisted him.

Why should you be concerned with whether a sentence is simple, compound, complex, or compound-complex when you are analyzing someone else's writing or planning your own? The answer is that function grows out of form. When you need to make a succinct point, often a short, simple sentence will do so effectively. A short, simple sentence can suggest to a reader that you are in control, that you *want* to make a strong point. If you're trying to show how ideas are balanced and related in terms of equal importance, a compound sentence can convey that to the reader. A single compound sentence or a series of them in a composition can suggest to your reader that you are the kind of person who takes a balanced view of challenging issues, that you want to give equal weight to more than one side of an issue. If you want to show more complicated relationships between ideas, then complex and compound-complex sentences can communicate the intricacies of your thinking. A single complex or compound-complex sentence or a series of them can cue a reader that yours is a mind that willingly takes up complicated issues and tries to make sense of them, both for yourself and for your readers.

A second method of analyzing sentences looks at them in terms of another important structural distinction—as **loose sentences** or **periodic sentences.** Just as writers can vary the number and type of clauses in a sentence according to the subject they are treating and the effect they are trying to have on readers, so can writers vary sentences along the loose-periodic continuum to achieve similar goals.

Sentences vary along the loose-periodic continuum according to how they incorporate extra details in relation to basic sentence elements. As you know, the basic elements of every sentence in English are subjects, verbs, and complements. Here is a sentence with just two basic elements:

> Abraham Lincoln wept.

A loose sentence is a basic sentence with details added *immediately at the end* of the basic sentence elements:

> Abraham Lincoln wept, fearing that the Union would not survive if the southern states seceded.

A periodic sentence is a sentence in which additional details are placed in one of two positions, either *before* the basic sentence elements or *in the middle of them.* Here is a periodic sentence that results from putting additional details before the basic sentence elements:

> Alone in his study, lost in somber thoughts about his beloved country, dejected but not broken in spirit, Abraham Lincoln wept.

And here is a periodic sentence that results from placing additional material in the middle of the basic sentence elements:

> Abraham Lincoln, alone in his study, lost in somber thoughts about his beloved country, dejected but not broken in spirit, wept.

Understanding the concepts of loose and periodic, you can achieve sentence variety by writing sentences that move along a loose-periodic continuum. The next sentence tends more toward loose than periodic:

> Abraham Lincoln considered the Union an inviolable, almost eternally inspired, concept.

And the next one tends more toward periodic than loose:

> Abraham Lincoln, a self-taught philosopher, a political scientist even before there was such a field, considered the Union an inviolable, almost eternally inspired, concept.

You can hear the differences in these sentences—in what is emphasized, as well as in how quickly a reader reads them. Writers use these types of sentences to effect changes in meaning. Readers use them to understand meaning more clearly. Since, as we just mentioned, the most emphatic position in a sentence is often at or near the end, and since the second most emphatic location is the beginning, recognizing and creating loose and periodic sentences enable the reader and the writer to make wise decisions about varying sentence structure for emphasis. Even more importantly, the structure of a sentence affects the pacing of a text. A loose sentence moves quickly, and a succession of loose sentences can make a piece of prose fairly gallop along. A periodic sentence works with delay—it postpones completing the sentence until after it has provided the details. In passages where a writer wants to sound crisp, businesslike, and efficient, the loose sentence will serve the writer well. In passages where a writer wants to sound balanced, deliberate, and thoughtful, a periodic sentence will be a useful tool.

Good writers make informed decisions about sentence structure. They know their sentences not only carry meaning but also affect readers, causing them, often subconsciously, to evaluate the ethos of the writer and empathize with the writer's position. Sentence structure says much about the writer and his or her purpose, credibility, and goals.

Activities

1. Do you think the following sentence from Booker T. Washington's *Up from Slavery* is loose or periodic?

   > In order to defend and protect the women and children who were left on the plantation when the white males went to war, the slaves would lay down their lives.

   Rewrite the sentence in a couple of ways, experimenting with making it more loose and more periodic. In a small group, discuss how changes affect tone, purpose, and the ethos of the speaker.

2. Change the first sentence of an essay you are working on to make it more periodic or more loose. What difference does the change make in your piece or in your voice?

Parallel Structure

One particular feature of style that good writers know how to use and careful readers frequently notice is **parallelism,** or parallel structure. The basic principle of parallel structure is quite simple: When a passage, a paragraph, or a sentence contains two or more ideas that are fulfilling a similar function, a writer who wants to sound measured, deliberate, and balanced will express those ideas in the same grammatical form—words balance words, phrases balance phrases, clauses balance clauses, and sentences balance sentences.

One way to learn about parallel structure is to recognize passages or sentences that violate it. Consider, for example, the following sentence from a student's paper about a short story by Larry Kramer:

> In these moments, Rivka discovers the bitter truth about her husband's hidden life, her son's death, and that Herman was not sending her the letters all along.

This sentence, as you can see, contains three elements, all serving the same function—they are all the things that Rivka "discovers the bitter truth about." The sentence doesn't work stylistically, though, because not all three elements are in the same grammatical form. The first two are noun phrases—a noun preceded by modifiers—while the third is a clause, a group of words with a subject and verb. There are two ways to revise the sentence to achieve parallel structure, both of which make the writer sound more careful, deliberate, and in control:

> In these moments, Rivka discovers the bitter truth about her husband's hidden life, her son's death, and Herman's deceit about the letters. [a revision making all three elements noun phrases]

> In these moments, Rivka discovers the bitter truth about how her husband had lived, her son had died, and Herman had deceived her about the letters. [a revision making all three elements clauses]

> In these moments, Rivka discovers the bitter truth that her husband had led a hidden life, her son had died, and Herman had not sent her the letters all along. [an alternative revision with three clauses]

Here's another example of a breakdown in parallel structure, this one from a published magazine article:

> What happens to a leading writer after he gets a MacArthur genius grant, a Getty fellowship, and his new book hits number one on the nonfiction bestseller list?

Notice the three elements serving the same function in this sentence—three things that happen to this "leading writer." The sentence is a stylistic clunker, though—the writer sounds less deliberate and balanced than she might—because the three elements are not in the same grammatical form. Look at how the sentence might be revised:

> What happens to a leading writer after he gets a MacArthur genius grant, wins a Getty fellowship, and has a book in the number-one position on the nonfiction bestseller list? [three elements as verbs followed by direct objects and modifiers]

> What happens to a leading writer after he gets a MacArthur genius grant, a Getty fellowship, and a number-one ranking on the nonfiction bestseller list? [three elements as noun phrases serving as objects of *gets*]

With practice, you'll learn to notice parallel structure in sentences you read, to change nonparallel elements as you read, and to create parallel structures in your own compositions. (Notice the parallel structure in that sentence? Three things fulfilling the same function, all signaled by the infinitive *to*.) An even greater challenge than working with parallel structure at the sentence level, however, is to analyze it in longer passages you might read and to create such a passage in your own writing. Abraham Lincoln was a master at the parallel construction. His most famous work, the brief but eloquent Gettysburg Address, ends with a paragraph that is a tour-de-force of parallel structure.

> But in a larger sense, we cannot dedicate, we cannot consecrate, we cannot hallow this ground. The brave men, living and dead who struggled here, have consecrated it far above our poor power to add or detract. The world will little note nor long remember what we say here, but it can never forget what they did here. It is for us the living rather to be dedicated here to the unfinished work, which they who fought here have thus far so nobly advanced. It is rather for us to be here dedicated to the great task remaining before us—that from these honored dead we take increased devotion to that cause for which they gave the last full measure of devotion—that we here highly resolve that these dead shall not have died in vain, that this nation under God shall have a new birth of freedom, and that government of the people, by the people, for the people shall not perish from the earth.

Notice the sense of measured balance in this paragraph created by the repeated parallel structures. In the first sentence, Lincoln creates a strong triplet of clauses, all with the same direct object:

> we cannot dedicate, we cannot consecrate, we cannot hallow this ground

In the third sentence, he balances two verbs, each modified by an adverb:

> The world will little note nor long remember

The final sentence brings the speech to a powerful conclusion with two sets of parallel structures: a set of three clauses beginning with *that*

> that we here highly resolve, that this nation under God shall have, and that the government of the people

plus the triad of three of the most famous prepositional phrases in the English language

> government of the people, by the people, and for the people

Activities

1. Consider the following passage by Patricia Williams, a prominent lawyer and legal theorist. In a small group, point out Williams's use of parallel structure, and discuss how it appeals to readers.

   > Money buys self-esteem. If you're poor, you can't be happy because you're the object of revulsion and ridicule; if you're poor, you can't accept it as fate because poverty is your fault; and if you're poor, you have to resent the

upper classes because competition—or economic revenge—is the name of the game, the only way out.

2. Using parallel construction, write the first sentence for one of these stereotypical first-day-of-class assignments:

>   My Favorite Hobbies
>
>   Summer Vacation
>
>   When I'm Fifty

Words

When skillful writers make decisions about style and when perceptive readers analyze the style of a document they read, they pay careful attention to diction, or the choice of words. *Diction* strikes some people as an odd term to refer to word choice—to many people, diction means "pronunciation." The word *diction* comes from Latin *dictio,* which means "style of speech." In ancient Greece and Rome, when rhetoricians were more concerned with speaking than writing, *dictio* meant "choice of words," and *pronunciatio* referred to the actual speaking of them. When this book uses *diction,* it reflects the classical meaning.

As with sentences, a study of diction depends on situation and genre. In other words, when you are writing a paper and you wonder about using a certain word in a sentence, you need to ask yourself first of all, "What is my purpose, who is my audience, and what kind of text am I writing?" Then ask, "Is it *appropriate* to use the word?" A word that might work perfectly well in one situation and in one type of writing could be completely out of place in another situation and genre.

To make these considerations more real, think about three different types of compositions you might be called upon to produce about the same subject. We'll carry this hypothetical set of writing tasks through the chapter to give some illustrations of the terms we bring up. Imagine you are writing about recreational sports at your school—not organized or competitive sports but activities such as intramural sports teams, recreation nights for the community, and clubs. Think about the kind of document you'd produce in three different settings, or contexts.

- In a public-health class where research is important, you'd produce a researched, documented position paper about the benefits of recreational sports.
- For a Web site sponsored by a real-estate company, you'd write informative pages about the types of recreational sports the schools offer to students and to citizens who live in the community,

■ In a letter to a friend, you'd write about your own participation in recreational sports.

Imagine that in each case you'll have a section in the document to explain the advantages of participating in recreational sports—improved physical health, improved mental health, improved coordination, and social benefits. In each piece, you'd vary your word choice to describe those advantages.

Activity

Write the first sentence of your imaginary piece on recreational sports in each of the three settings.

General Versus Specific Words

The famous twentieth-century language expert S. I. Hayakawa in his book *Language in Thought and Action* described a phenomenon he called "the ladder of abstraction." At the top of the ladder were general, often quite abstract terms, like *transportation* and *justice;* near the middle rungs were slightly more specific terms, like *automobiles* and *juvenile court;* and near the bottom of the ladder were specific, concrete terms like *my 2001 green Subaru Forester* and *the offender's five-year probation sentence for shoplifting.* A good writer, Hayakawa claimed, is able to move up and down the ladder of abstraction like a monkey in a tree.

Notice how you could use the ladder of abstraction to vary the key terms in your explanation of the benefits of participating in recreational sports. Just considering one of the four benefits at the abstract, general level, you could refer to *physical health benefits.* Slightly more specifically, you could refer to the same thing as *cardiovascular health benefits.* Slightly more specifically, you could write about *benefits to the heart.* Near the bottom of the ladder of abstraction, you could concentrate on *the benefits to the small blood vessels around your heart.* But why, you might wonder, would any writer want to vary his or her diction in this way? The answer lies in the situation and the genre. A community of scholars in public health might look in a research paper, like the hypothetical one you're writing, for information about *cardiovascular health benefits.* Readers of a Web site about schools might simply want to see that your school's recreational sports program emphasizes general *physical health benefits.* Your distant friend, to whom you have written an e-mail about participating in your school's intramural sports program, might be most interested to know that a strenuous game of volleyball can strengthen and create *small blood vessels around your heart.* You vary the generality or specificity of your diction in order to address your readers in terms most useful to them.

Formal Versus Informal Words

Varying your diction on this dimension is like going to a dance. For an informal occasion at someone's house or a local club, the dress is casual—jeans, T-shirts, and so on. But for a formal dance like a prom, the dress is formal—tuxedos and gowns. Your writing situations can be seen as occasions that require an understanding of the level of formality, and your diction ought to suit the occasion.

What are some of the ways in which diction varies in formality? Some of the ways to make your diction more formal will be considered in the following sections, which take up Latinate or Anglo-Saxon words and slang or colloquialisms. For now, let's consider just two areas that raise formal-versus-informal concerns: contractions and pronoun reference.

A research paper for an academic class, such as the hypothetical one you're writing for your public health class, represents a formal writing occasion, and in such a paper, you should probably prefer *have not* to *haven't*, *would have* to *would've*, and *is not* to *isn't*. Your contribution to the Web site about the recreational sports program at your school is a slightly less formal writing occasion than the research paper; nonetheless, you might prefer the full words instead of the contractions. The e-mail to your friend, however, would be informal, so contractions would be more appropriate. (Notice that we, the two authors, consider this book to be somewhere in the middle of this formal-to-informal continuum, so we feel free to use contractions.)

Is it appropriate to use first-person references (*I, me, my, mine, we, us, our, ours*) in a paper? Like most other stylistic decisions, situation and genre determine appropriateness. Most teachers and editors prefer that writers do not write in the first person in formal writing situations such as the one calling for the research paper. The Web site might effectively use first-person pronouns if you were describing your personal involvement in the recreational activities. And, of course, a friend would worry if you didn't use first person when you e-mailed.

The question of pronoun use in formal and informal papers raises two additional issues. The first is the use of the impersonal *we* in formal papers. Consider three sentences that might go into your hypothetical research paper:

> I develop multiple intelligences by participating in recreational sports.
> We develop multiple intelligences by participating in recreational sports.
> Participating in recreational sports helps develop multiple intelligences.

The first would probably not be appropriate since the aim of research is to investigate the subject rather than the writer. The second sentence also seems inappropriate since the *we* is unspecified. The impersonal *we* is used most frequently in newspaper editorials or in documents where the writer can actually be sure he or she is writing on behalf of a collective body—such as the editorial board of the newspaper, the governing board of the corporation, or the leaders of the political party. Although there are exceptions, in some science research, for example, you're probably on safest ground using the third sentence in formal research essays, the one with no pronoun reference at all.

The second issue involving pronoun reference is the grammatical concern of pronoun-antecedent agreement. In formal grammar, a pronoun is supposed to agree in number and gender with the word it refers to, its antecedent, and the phrase *a person* is a singular construction. If you were to write

> A person learns to take advantage of a different part of their intelligence than they normally use

your pronoun and antecedent won't agree. How could you write the same sentence and stay within the boundaries of the rule? You have several options. One is to use singular pronouns:

> A person learns to take advantage of a different part of his intelligence than he normally uses

OR

> A person learns to take advantage of a different part of her intelligence than she normally uses.

If you choose to follow this option, you should make an effort to *alternate* the use of the singular pronouns, sometimes using the masculine and sometimes the feminine.

A second option is to use *he or she,* or *him or her.* Alternatively, you may use a hyphenated or slashed phrase that includes both the masculine and the feminine in your reference:

> A person learns to take advantage of a different part of his/her intelligence than he/she normally uses.

This option takes care of pronoun-antecedent agreement and includes both the masculine and feminine reference but is stylistically awkward and reads poorly. A third option pluralizes the antecedent, allowing you to make your pronoun and antecedent agree:

> People learn to take advantage of a different part of their intelligence than they normally use.

Latinate Versus Anglo-Saxon Words

Historically, English is something of a mongrel language. The ancestor of the English we speak and write today was called Old English, which was a Germanic language. The Old English spoken in the British Isles from around the fourth century to the eleventh century C.E. has been labeled Anglo-Saxon English because the two tribes of people who spoke it were the Angles and the Saxons. But around 1100 C.E., the language began to change. In 1066 C.E., England was invaded—and the English king overthrown—by a French king, William of Normandy. The Norman Invasion opened the door to a substantial infusion into English of words and phrases from the languages spoken in western Europe, notably France, Spain, and Italy. French, Spanish, and Italian are historically **romance languages,** so called because of their common roots in Latin, the language spoken in ancient Rome. After the Norman Invasion, and throughout the Renaissance, English came to acquire more and more words and phrases that had their origins in Latin. And because the people who helped bring this Latinate influence into the language tended to be the powerful nobility, the use of what is called **Latinate diction** has come to be associated with writing in more formal situations, while the use of what is called **Anglo-Saxon diction** has come to be linked with writing in more informal situations.

In general, you can recognize Latinate words by their multisyllabic construction in contrast to monosyllabic Anglo-Saxon words. A Latinate word usually consists of a root, derived from Latin, plus a prefix that qualifies the meaning of the root, a suffix that designates what part of speech the word is, or both. Consider, for example, the word *magnanimous.* The root is *anim,* which means "soul" or "spirit." The prefix is *magn,* which means "large." The suffix is *ous,* which indicates that the word is an adjective. Thus, magnanimous is an English word, with Latinate word parts, meaning "kind, noble, or honorable." Notice that the brief, Anglo-Saxon word *kind* is simpler and seems more direct, and in many writing situations, you might use *kind* instead of *magnanimous.* In others, you'd choose the longer word for its appropriateness to the situation and genre or for the subtle difference in meaning between the two words.

How might the Latinate versus Anglo-Saxon distinction affect your writing of your three pieces about recreational sports? You could refer to the activity as *participating* (a Latinate word) in recreational sports or *playing* (an Anglo-Saxon word) recreational sports. You could claim that "participating in recreational sports employs multiple intelligences" (several Latinate words), or you could say that "playing recreational sports uses different parts of your mind" (several Anglo-Saxon words). You could assert that "participating in recreational sports facilitates social interaction" (several Latinate words), or you could write that "playing recreational sports helps you make friends" (several Anglo-Saxon words). The Latinate constructions seem more formal and might be more appropriate in the research paper than on the Web site or in the e-mail to your friend.

Activity

Consider several pairs of terms that illustrate both Latinate diction and Anglo-Saxon diction in English:

- *Facilitate* **(Latinate) versus** *help* **(Anglo-Saxon):** both words mean "to make easier."
- *Manufacture* **(Latinate) versus** *make* **(Anglo-Saxon):** the roots of *manufacture* suggest that it means "to make by hand," but over the centuries, it has come simply to mean "to make."

- *Interrogate* **(Latinate) versus** *ask* **(Anglo-Saxon):** *interrogate* derives from both the Latin for "to ask," *rogare,* and the prefix *inter,* meaning "between or among."
- *Maximize* and *minimize* (Latinate) versus *grow* and *shrink* (Anglo-Saxon).

In a small group, talk in specific terms about what kinds of writing situations would call for the more Latinate diction and what kinds of writing situations would call for the more Anglo-Saxon diction. Explain the difference in meaning and effect between the two words in each pair.

Common Terms Versus Slang or Jargon

Slang and jargon generally get a bad rap. Just look at how a popular online reference source, *Merriam-Webster's Collegiate Dictionary,* defines these two terms. **Slang** is either "language peculiar to a particular group" or "an informal, nonstandard vocabulary composed typically of coinages, arbitrarily changed words, and extravagant, forced, or facetious figures of speech." If you were to encounter the following sentence in a novel, you would probably recognize it as slang from the 1920s, known in America as the Jazz Age:

> I'd say let's ankle to the joint, but I got a gimp. Other than that, everything's jake.

What the character is saying is,

> I'd say let's walk to the restaurant, but I'm limping. Other than that, everything's fine.

Jargon is "confused, unintelligible language"; "a strange, outlandish, or barbarous language or **dialect**"; "a hybrid language or dialect simplified in vocabulary and grammar and used for communication between peoples of different speech"; "the technical terminology or characteristic idiom of a special activity or group"; or "obscure and often pretentious language marked by circumlocutions and long words." If you were to use the terms *drop-down menu* and *DKDC,* you would be using jargon common to online writing among Internet aficionados. A more common way to refer to these terms would be "a screen menu that drops down from a term when you point the cursor toward the term" and "don't know don't care."

Should you use slang or jargon in any of the hypothetical papers you are writing about recreational sports? A sentence such as the following would be out of place in the researched paper or the informative Web site:

> While some folks think playing volleyball is way old skool, others know it's a way to meet some phat friends and escape the rents for a couple hours.

That sentence might work in the e-mail to the friend, assuming the friend understands the slang terms. A sentence like this might work in your research paper:

> Some critics of intramural recreation programs find fault with their social hegemonic nature

while readers of the Web site or your friend might be confused or put off by the social-science jargon.

Both slang and jargon seem like dangerous territory for a writer because both employ language that might obscure a writer's message rather than clarify and simplify it. To a certain extent, that is true, and savvy writers ought to be aware of the simpler, more direct, more common words they could use. But, as with all questions involving style, a writer's decision about whether to use slang or jargon depends on the situation in which he or she is writing. As always, the question is this: "Given this subject matter, this purpose, this audience, and this type of writing, would slang or jargon be *appropriate?*" Sometimes the answer is yes. The use of slang or jargon can signal to your readers that you are a member of their group, that you are in solidarity with them, and that you have done your homework about a particularly complicated topic that is important to the community.

Denotation Versus Connotation

Intuitively, we all know that words can be loaded. A careful reader always notes how a text capitalizes on the multiple meanings of words, and a careful writer chooses and arranges words so that the reader catches subtle, suggested meanings.

Consider these two simple sentences:

> Wilbert Newton is a perfect example of a statesman.
> Wilbert Newton is a perfect example of a politician.

This Newton fellow would probably be pleased if someone said the first sentence about him. *Statesman* suggests responsibility, intelligence, and high-mindedness. But he might be unhappy if someone said the second sentence about him, since *politician* often these days suggests self-serving or unprincipled behavior. The differences in meaning in these two sentences illustrate what scholars of language refer to as **denotation** and **connotation.** Denotation refers to a literal meaning of a word, while connotation refers to an association, emotional or otherwise, that the word evokes. Both sentences above use words that might have the same denotative meaning—elected official—but carry quite different connotations.

Figures of Rhetoric: Schemes and Tropes

One of the most time-honored methods of elaborating one's style is to employ **figures of rhetoric** in a piece of writing. A critical reader will learn to recognize when a writer is using one or more of the figures, just as a good writer will learn how to incorporate them effectively in a composition.

People have been teaching and learning about the figures since ancient Greece and Rome, when rhetoric began to be studied as an organized subject. In general, the classical rhetoricians divided the figures into two broad categories: schemes and tropes.

- A **scheme** is any artful variation from the typical arrangement of words in a sentence.
- A **trope** is any artful variation from the typical or expected way a word or idea is expressed.

In ancient Rome, and later in the European Middle Ages and Renaissance, scholars developed substantial lists of figures, categorizing them under these two general labels, and schoolchildren had to learn the definitions and find examples of the figures in literary works and public discourse. It would not have been unusual, for example, for a grammar school student in Renaissance England to be given a list of 300 or so names of schemes and tropes and to be required to memorize the definitions and produce an example of any one of them on demand. Students undertook this task not simply to learn how to vary their words, phrases, and sentences. They did so because their teachers believed that a different way of *saying* something about the world was also a different way of *seeing* something about the world. In other words, they taught that using figurative language to express ideas helped to clarify and sharpen a person's thinking—not a bad lesson for students even today.

You don't have to memorize 300 definitions to use figures. (You can consult any number of excellent handbooks and Internet sites. One particularly helpful resource is Professor Gideon Burton's Web site at Brigham Young University called *Silva Rhetoricae,* literally "the forest of rhetoric" at http://humanities.byu.edu/rhetoric/silva.htm.) But you can learn to recognize schemes and tropes by their functions and understand their effect on readers.

Schemes Involving Balance

The most common scheme involving balance is parallelism, which uses the same grammatical structure for similar items (see pages 63–66). Readers understand the equivalency of items in parallel construction and exercise the logical, systematic thinking abilities. In your sports paper, you might write parallel sentences like the following:

- **Parallelism of words:** Exercise physiologists argue that body-pump aerobics sessions benefit a person's heart and lungs, muscles and nerves, and joints and cartilage.
- **Parallelism of phrases:** Exercise physiologists argue that body-pump aerobics sessions help a person breathe more effectively, move with less discomfort, and avoid injury.

- **Parallelism of clauses:** Exercise physiologists argue that body-pump aerobics is the most efficient exercise class, that body-pump participants show greater gains in stamina than participants in comparable exercise programs, and that body-pump aerobics is less expensive in terms of equipment and training needed to lead or take classes.

Coincidentally, each of these three parallel schemes is also called a **zeugma,** a figure in which more than one item in a sentence is governed by a single word, usually a verb. Each of the three examples of parallelism involves a single verb, *argue,* that introduces a list of three words, phrases, or clauses.

A related scheme involving balance is **antithesis,** in which parallelism is used to juxtapose words, phrases, or clauses that contrast. With an antithesis, a writer tries to point out to the reader differences between two juxtaposed ideas rather than similarities. Here are three antitheses (note how to spell the plural) that might be appropriate in your sports research paper:

- **Antithesis of words:** When distance runners reach the state they call the zone, they find themselves mentally *engaged* yet *detached.*
- **Antithesis of phrases:** When distance runners reach the state they call the zone, they find themselves mentally *engaged with their physical surroundings* yet *detached from moment-to-moment concerns about their conditioning.*
- **Antithesis of clauses:** When distance runners reach the state they call the zone, they find *that they are empirically engaged with their physical surroundings,* yet *they are also completely detached from moment-to-moment concerns about their conditioning.*

A famous example of antithesis in clauses is "To err is human; to forgive, divine."

Another scheme that looks a great deal like antithesis is an **antimetabole** (anti-muh-**TI**-boh-lee), in which words are repeated in different grammatical forms. Well-known examples of antimetabole are "When the going gets tough, the tough get going" (adjective becomes noun; noun becomes verb); "You can take the kid out of the country, but you can't take the country out of the kid"; and the famous line from President John F. Kennedy's inaugural address: "Ask not what your country can do for you—ask what you can do for your country."

Schemes Involving Interruption

Sometimes, a writer needs to interrupt the flow of a passage in order to provide necessary, on-the-spot information or ideas to readers. Two schemes are especially useful for this purpose. The first goes by the name of **parenthesis** (the same word as the singular of parentheses, the punctuation marks). Here is a parenthesis embedded in a sentence from your hypothetical letter to your friend:

> Sports night at the school always brings out the would-be jocks—who would expect any different?—ready to show that they're potentially as good as the varsity players.

Notice that this parenthesis is set off by dashes, the punctuation marks most commonly used to set off an interruptive word, phrase, or clause. When you use dashes to set off an interruption, be sure to include them at the beginning and the end of the interruption. A parenthesis, however, can also be set off from the remainder of the sentences with parentheses:

> Sports night at the school always brings out the would-be jocks (who would expect any different?) ready to show that they're potentially as good as the varsity players.

Notice that a parenthesis in the form of a question, as in the example above, needs to be punctuated with a question mark. The same would hold true for a exclamatory word, phrase, or clause

> When sports night is canceled—oh, sorrowful day!—all the would-be jocks get a case of show-off withdrawal

but not for a simple declarative sentence:

> Sports night supervisors have to stop people from trying to slam dunk—this is the ultimate showboat move—for fear that one of the would-be jocks might hurt himself.

A second scheme useful for setting off additional material is an **appositive.** An appositive is a construction in which two coordinating elements are set side by side, and the second explains or modifies the first:

> Joe Weider, *a pioneer in personal weight training,* would marvel at the facilities open to today's student athletes.

Schemes Involving Omission

A writer occasionally needs to omit material from a sentence so that its rhythm is heightened and often accelerated and so that the readers will pay close attention to the potentially dramatic effect of the prose. Two schemes useful for this purpose are ellipsis and asyndeton (uh-**SIN**-duh-ton). An **ellipsis** is any omission of words, the meaning of which is provided by the overall context of the passage:

> In a hockey power play, if you pass the puck to the wing, and he to you, then you can close in on the goal.

The phrase *and he to you* omits the words *passes it,* but a reader can clearly infer the meaning. An **asyndeton** is an omission of conjunctions between related clauses:

> I skated, I shot, I scored, I cheered—what a glorious moment of sport!

Schemes Involving Repetition

Beginning writers are often warned not to be repetitive. That's good advice, as far as it goes; but it actually should be "Don't be repetitive, but use repetition." Several schemes involving repeating sounds or words can actually lead the reader to pay closer attention to the prose and to see the writer as a purposeful, forceful, even artistic writer. Some of these schemes will be familiar to you from studying literature.

- **Alliteration:** repetition of consonant sounds at the beginning or in the middle of two or more adjacent words:

  Intramural hockey is a strenuous, stimulating, satisfying sport.

- **Assonance:** repetition of vowel sounds in the stressed syllables of two or more adjacent words:

  A workout partner is finally a kind, reliable, right-minded helper.

- **Anaphora** (uh-**NA**-fuh-ruh): repetition of the same group of words at the beginning of successive clauses:

  Exercise builds stamina in young children; exercise builds stamina in teenagers and young adults; exercise builds stamina in older adults and senior citizens.

- **Epistrophe** (e-**PIS**-truh-fee): repetition of the same group of words at the end of successive clauses:

  To become a top-notch player, I thought like an athlete, I trained like an athlete, I ate like an athlete.

- **Anadiplosis** (a-nuh-duh-**PLOH**-suhs): repetition of the last word of one clause at the beginning of the following clause:

  Mental preparation leads to training; training builds muscle tone and coordination; muscle tone and coordination, combined with focused thinking, produce athletic excellence.

- **Climax:** repetition of words, phrases, or clauses in order of increasing number or importance:

  Excellent athletes need to be respectful of themselves, their teammates, their schools, and their communities.

Anadiplosis and climax are closely enough related that some teachers of the figures refer to the two schemes together as **climbing the ladder.**

Activity

Reread carefully a paper you are working on. Identify a passage where you can consciously use one or more of the schemes that affect balance, and add them.

Tropes Involving Comparisons

The most important trope in this category, the one upon which all the others in this group are based, is metaphor, an implied comparison between two things that, on the surface, seem dissimilar but that, upon further examination, share common characteristics:

> Many an athletic contest is lost when the player's mind is an idling engine.

Clearly, an athlete's mind and an automobile engine are dissimilar. Yet the metaphor here suggests that, to be successful, an athlete must put his or her mind to purposeful work, just as a driver puts an automobile engine in gear to drive the car. A **simile** resembles a metaphor except that with a simile, the comparison between the two things is made explicit with the use of the word *like* or *as*, rather than remaining implicit, as it does in a metaphor:

> An athlete's mind must be like a well-tuned engine, in gear and responding to the twists and curves of the contest.

Notice that this sentence, which begins with a simile, ends with an **implied metaphor**—the athletic contest is compared to a twisting, curving road.

Other tropes involving comparison include the following:

- **Synecdoche** (suh-**NEK**-duh-kee): A part of something is used to refer to the whole.

  > We decided we could rearrange the gym equipment if everyone would lend a hand.

  (Obviously, everyone needed to use hands, arms, legs, shoulders, and so on, but *hand* stands for them all.)

- **Metonymy** (muh-**TAH**-nuh-mee): An entity is referred to by one of its attributes.

  > The central office announced today new regulations for sports night.

  (The central office can't speak, of course, but the noun is an attribute of the person or an association with the person who works in the central office.)

- **Personification:** Inanimate objects are given human characteristics.

  > After almost three periods of searching, the puck finally found the goal.

■ **Periphrasis** (puh-**RI**-frah-suhs): A descriptive word or phrase is used to refer to a proper name.

> The New York Rangers and the New York Islanders vie to be the best hockey team in the Big Apple.

Tropes Involving Word Play

Some writers like to entertain (and enlighten) their readers simply by playing with the sounds and meanings of words. The most common trope for doing so is the **pun,** a word that suggests two of its meanings or the meaning of a homonym. Puns have a bad reputation—and it's often well deserved. But sometimes a good pun can really attract a reader's attention:

> The tipped-but-caught third strike, ending a bases-loaded rally, was a foul most foul.

Two additional wordplay tropes are:

■ **Anthimeria** (an-thuh-**MEER**-ee-uh): One part of speech, usually a verb, substitutes for another, usually a noun.

> When the Little Leaguers lost the championship, they needed just to have a good cry before they could feel okay about their season.

■ **Onomatopoeia:** Sounds of the words used are related to their meaning.

> The puck whizzed and zipped over the ice, then clattered into the goal.

Tropes Involving Overstatement or Understatement

A writer, ironically, can help readers see an idea or point clearly by overstating it or understating it. The trope of **overstatement** is called **hyperbole** (hye-**PUHR**-boh-lee):

> He couldn't make that shot again if he tried a million times

while the trope for **understatement** is called **litotes** (**LYE**-tuh-tees):

> Shutting out the opponents for three straight games is no small feat for a goaltender.

Tropes Involving the Management of Meaning

Some tropes can be seen as techniques that simply allow a writer to play with the meaning and development of ideas in strategic ways.

■ **Irony:** Words are meant to convey the opposite of their literal meaning.

> Their center is over seven feet tall—where do they come up with these little pipsqueaks?

When irony has a particularly biting or bitter tone, it is called **sarcasm.**

- **Oxymoron:** Words that have apparently contradictory meanings are placed near each other.

   When you have to face your best friend in competition, whoever wins feels an aching pleasure.

- **Rhetorical question:** A question is designed not to secure an answer but to move the development of an idea forward and suggest a point.

   Hasn't the state of intercollegiate athletics reached the point where the line between professionalism and amateurism is blurred?

Activity

Turn again to a paper you are currently working on. Find a section into which you can incorporate one or more of the tropes described above. Do so, and then discuss in a small group whether your rewritten version is appropriate for the audience and purpose of your paper.

Memory

Today, most of the important work that advances the collective knowledge of the world's communities is done in writing. Scholars write books and articles; journalists write columns; government workers write white papers; and specialists in many fields write reports, case studies, feasibility analyses, and project plans. Our culture places great emphasis on getting things in writing.

In ancient Greece and Rome, when citizens were often asked to speak for themselves in public forums and writing was not so widespread in the culture, teachers included memory as one of the canons of rhetoric. Would-be public speakers were taught various techniques (called **mnemonic devices,** derived from the Greek word for memory, *mnesis*) to memorize their speeches so that they could deliver them without notes or a script. The most commonly taught mnemonic device was the **house analogy.** Speakers were taught to associate different parts of their speech with specific locations in their houses—for example, the introduction of their speech was like the entrance way, the developmental sections of their speech became like various rooms that they could move into one after the other, until they reached the conclusion and exited from the back door of the house. In a primarily oral culture, it was as important for an effective communicator to learn the art of memory as it was to learn about the strategies of invention, arrangement, and style.

In our writing culture, the significance of memory in a person's rhetorical abilities—indeed, the way memory is actually defined in rhetoric—has shifted. Memory in contemporary thinking about rhetoric has to do in part with how much knowledge, information, and data a writer can access electronically or otherwise and then use judiciously. Memory also has to do with the cultural memory of a writer; that is, what the writer knows about history, art, science, and literature. Both contemporary meanings of memory suggest that successful writers and speakers tap into the memory sources available on computers, in books, and in the culture at large. Memory today also refers to the reader-writer connection. To use a phrase, **allusion,** or topical event highlights the role of memory for both reader and writer.

Delivery

As was the case with memory, delivery, the fifth of the traditional canons, assumed its place in the rhetoric curriculum because ancient Greece and Rome were primarily oral cultures. Speakers who wanted to excel in politics and public affairs needed to learn how to use their voices effectively, how to enunciate clearly, and how to use their bodies to gesture appropriately while they were giving a speech. One of the most famous stories in the lore of rhetoric, indeed, involves Demosthenes, a celebrated orator in fourth-century B.C.E. Athens. As a youth, Demosthenes had a speech impediment, so to perfect his craft, he practiced enunciation with his mouth full of pebbles, he recited speeches while he was running, and he declaimed at the seashore, strengthening his voice by speaking over the roar of the waves. When asked which was the most important of the five canons, Demosthenes is reputed to have answered, "Delivery, delivery, and delivery."

In our culture, where written documents tend to do more knowledge work than speeches, delivery has taken on new meanings. Delivery now refers to how the written text is, well, delivered. Among the many questions a contemporary student can ask now in analyzing delivery, or in planning his or her own, are these:

- Does the writer choose an electronic or print format?
- If the former, does the writer choose to include any hypertextual links? How effective are they?
- Does the writer use any photographs or other kinds of images to accompany the written text?
- Does the writer choose to put a cover of any kind on a printed text?
- How does the writer use such features as font sizes and styles, bullets or numbered lists, and white space?

Delivery may also include stylistic choices that let readers hear some words more loudly than others—setting off words in a paragraph, for example, with hyphens or ellipsis marks, or capitalizing words or making all lowercase.

Re-creating dialect in spelling or word choice is another decision that affects delivery. Delivery has to do with how a text looks, but it also has to do with how it's heard. All of these features, and others that involve the delivery of the text, affect how clearly the writer conveys the central ideas of a piece and what kind of credible, trustworthy person the readers perceive the writer to be.

Activity

Write the paragraph above or another one of your choice in slang or dialect, using punctuation, typeface, paragraphing, or other format changes to highlight how the paragraph sounds or how it would be spoken.

Interchapter

2

- The five traditional canons of rhetoric—invention, arrangement, style, memory, and delivery—suggest strategies for creating clear, compelling texts. Such compositions appeal to logos, ethos, and pathos. You can analyze the five canons in a writer's work or plan to use them in your own.

- The canon of invention comprises strategies—both systematic and intuitive—that writers can use to generate abundant material for texts.

- The canon of arrangement offers techniques that writers can use to give appropriate and effective order and structure to texts.

- The canon of style represents an extensive array of strategies that writers can use to craft their sentences, phrases, and words in ways that are appropriate and effective in the particular writing situation.

- The canon of memory today guides writers to try to tap into the "cultural memory" of their readers effectively.

- The canon of delivery today helps writers decide how to format their compositions, either in print or electronically, in a way that is most effective for readers.

Activities and Discussion Questions for Chapter 2 Use these questions and comments as guides for your own discussion and writing about these works.

Henry David Thoreau, "An Essay on Civil Disobedience" (published 1849) The text appears on pages 209–225. In a discussion with a group of your classmates, or in a well-developed essay, address one or more of the following questions.

1. State and explain what you see as the central enthymeme in "Civil Disobedience." Then describe and explain what you see as one of the subsidiary or supporting enthymemes.

2. Point out and explain a way you see Thoreau using the topics as a strategy of invention.

3. Using the six numbered questions on pages 53–54, divide "Civil Disobedience" into functional sections. Then, using the bulleted questions on pages 55–56, analyze the effectiveness of arrangement in *one* of the functional sections.

4. Select one specific paragraph that you believe represents the most interesting, most vivid passage in "Civil Disobedience." Describe as much about the style of that passage as you can. For every stylistic feature you notice, explain what you see as its effect on the appeal of "Civil Disobedience" to the development of the central idea, to the credibility of Thoreau, or to the emotional power of the piece.

5. Point out some ways you see Thoreau tapping into the "cultural memory" of his readers. To what does the text refer or allude with the expectation that readers will know the reference or allusion? How do these references and allusions affect the appeal of readers today?

Eavan Boland, "It's a Woman's World" (published 1982)

The text appears on pages 226–227. In a discussion with a group of your classmates or in an essay, address one or more of the following questions:

1. Is there a central argument in "It's a Woman's World"? If so, what is it? Using the structure of an enthymeme, state and analyze the argument.

2. Does the poem move from general to specific or specific to general, or are specific references and general claims mixed? What is the effect of the arrangement of general claims and specific details in the poem?

3. Paying careful attention to schemes of repetition and balance, analyze what you see as the major stylistic effects of "It's a Woman's World."

4. Describe and analyze the delivery of the poem on the page. How do the line lengths and the stanza divisions influence the effectiveness of the poem?

Alice Walker, "Everyday Use" (published 1973)

The text appears on pages 228–234. In a discussion with a group of your classmates, or in a well-organized essay, address one or more of the following questions:

1. Is there a central argument in "Everyday Use"? If so, what is it? Using the structure of an enthymeme, state and analyze the argument.

2. How does Walker use time as an ordering device in "Everyday Use"? Consider the events mentioned, even in passing, in the story, and arrange them in an exact chronological order. Then contrast the chronological order with the order Walker uses, and explain the effect of Walker's choice of arrangement.

3. Look carefully at the section of "Everyday Use" where Dee/Wangero shows up at the house with Asalamalakim. Describe how the order of details contributes to the effectiveness of this arrival scene.

4. Describe and analyze the way Walker uses diction to create the character of the narrator of the story, the mother.

5. Do you see "Everyday Use" in any way as a story about cultural memory? If so, explain how. How do these references and allusions affect the appeal of readers today?

Rhetoric and the Writer

"Let's say you want to write an award-winning short story—you just push this key, here . . . "

Working your way through the first two chapters of this book, you have assembled a considerable storehouse of new ideas and strategies to use as a reader, writer, speaker, and thinker. You know now that rhetoric is a set of strategies you employ every day as you use language in your roles as a student, a family member, and a participant in your community, nation, and world. What's more, you have acquired at least a beginning sense of how those strategies work to accomplish a purpose. And you know now that these strategies can be classified under the five canons of rhetoric: invention, arrangement, style, memory, and delivery.

As you consider all this information, you may be wondering how you might use all these definitions, strategies, and techniques. How can you make your understandings about rhetoric work for you? The aim of this chapter is to help you understand how to make rhetorical choices—choices involving invention, arrangement, style, memory, and delivery—in a writing process that is guided by your developing purpose, or intentions, as a writer. In this chapter, we will show real writers at work—writers much like you—and show how these writers understand the rhetorical situation they have at hand, make the situation their own by discovering their own intentions within it, and respond to the situation and their own purposes effectively. We offer real stories of writers making choices about the processes they engage in, the material they decide to incorporate, the organizational strategies they employ, and the language they use.

Before moving to these writers' stories—and to give us some common language to use in examining them—we need to review some terms and concepts that you have probably studied before, definitions of the writing process and its components. But we hope your new perspective on rhetoric can help you examine the writing process in a considerably different light. The writing process, as we will explain below, is most usefully seen not as a set of isolated moments but instead as a collection of strategic moves designed to help a writer achieve a purpose for an audience. In other words, the writing process is ultimately a rhetorical process.

Writing as Process: Making the Right Moves for Context

Every good writer knows that writing involves a series of processes. It would be nice if you could simply sit down at the word processor or with a pad and pencil and, voilà, the words magically appeared on the screen or the page. It doesn't work that way. Instead, writers must generate good writing: build it, cook it, incubate it, massage it, live with it, whatever-growth-metaphor-you-choose with it.

When teachers and students talk about generating good writing over time, they frequently name their activity "following the writing process." But even though it's usually referred to in the singular, *the* writing process is actually *several* processes; different people use different labels to describe them.

Since what gets called the **writing process** can be described in many ways, bear in mind that seeing writing as a process means understanding that what all writers do, repeatedly and simultaneously, is invent and revise. Think back over something you have written that you were proud of, and try to remember what it felt like when you were deep into the process. It's probably hard to remember a moment in your work on this piece when you were not thinking up new material—ideas, specific sentences, phrases, and words—and, at the same time, evaluating its quality and making appropriate changes. You were almost simultaneously inventing and revising. While acknowledging that the heart of writing as process is this continual interplay of inventing and revising, we nevertheless provide a seven-term overview of writing processes—not only to do justice to the complexity of writing but also to suggest how this inventing-revising interaction works. If writing processes did not occur so interactively, we might say that the first three of the points in the process could be subsumed under inventing, while the last three could be considered as **revising,** with the middle process, **drafting,** considered under both labels.

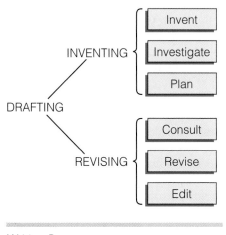

Writing Processes

But we can't make this claim because the processes are fluid. Good writers allow themselves to move among the processes as the need arises.

Writing as a Rhetorical Process

In a substantial writing project—one that requires research, rethinking, taking on more than one perspective, experimentation, and so on—good writers almost always engage in these acts within their writing process, knowing that the rhetorical context will help them decide how to proceed through each **act** and how much time and energy to devote to each one—to inventing, investigating, planning, drafting, consulting, revising, and editing.

Inventing

Inventing is the general term for the activities that writers undertake to extract information from the "database" of their memories or experiences and to evaluate and reflect on what they've uncovered for its usefulness in the writing task at hand. As you recall, invention is the first of the five canons of classical rhetoric. You've practiced invention activities in Chapter 2.

Investigating

Investigating is the general name for the activities people undertake to discover information and generate a fund of knowledge about which they will write. Not everyone includes investigating in the *writing* process; some teachers consider it instead a process that precedes the actual writing. There are good reasons, however, for including it. The rhetorical situation, as outlined in Chapter 1, including the kind, or genre, of writing a writer aims to produce, influences the nature of a writer's investigation.

Consider this rhetorical situation, for example: You have to write a paper for a psychology class analyzing how preschool children behave after their parents drop them off at a day-care center. Your audience consists of the other students in your class and your teacher, but your teacher has urged you to write a paper that would speak to the intellectual and professional interests of child psychologists and that would particularize your study, as well as prevent you from making too general a claim. How might you investigate this topic? You might read books and articles about children's behaviors or consult your parents about your own behavior in day care. An effective investigation might well begin with actual observation in a day-care facility. Especially if your psychology class has studied experimentation and observation, this kind of investigation will be appropriate as a beginning for your thinking about the topic.

Activity

Read several essays on the opinion page of a major daily newspaper. In a small group, discuss these editorial pieces, and then, with your group, write just the beginning of two essays analyzing the editorials. Assume one essay is for an English class and one for a political science or U.S. government class. What do you need to investigate to write each of these pieces?

Planning

Planning occurs when a writer determines (1) who the audience for the writing might be and (2) what purpose or purposes the paper can accomplish, given its contexts and constraints, and then decides how to state and reflect on ideas most effectively.

Planning might better be labeled **brainstorming.** When writers plan, they must be keenly aware of the occasion for writing, the subject, the purpose, the audience, as well as the genre and the length considerations.

Consider this rhetorical situation: You have been assigned to write a paper for your U.S. government class about some issue relating to government and education. Your preliminary planning or brainstorming looks, or perhaps *sounds,* something like this:

> Writing a paper that my U.S. government teacher will read. I want to convince her that the federal government hasn't really considered the drawbacks of too much standardized testing. But my teacher is just one person of a larger group interested in the politics of education, so I might consider other possible readers too. With this audience and purpose, how should I begin? With an **anecdote** about how many days every school year are given over to standardized testing? Then I can talk about the brain-numbing effect those days have. I could tell a story here—or maybe that's not going to be good evidence. It is supposed to be formal. I'll ask the teacher. Then I can try to show how legislators think only about the bottom line of standardized testing and don't consider how it actually affects education day to day. I want to make clear what students, parents, and interested citizens can do to change the testing environment in schools. But I know I'll need to suggest my main ideas up front. What sections should I have?

Planning is an incredibly active process. It's not just imagining an audience and achieving a purpose; it's understanding and working with the *interaction* of audience and purpose; it's capitalizing on the *synergy* that this subject-audience-purpose dynamic creates; it's thinking aloud, sometimes to yourself and sometimes to a writing partner or group, about the possible directions a paper might take to be persuasive with an audience.

Activity

Imagine that you were asked to write a piece for the op-ed page of your local newspaper describing the *best* thing that happens at your school to improve students' educational opportunities. With a partner or in a small group, plan this piece, considering all ideas about what *is* best. Think about your audience (your local community), and consider why you're writing to this audience (and why the paper might have asked you to write). Your plan might be reflective notes, as above, or a list or an outline.

Drafting

Drafting is the process by which writers simply get something written on paper or in a computer file so that they can develop their ideas and begin moving toward an end, a start-to-finish product. Good writers realize that no piece of writing emerges immediately in finished form. They see a draft as raw material for what will become the final product, and they know this raw material will need expanding, reducing, rearranging, and rethinking. When they draft, many successful writers tell themselves (perhaps subconsciously, but forcefully), "For the time being, stop investigating, stop planning, and stop inventing. Don't worry about perfection. Just write."

How a writer produces a draft is influenced by how familiar he or she is with the rhetorical situation. Writers in English classes who regularly write one-page response papers, in which they reflect informally on the texts they read, and use these papers to begin class discussion, might write a draft that appears in nearly final form. Their familiarity with the rhetorical situation—the fact that the paper won't be graded, that it's quick, and that they can use it to speak from—helps the draft develop. But writers in that same English class who are asked for the first time to write up research on a recurring theme in literature over several historical periods and to assume an audience of literary scholars can expect less ease in the drafting of their papers.

Activity

With a partner or in a writing group, discuss a paper you have written in the past that you found easy to draft and one that you found difficult and time consuming to draft. How can you account for the difference?

Consulting

Sometimes referred to as **peer review, consulting** is the activity of seeking the help of a "fresh" reader and asking him or her to tell you what is good about a draft, what is questionable, and what definitely needs change and improvement. There's an old saying that circulates in the hills of Appalachia, where both of the authors of this book grew up: "There's no child so homely that its mother doesn't love it." There's an analogy to writing here. When you write something, especially something you have worked very hard at drafting, you justifiably feel proud of it. It's part of you—your ideas taking shape as words on the page. But for important pieces of work, it's vital to get someone else to read your work and be frank and honest in appraising it.

Notice that working with a consultant does not mean finding someone to proofread, edit, or correct your writing. It means finding someone to read your work once you have produced a comprehensible draft, not a final product. Consulting readers of your drafts can be representatives, either actual participants or role-playing stand-ins, of the rhetorical context at hand; that is, they can say, "As a reader, here's my honest reaction to the way you have developed your idea to achieve the purpose you have in mind for your audience." Consulting readers can give you their opinions about the good, the bad, and the questionable in your draft. In the task we mentioned above, to write up research on literary themes over time, consulting readers with greater experience and expertise in genre, methods, and evidence—teachers, avid readers of literature, and/or students who are writing about similar research—can be invaluable.

Working with a consulting reader often requires that you take a big gulp, swallow your pride momentarily, and put your ego aside. You may hear responses to your draft that you had not expected and do not necessarily enjoy. On the other hand, you will probably discover things about your draft that you never expected to find out. It will be up to you whether to actually do anything in response to your consulting readers' comments. But getting someone to consult with you about a draft affords you an objective person's (or persons') views of how your work is shaping up.

Revising

When writers return to their drafts, reread and rethink them, and then decide what to change in order to improve them, they are revising. Revising is a process that activates other processes. For example, when you revise, you may engage in planning: "How can I approach my audience better to make my purpose clearer?" When you revise, you may return to investigating: "Do I need to read more to be convincing? Is there a place I should visit and observe?" When you revise, you may engage in more invention strategies: "I know I need more examples. Let me think of stories I've heard." When you revise, you almost always realize that the draft isn't quite finished. And you often realize that it has not "settled" into its rhetorical situation yet—it's not doing all it can do to achieve its purpose with the audience at hand. So you revise—literally, you "resee" and then rethink the piece—the composition as a whole, as well as its sections.

Activity

With a partner or in a small group, revise a short piece you've written recently in class. Follow these steps: (1) write a note about what you'd like to add or change, (2) read the piece aloud, (3) ask the group to suggest changes and discuss reactions, and (4) make a note about their responses.

Editing

This is your final interaction with your composition before you submit it to the audience—publisher, peers, teachers—for response and evaluation. **Editing** occurs when writers read over their texts slowly, looking for lapses in usage, in sense or coherence, and in spelling or punctuation. As with the other processes, the rhetorical situation strongly influences how a writer edits. If you know your audience holds standards of excellence in spelling, grammar, mechanics, and punctuation, and you want your paper to make a strong statement to this audience, it has to meet those standards. If an audience expects a draft of a work in progress, you will edit less strenuously.

Activity

Take a careful look at a paper you have recently written for a class, and select two paragraphs from the middle of this paper. Read one of these paragraphs aloud. Then read the other aloud, but backward, starting with the last word and moving to the first one. Edit both paragraphs. What do you notice about the different levels of attention you pay to individual words and punctuation marks in the two reading experiences? Does reading backward help you edit?

Real Writers at Work: Cases for Studying Writing and Rhetoric

Rhetoric is not some disembodied academic pursuit. Rhetoric involves real readers, writers, speakers, and listeners in real situations. In the rest of this chapter, therefore, we present four cases: stories about real writers like you who are working hard to become the kinds of rhetorically effective, perceptive writers and readers who succeed in school and beyond. Each case begins with a series of focusing questions, then follows a **narrative** of the writer at work. Within the narratives are activities that you can do alone or in a small group. Working through each of these cases, and then taking on a case of your own, you will put into play what you have learned about understanding rhetorical purpose, operating within context, employing the appeals, using the canons, and seeing the writing process as a rhetorical one.

Erica: Slow Starter

As you study Erica's case, keep the following questions in mind. Discuss them with your group when you can.

1. What does Erica need to do to clarify the rhetorical purpose?
2. What does Erica need to do to understand her audience more thoroughly?
3. What does Erica need to do to invent material for her new composition?

4. How might Erica go about planning her new composition?

5. How might Erica get started drafting her composition and keep the drafting process going?

"I don't know where to start," Erica tells her teacher as she's explaining her problem in writing a paper. "I know what I want to say, sort of, but I don't know how to say it."

The student's frustration is probably familiar to you. We all have moments, usually at the beginning of writing something, when we just can't think how or where to start. It's hard to put fingers to the keyboard or pen to paper when we can't figure out what should go first or why. Sometimes, that feeling is enough to make a writer put away the pen or get up from the computer and delay the start of the process for as long as possible. When words do begin to come, it's because they're being forced out under the pressure of a nonnegotiable and usually very immediate deadline.

Erica's assignment is to analyze one essay from a collection of articles on identity and cultural diversity. She has picked a good essay, but a difficult one, on stereotyping. She has shown herself in earlier assignments to be a careful and adept writer, and the first question her teacher has for her is why the paper she had completed the week before—a paper about her first name—hadn't presented her with problems. "Well, it was about me," she smiles. "I got to talk about my name and where it came from. I knew about that stuff."

"But how did you know how to begin?" the teacher asks.

"It's the funniest thing about the name. Where it came from."

This was the first line of her piece: "I am named for a cow." It was a funny and poignant essay about her mother's friendship with a German neighbor who kept a cow in her backyard. Erica had known how to begin because, as she said, she knew about herself and her story. But it was also because she felt confident about the way it should be told, perhaps because she had told the story often before. She felt sure of her audience too, students in her class who she knew would like the opening, its quickness, its unexpectedness. She was right. When she read it aloud to her classmates, they all laughed, and, after she finished reading, they commented on how effectively she had written.

One other factor seems important to explain why Erica had little problem in beginning her essay on her name. The class had already been talking about the issue that Erica would explore: the importance of names and of naming something. They had read the beginning section of Sandra Cisneros's *House on Mango Street*, which begins, "My name is Esperanza."

MY NAME

In English my name means hope. In Spanish it means too many letters. It means sadness, it means waiting. It is like the number nine. A muddy color. It is the Mexican records my father plays on Sunday mornings when he is shaving, songs like sobbing.

It was my great-grandmother's name and now it is mine. She was a horse woman too, born like me in the Chinese year of the horse—which is supposed to be bad luck if you're born female—but I think this is a Chinese lie because the Chinese, like the Mexicans, don't like their women strong.

My great-grandmother. I would've liked to have known her, a wild horse of a woman, so wild she wouldn't marry. Until my great-grandfather threw a sack over her head and carried her off. Just like that, as if she were a fancy chandelier. That's the way he did it.

And the story goes she never forgave him. She looked out the window her whole life, the way so many women sit their sadness on an elbow. I wonder if she made the best with what she got or was she sorry because she couldn't be all the things she wanted to be. Esperanza. I have inherited her name, but I don't want to inherit her place by the window.

At school they say my name funny as if the syllables were made out of tin and hurt the roof of your mouth. But in Spanish my name is made out of a softer something, like silver, not quite as thick as sister's name—Magdalena—which is uglier than mine. Magdalena who at least can come home and become Nenny. But I am always Esperanza.

I would like to baptize myself under a new name, a name more like the real me, the one nobody sees. Esperanza as Lisandra or Martiza or Zeze the X. Yes. Something like Zeze the X will do.

Cisneros's narrator translates her name, talks about its derivation and its connection to her family's past, and considers her feelings about it and her grandmother, the person she is named for. You might hear the echo of Cisneros's opening in Erica's "I am named for a cow." Its simplicity, its brevity, its no-nonsense tone strike a note similar to Cisneros's sentence. Erica had known how to begin in part because she had already heard a beginning that sounded like something she might try herself. And it worked.

So Erica's success in inventing, planning, and drafting her name paper came about because (1) she knew her subject well, (2) she knew how her audience might respond to the subject, (3) she had experience and examples that she could use to develop her writing, and (4) she understood why she was writing. All these elements made Erica feel sure of herself as she completed a draft. She revised extensively after working with her small group, who talked with her about how to make her intention—to tell a funny story and to honor her mother and her friend—most effective for them.

But what about the problem with the second assignment? With this task, Erica seems to have none of the understandings that had allowed her to gather ideas and begin so easily when she wrote about her name. She fears her subject (she asks herself silently, "Do I really understand the point of this essay?"). She ignores her audience (she asks herself, "If I don't understand it, how do I expect anybody else to?"). She doesn't trust any of her own experiences and doesn't think of any examples that might help her (she frets to herself, "I don't know how I'm supposed to sound"). And, most of all, she doesn't understand why she is writing.

The topic she is supposed to be writing about is one similar to many school assignments. It asks for an analysis of a text and requires careful reading of the text, cogent assessment of details in the text, and well-supported conclusions about it. Erica is focusing much more on the possibility of being wrong about what she says and the way she says it than she did in her first essay, and her worry has begun to prevent her from writing at all.

In brief, Erica isn't clear about her *intention* (other than her intention to complete the assignment). She is stymied. So what does Erica need to do?

Activity

Think carefully about two papers you have written in the past, one for which you felt a strong sense of intention and another for which this sense was largely absent. In your group, discuss how the processes of drafting and revising seemed different to you for each of these papers. Or write about an assignment that gave you the kind of trouble Erica faces. What was the assignment? How did you resolve the problem? Share your response with your small group.

Erica's Intention and Invention

Recently, high school students in an advanced-placement English class discussed what they found most difficult about the process of writing. Five or six explained that the thesis presented the most difficulties for them; several mentioned form; and two more talked about gathering enough details. Only one said, "Getting started! That's the hardest thing for me." But when she spoke, almost all of the students nodded their heads. "Oh, yes. It's just jumping in. I put it off for as long as I can." Or "I start over and over again trying to get it right." What the students found as they talked was that the beginning of the process, particularly invention and drafting, presented the most challenges and frustrations for them. "Sometimes I wait so long that I don't have time to revise. I just turn it in and hope for the best," one admitted.

To begin inventing—considering ideas and scenarios, gathering material, and thinking through possibilities—a writer has to believe there's a reason to write. The writer has to believe in an *intention* for the text. After all, people write best when there's a reason to do so. But the reason must not be simply *extrinsic*—something outside, like a teacher or an assignment or a grade—that compels the writer. Rather, the reason should be at least in part *intrinsic*—something within the topic or the argument that compels the writer.

But here's the problem: A writer may not feel a sense of intention when starting work on the composition. Intention often emerges *while* the writer is in the process of writing. In other words, a writer's intention will, and should, change as he or she finds material or considers alternatives or uses a particular story or metaphor to explain a point.

How might Erica gather intention and thus improve her ability to invent ideas on the topic she is exploring? First, she might consider what she knows already. Interestingly enough, her name paper can give her background information and experience for examining the article on stereotyping and cultural diversity that she is trying to analyze. Stereotyping is a kind of naming. And knowing the importance of her own name to her can help Erica think through the issues about being called a name that doesn't fit or that hurts or that carries lots of negative associations. Finding out that she brings something to the assignment improves her confidence immediately and makes her able to look at the text more closely, discovering the details that begin to support her feeling about the power of naming. As her intention becomes clearer, her ability to talk with others about what she's thinking develops, and she brings to her group the following, a potential beginning paragraph:

> Words, especially names, make a difference. What a person is called gives her an identity, a kind of place. In Sandra Cisneros's story, the main character dislikes what she's called because she doesn't want the identity that goes with it. Her grandmother lived a sad life, and Esperanza fears that her grandmother's identity, as well as her name, might be passed down to her. In the article "The Function of Stereotypes," the author shows how defining people with stereotypes misrepresents them and gives them an identity that is so hard to escape.

Erica has found a way into her text analysis by linking her task in this assignment to issues she's already thought about, to experiences she already knows. She is beginning to discover her intention and beginning the process of analyzing the argument in the article. She changes some of that first paragraph later, after she's written more, but she retains the connections to the Cisneros story in her later version. She's been able to hear her own voice more clearly because she feels more assurance about her position on the article, so she can find the details in the article that support her own emerging argument.

Activity

Write your whole name, or a nickname, and then jot down some ideas about it. Are you named for someone? Do you like your name? Is there a funny story associated with your name, how it's pronounced, or how it's spelled? Are there things you don't know about your name—why your parents gave it to you or what the word means? Write those questions too. Write quickly without stopping much to consider how you sound or where you're headed. The idea is to get your initial thoughts on the page or screen where you can see them.

Apply Erica's Solution

You've begun to search for **rhetorical intention** now, with your notes and questions. You already know a lot, but you may find that there are things you still need to know before you might write a whole essay about your name.

You might need to investigate a little, talking to a family member or looking up the derivation of the name. You might need to plan where you will tell a story about being named or how you'll argue that your name fits you or doesn't.

Your notes and comments may seem chaotic as you look back at them. How might they fit together? What's your point in writing them? But chaos is not necessarily bad. In fact, for a writer it's a necessary step in the process. Generating ideas and considering possibilities are both chaotic. At first, there seem to be too many choices. One reason that writers fear beginning a writing task is their apprehension about the chaos of ideas that inevitably comes with invention. But, as the writing teacher and theorist Ann Berthoff says, "Chaos begins the forming." The questions and comments you've jotted down, the memories you've stirred with the words you've written, and the ideas you've begun to consider are not simply chaotic; they are generative. They help you begin the process of formulating ideas into a plan, an approach, and a direction.

That direction gets set as writers understand more about rhetorical situations—the interaction of the subject with the audience and the purpose. If you are writing your piece for your family, you'll no doubt begin differently than if you're writing for the school newspaper. If you're writing about your name because your teacher has given you the assignment, you'll approach it somewhat differently than if you came up with your own idea for a discussion of names. If you want to make an argument that people should be more careful about what they call others, you might add details that wouldn't appear if you were writing to explain how names get changed. Your readers, your purpose, and your context will affect your persona, the type of person you present yourself to be to your readers. All the elements of Aristotle's triangle, as we explained in Chapter 1, will direct the way you come up with ideas and details as you write.

Recall that in Chapter 2, we set out a wide range of systematic invention strategies, techniques you can use to analyze how a writer comes up with ideas for a composition and to plan how to generate ideas for your own papers. Erica's story provides the raw material for using these techniques. It illustrates the individual sources writers can tap into to discover the material for their work. As Erica's story suggests, writers generate ideas from all kinds of sources. They invent by using what's available to them, both from their own backgrounds and from what they're able to investigate. Remember Aristotle's definition: Rhetoricians observe the *available means* in order to effect their purpose, in order to persuade their readers. As you examine the following "available means," think about how Erica (or you) could use each of these sources to invent material through the journalist's questions, Burke's pentad, the topics, or the enthymeme.

- **Experience.** The writer's life in a family, in a school, or in the community can be useful both to understand situations he or she reads about and to employ as an illustration or as a narrative to provoke or connect with readers. Cisneros's character Esperanza speaks of her past and present to explain the power of names. Erica uses the story of her mother's friendship with a neighbor to make a connection with her readers. Some subjects lend themselves more easily than others to the overt use of past experience in an essay. But experience is always important as people read and write. If you've read a John Updike novel in the past, you'll carry attitudes about his style that will affect the way you read any other Updike story. If you are assigned to write about the grocery boy narrator in Updike's short story "A&P," you'll connect what you know about being a grocery bagger in your local market to the character even if you never write about your own experience in your final text.

- **Observation.** All good writers are good observers. They watch the world around them as well as participate in it. They learn about what motivates people, what scares them, what entertains them—because they take note of the world around them. They use their understandings as they write to make connections with their readers. In other words, they pay attention to what they see and hear. Aristotle spoke of how to appeal to various kinds of audiences—old men, soldiers, young people, politicians—giving advice about approaches to subjects that would work best with each group. He had obviously observed the reactions and understood the motivations of these men.

- **Research.** Both observation and past experience represent kinds of research. But research also means the writer's investigation of sources outside the self and outside direct observation. Library and online research in a variety of sources—newspapers, journals, books, and documents—helps writers gather information that contributes to the strength of their arguments or the development of their explanations. Talking to experts—people who are knowledgeable about a particular issue or event—is a different kind of research. Becoming a recorder and observer in a scene, doing what's called *ethnographic* research, is yet another method of accomplishing research.

- **Sharing.** Talking about issues, ideas, and emerging opinions with others is useful for all writers. Listening to objections to an opinion prepares writers to counter those objections when they write or helps them qualify or complicate their positions. When writers articulate what they're thinking about a subject or about a text they have read, they are generating ideas about that subject or text. And, as a small group or a conversation partner asks questions or gives an alternate opinion, writers rethink and reform their own thinking.

- **Reading.** Reading, of course, is a kind of experience and a kind of research. We separate it here to highlight the importance of reading widely from popular magazines and Internet Web sites, from letters and journals, and from textbooks. Reading for pleasure as well as for information gives a writer a rich mine from which to draw ideas and explore new directions. And reading allows writers to sharpen their own ears, to hear voices and styles that can strengthen their own.

Activity

Think about something you've written recently, and consider how you've made use of the possibilities described above—experience, observations, research, sharing, and reading—for inventing ideas. With a partner or in your group, discuss whether there are possibilities you might have explored but didn't.

Chan: Confused About Context

As you study Chan's case, keep the following questions in mind. Discuss them with your group when you can.

1. How does the context affect the way Chan engages in invention strategies?

2. How does the context affect the way Chan investigates a subject in order to write about it?

3. How does the context affect the way Chan goes about planning a composition?

Our second case is about Chan, and his story leads us to think about how the context of a writing project affects the ways a writer goes about completing it. In much of the writing you do in school, the assignment provided by the teacher is the informative clue about the context. In some ways, Chan's story is the mirror image of Erica's. Erica felt a sense of intention with a topic of her own choosing and had difficulty with one assigned to her. Chan, on the other hand, finds it difficult to come up with a sense of intention when the teacher does not assign a specific task or subject.

Chan is a transfer student, moving into a new school at the semester break, and he is fairly confident that he will be able to continue doing well in his new writing course. In the course he took at his previous school, he had usually done well on the assignments, which required students to read short stories, identify important themes or issues in them, and then write three- to five-page compositions demonstrating how the identified themes and issues might be relevant in contemporary life. Chan had interesting insights on this literature-life connection, and his teacher both praised him for his incisive readings and helped him learn more about how to write about them clearly.

But the first assignment that Chan faces in his new writing class throws him for a loop. Here is the assignment:

WRITING PIECE #1

Make your argument. State your claim. Have your say.

One of the biggest, most popular areas of nonfiction writing is the personal opinion piece. Take a look at the last page of *Time* magazine at the "My Turn" essay.

Look at the editorial writers' pieces on the last inside pages of the front section of the *News and Record*. (I'm including one of these for you to examine.) Look at collections of columns from writers like Dave Barry, Ellen Goodman, Katha Pollitt, William Raspberry, and Molly Ivins. Think of writers in past decades or centuries who wrote commentary that expressed personal opinion on some matter of the day; writers from Jonathan Swift to Mary Wollstonecraft to Oscar Wilde all wrote opinion essays, or what you might call argument.

Your task is to discover your own argument and have your say. What do you want to have a say about? Something funny like why Harris Teeter has stopped carrying Golden Fleece pot cleaners? (I bet you don't know what that is!) Something serious like why states are executing innocent men? You can comment on an event, a cultural phenomenon (why were we glued to the TV to watch the Survivors eat grubs?), a societal problem, or a coming change in local or national life. Once you have your idea, you'll begin to discover form and tone. The writers above vary wildly in terms of style and format. Some use humor; others use anger, irony, or compassion to get across their views and to persuade others to agree with their point. Think about how you will best convey your idea and make an appeal to your reader. Notice that most personal opinion pieces are relatively short; you should consider length as you write. Your piece should probably be not less than two pages and not more than five.

Have fun. Have a point. Have a title.

Chan feels quite uncomfortable when he starts to work on this assignment. Why is it so long? What is he supposed to make of the distinctive teacher voice that he hears in the assignment? What idea should he choose when the topic is not even indicated? What kind of voice and tone would be appropriate? What form should the paper take? Chan needs to imagine his task differently from the writing-about-literature assignments he wrote at his previous school, and, frankly, he isn't prepared to do so. Working through this difficulty, Chan discovers the responsibility that attends writing: that good writers not only complete the assignment but also make it their own.

Take another look at the assignment, and notice which elements of the rhetorical situation Chan might connect with.

- First of all, the context that surrounds this writing task assumes an ongoing class discussion. Are there things you don't understand when you read the assignment? (Why the mention of Golden Fleece pot cleaners?) It's in the context of that discussion that the assignment occurs, so it will help Chan, as he starts to work, to re-create mentally the classroom conversation. The voice of the teacher, the one who has initiated the assignment, is low-key, conversational, and humorous; the teacher deliberately chose that voice to make writers feel relaxed rather than pressured.

- Second, the assignment makes it clear that students should read published personal opinion pieces from a variety of sources that will give them some ideas—about form, voice, and details—and that writers should feel encouraged to use their reading as guides to genre considerations or to subject matter as they begin their own pieces.

- Third, the assignment indicates a presumed audience as well: not only the teacher who will read students' writing but also regular readers of columns like "My Turn," so it might benefit Chan to examine a column like this to see how it approaches audience.

- Finally, the persona the writer develops in the piece is implied when the assignment suggests that the writer should have a real stake in the writing, should explore an issue that means something personally and that he or she wants to share an opinion about.

What's missing from this context is the subject, and that's what perplexes Chan the most. In this assignment, students have to find their own subjects, the issues and ideas that they have experienced and want to investigate on their own.

Activity

In your group, brainstorm for ten minutes on this assignment: "You must teach a class session about some literary technique." Then, again in your group, brainstorm for ten minutes on this assignment: "You must teach a class about the definitions of *hero* and *villain* in literary works." After you have finished brainstorming, talk in your group about the differences in the two planning experiences.

Chan, Context, and Notes

Chan feels considerably more at home with the next assignment, when the class begins reading a novel and is asked to write about it. Many students share Chan's comfort with this kind of assignment because they are more familiar with one in which the subject matter and rhetorical requirements are fully described. Here is the next assignment that Chan gets:

ESSAY ON *THE SCARLET LETTER*

Write a two- to three-page description of the real villain in *The Scarlet Letter*. Remember that you'll have to decide for yourself who the real villain is and prove it in the way you support your idea with details and examples from the text. Be careful not to simply summarize the plot. Making use of quotes from the novel will add to the specificity of your examples and your argument.

Notice that this assignment indicates much of the rhetorical situation for Chan to use as he begins to invent ideas for the paper. Length is specified, suggesting that Chan needs to understand something about the depth he should go into in his description of the villain. If the paper were to be longer, he might add short descriptions of the other characters or include criticism from some outside source that would add to his claim, but the brevity called for in the assignment tells Chan that he needs to get to the point quickly and clearly.

The form that the paper should take is also indicated by the request to add details and examples and by the direct suggestion that quotations will make papers more effective. We don't know much about the actual classroom context for the assignment, but it's fair to say that the teacher expects Chan and the other students to know already something about how to use details to support a position. And they have obviously already read the novel, so they can use their reading experience to help them make a decision about the villain. One other thing: the assignment implies that the identity of the villain is open to question, that it's a matter for debate. Chan won't be judged to be incorrect if he chooses a character who may not be the most obvious evil character in the novel.

In deciding upon the character to describe, Chan needs to find his own angle on the assignment. Clearly, the fact that he has been reading *The Scarlet Letter* in order to write a paper about it has affected the way he reads—a person reads fiction with a different eye if he or she is reading for pleasure rather than performance. Chan's invention strategies for the paper will depend on what he has been thinking as he's been reading about the characters and their actions. He might use the journalist's questions (page 36) or Burke's pentad (page 39) to generate insights about characters and motives. He might consider one of the classical topics of relationship, comparison and contrast (page 46), as a perspective for considering varying motives and actions. His strategies will depend on what's been discussed in class and in small-group discussions about morality and revenge and hypocrisy, all issues for the characters in the novel. Since the teacher has indicated an audience of classmates and interested readers, Chan's planning strategies—considerations of who will be reading his work and how he needs to support his points—will be affected by class discussions as well.

As he reads the assignment, Chan already knows the character he'll choose based on his reading and discussion, and his aim for the essay will center on how to be most convincing about his choice.

Here are sample notes that Chan makes as he starts working on the assignment.

> Hester: obvious guilt with the A on her dress. More than that?
>
> Chillingworth: her husband and angry about what she's done. Mean and gets uglier throughout the book. The way somebody looks is sometimes a key to how they are inside (check).
>
> Dimmesdale: well, he's just a coward. Makes me mad that he lets Hester carry it all.

These notes show Chan figuring out which of the characters he finds most guilty or evil. He hasn't quite decided, perhaps, but you can tell from his notes that he leans toward Dimmesdale, the one who "makes me mad."

Chan's method here is worth emulating. Writing notes to yourself at the very beginning of a writing task is a good way to begin the invention process without much pressure. If they're just notes, you're not held accountable for them, and they won't be the first sentence of your final essay. This kind of thinking on paper or computer helps you formulate ideas quickly and allows you to continue writing and thinking rather than procrastinating because you feel too much pressure to perform.

Once Chan establishes his opinion, he can begin the data gathering that will constitute his evidence. Lines from the book, events and their consequences, and other situations from Chan's own experience or other reading all might help with the argument he intends to make. Notice that even in the early notes, above, Chan has shown why he leans toward Dimmesdale as the villain. "He's just a coward." That reaction might help Chan as he looks for evidence in the text (Where does Dimmesdale show his cowardice? What happens because of it? How does his cowardice affect others?) and sustains a developing argument about Dimmesdale's character.

One invention technique Chan's teacher suggests that he begin to use is keeping a journal. Following up on this suggestion helps Chan discover the seeds of lots of good ideas for his assignment on the villainous character and later on, for that matter, for essays on any number of topics.

A **reading journal,** a log that the reader uses to trace and monitor developing ideas and reactions to the reading, is a fine way to stimulate invention. Readers write about the characters in a book ("Interesting that Hawthorne compares Hester to a Madonna"), their own connections to the themes or context ("I went to Boston once, and it still feels like a Puritan place"), what they like or dislike, what they don't understand, and what they predict. The reading journal becomes a record of ideas developing and a source of pleasure as readers give voice to their reactions in ways they sometimes aren't able to in classroom discussion.

The best thing about journals kept by writers in a classroom or on their own is that in the journal the writer feels free of many of the rhetorical constraints that are present in assignments like the two given above. The audience may be a teacher or a reading partner, but that audience is not evaluating or judging the journal; instead, the journal is operating as a kind of sounding board for ideas. The subject is the book at hand, but, within that constraint, readers choose any topic that occurs to them to comment and reflect on. The persona of the writer in the reader's journal is determined by the writer's own mood and inclination, not by the demands of correctness or of overt persuasion. The language of this kind of journal is exploratory, with an aim of discovery and explanation to the self rather than to an outside *other;* it is concerned with speculating on possibilities rather than with right or wrong responses. Here is a portion of Chan's journal that he wrote while working on the *Scarlet Letter* assignment:

> I've got to say I just don't get it when Hester refuses to tell everybody who the father of her baby is. If she would just tell, then everybody would have to face up to things, including the fact that people we want to think are so great—pillars of the community, ministers—are just like the rest of us. I wish she'd be braver. Why do people always think it's so brave not to tell on somebody? Sometimes that's the bravest thing.

Apply Chan's Solution

The freedom of thought offered by the journal often results in fluent, interesting, and perceptive writing. Writers who feel free to voice opinions and questions, who aren't burdened by demands for particular forms or length requirements, demonstrate confidence and skill, as well as creativity. And writing in a journal can transfer to other, more formal writing tasks. It's a habit all writers should get into, taking time to write ideas and questions in a journal.

Aristotle believed speakers could understand audiences well because speakers themselves were also audiences. In other words, the more speakers knew themselves, the more they inevitably knew about their listeners. Socrates's famous injunction, "Know thyself," becomes a command to writers who want to reach readers. Writing in a journal, about books or events or plans, is one of the most effective ways for writers to know themselves—and thus, as Aristotle tells us, to begin to know those we're trying to reach.

Activity

Keep a journal of your own for two weeks, writing three times a week. Write about what's going on in the news, what you feel about the work you're doing in class, and what you like or don't understand about the texts you're reading in school. When you're given an assignment, write a journal entry that speculates how you might go about it, what you think you'll need to do to accomplish it, and what you're worried about.

Tasha, Lewis, and Susan: A Group at Work on Writing

As you consider the case of Tasha, Lewis, and Susan, keep the following questions in mind. Discuss them with your group when you can.

1. Since thinking about who your readers are, what they know about your subject, and how you need to interact with them is such a vital part of planning, how does working in a writing group help you plan your writing?
2. How can you use the insights of the other members of a writing group to help you invent effective material for your writing?

As Aristotle taught his students, and as we've shown throughout this book, writers always invent, draft, and revise more effectively if they think carefully about their audience. Our next three writers—Tasha, Lewis, and Susan—show us not only how sharing ideas in a group discussion can help you know your audience better but also how such conversations help you generate more useful material for your compositions. These three writers are working collaboratively on a book review, and their teacher has told them that they should write to an audience of people like themselves—curious, educated students.

What exactly does thinking about an audience do for you as a writer? If you know who's listening or reading, you'll have a better idea of examples that will be effective, stories that will strike familiar notes, and evidence that will be compelling. You know something about how long you should go on because you can infer the tolerance level of your audience; you know something about what you should repeat or omit because you sense their level of experience or understanding.

An audience is much broader than simply who's in an auditorium listening to your speech or who's likely to read your essay in the school newspaper. An audience also has a part to play in helping give writers ideas and helping writers test those ideas. The small group is one place to find such an audience. The talk that students engage in when they're in a group fosters the development of ideas, as students learn both to articulate and to adjust as they speak and listen.

Here's a brief exchange from Tasha, Lewis, and Susan's preliminary discussions of collaboratively writing a review of the book they have just finished reading:

TASHA: I don't think we need to tell too much about her, do you?

LEWIS: You mean the writer? 'Cause I think she's really important to the whole thing. I mean, did you read that part where she talks about being a Quaker?

TASHA: Where was that?

SUSAN: In the intro; it wasn't even in the first chapter. And she never mentions it.

LEWIS: But now you can see why she's so worried about peace.

TASHA: Yeah, I thought, "Why is she talking about wars when it's education we're supposed to be reading about?" But, yeah, I see why we should put that into the report.

SUSAN: I think we should start with it, don't you?

This fragment of a conversation shows how one person's ideas and experience might alter the thinking of somebody else. Tasha begins by saying to her group that the author's life isn't important to the review. She's ready to move on to what she thinks is important: the book's ideas about education, which Tasha alludes to when she says, "It's education we're supposed to be reading about." Lewis has read the introduction, where the writer speaks of her Quaker background and its effect on her teaching; his knowledge changes the way the group sees its task. Tasha uses Lewis's information to reframe her thinking about the report the group is writing, and Susan begins to see the form the report will take, opening with the biographical piece of information that Tasha began the conversation by rejecting.

When a group produces a collaborative product—a report, a presentation, a review—each group member has a *writerly* investment in gathering ideas, presenting evidence, and deciding on organization. Everybody in the group has an idea about these matters because everybody engaged in a collaborative project is a writer of the project. That's one of the difficulties of writing with a partner or with a group, and also one of the benefits. Writers learn how to articulate ideas and decide on opening sentences, supporting details, and effective sentence constructions as they listen to others' writing decisions, and they learn how to negotiate, challenge, and alter ideas in that social context. In other words, their own writing is strengthened by their connection with others' writing.

The advantages of talk about writing in a group are particularly evident when writers are inventing ideas for writing. As in the conversation above, writers invent both what they will talk about and how by listening to each other and offering ideas. A writer can generate questions to discuss in a group by using the strategies of invention explained in Chapter 2: the journalist's questions (page 36), the pentad (page 39), the topics (page 46), and the enthymeme (page 42).

- **Hearing other perspectives.** Let's say that in the conversation above, one of the group members was a member of the Quaker faith. His perspective and experience would add both information and ideas to the discussion and might, in addition, change some group member's belief or opinion or strengthen it. Group talk about writing increases a writer's storehouse of information, and the interaction of several readers and writers creates new knowledge that every group member potentially can make use of.

- **Articulating thoughts.** When writers talk to others about plans or ideas for a piece of writing, they learn what they think about those plans and ideas because they have had to frame what might be unconscious or undeveloped thoughts into language that someone else can understand. The group asks questions such as "Why do you want to begin with a definition?" or "What will you say next?" In the act of responding, writers discover why they're making particular decisions and proceeding in certain directions. Writers become more conscious, in other words, of how they're generating ideas when they must account for those ideas within the group. The role of talk in helping writers make ideas conscious is similar to the way in which the journal can work by helping writers "see" what they think.

- **Understanding what works and what doesn't.** Effective group members let writers know when the decisions they're making seem appropriate and useful. They reinforce writers' ideas by adding information, suggesting details, questioning, and affirming. They also suggest changes or additions to a plan, or they question when they don't understand writers' intentions. In this way, writers become aware of how their own writing plans and decisions need to alter to accommodate a reader's needs. In later stages of drafting and revising, writers learn from talk in the group about how well evidence and logic work in their papers, how suitable their diction is, how clearly they move from point to point, and how effectively their voice carries.

Activity

Using the first chapter of Sandra Cisneros's *House on Mango Street* or any other piece you and your class have read recently, find one problem or issue that you think is important to discuss. It might be something about family from the Cisneros story, for example. Use one or more of the invention strategies from Chapter 2 to generate some ideas about the issue. Then write a paragraph that speculates about the issue. Try out your ideas in a discussion with your group. After the group discussion, rewrite the paragraph so that it incorporates in some way the perceptions, questions, or additions provided by someone in your group.

Nell: The Rhetorical Reviser

As you read Nell's case, consider the following questions and discuss them in your group when you can.

1. In general, what considerations seem most important to you when you're revising a piece of writing?
2. How is a writer's need to revise a piece of writing related to the need to do additional inventing, planning, or drafting?

So far in this chapter, we've been studying invention and revision, and looking at writers working alone or in groups, gathering ideas, and creating scenarios to make their ideas emerge. Now let's examine a writer who devotes a lot of attention to focusing her ideas, omitting what she sees as extraneous material, and changing her ideas. As you read about Nell's revision process, remember the point we made at the outset of this chapter: writers invent all the time during the process of writing, and they revise all the time too. That's why writing is called **recursive:** because it moves back and forth rather than in a straight line from beginning to end.

Nell is planning an editorial for the school newspaper about racial issues in her community, and she comes to talk to her instructor about her ideas: "I thought it would be useful to talk about the progress that's being made in our school on the issue of race. We hear so many bad things, and it's good sometimes to hear about the positive ones." She pauses. "So I thought I'd talk about what the student body did for Martin Luther King Day last year, when we had that special assembly." Her teacher nods. She continues: "But maybe I should start with all the problems we've had here in the past. I don't want to sound like I don't know about how prejudiced we've been."

Nell thinks out loud as she's talking to her teacher. As she's inventing possibilities, she's also revising out loud. She sets her aim—to demonstrate that progress has been made in racial issues at her school. She offers evidence—Martin Luther King Day assemblies—and she considers the audience, who she feels have heard "so many bad things" that they might need to hear something positive. But you can see that she's also revising her initial idea as she decides that she must acknowledge racial problems. She's considering her audience here as well; she doesn't want her readers to think that she isn't aware of problems or is trying to ignore past racial difficulties. All this invention and revision occur in the space of a minute or so of talk!

Although revision occurs during the entire writing process, it's when writers have put words and paragraphs down on paper that they most consciously consider purpose, audience, and voice. Once ideas have been shaped onto the page, a writer begins to decide more directly how those ideas work together, how the voice sounds in presenting them, and how readers might react to them. Writers begin the process of changing and adding and deleting as they invent new ideas, and they consider the effect of their language and organization on communication with readers and on their emerging aim.

The journal and the writer's group are both useful in this part of the writing process, too, when writers are rethinking or reseeing their work. As we've suggested, the journal is a way to speculate and explore, to try out ideas and voices. Writers who get stuck or "blocked" in the middle of writing a paper can use the journal to get unstuck. Writer's block often happens because writers feel sudden or intense pressure: the time is too short, they don't like the previous paragraph, they don't know what comes next, or they don't sound knowledgeable enough. These writers are feeling the rhetorical constraints of voice, subject, aim, or audience too intensely and find it hard to proceed.

Audience is the constraint that most often blocks student writers, since so often their audience is an evaluator who will grade or score their performance, who may or may not talk to them about it, and who seems to have in mind already what constitutes an acceptable writing performance. The journal, taken up in the middle of a writing assignment, can free writers once again to explore ideas even if they choose not to write about the issue at hand in their journal entry.

Next time you feel blocked in your own writing, write in your journal about your problems with the assignment. "I think I know where I'm going, but I don't seem to be able to get there. It's like I'm on a highway with no exit," one student wrote to his teacher about his trouble in completing a draft. Writing through his anxiety helped him continue. Or write about something totally unrelated to your draft: observe somebody in the hall, write a character sketch, or write about a funny moment in class. Any experience or speculation that you write about with some attention will work to build your confidence. And confidence is what writers who feel blocked need.

Activity

As quickly as you can, write a first draft of what you think would be a good first paragraph for the composition Nell is working on. Then, in your group, compare your first drafts, and talk about what you would do to revise them if you continued working on this assignment.

You Pull It All Together

As you work on this final case, consider the following questions, and discuss them in your group when you can.

1. How do you connect your own experiences to the texts you read when you're planning a composition?

2. How do you develop your own *persona* when you're also paying attention to the voices and positions from the texts you're reading?

3. How do you persuade an audience when you're writing about a controversial issue or one that provokes strong feelings?

Let's conclude this chapter with a flourish—with a project that asks you to practice some of the major considerations you take into account with a substantial writing project. Your writing processes here will include invention, drafting, and revising.

Following are two articles taken from the Greensboro, North Carolina, *News and Record*. The newspaper publishes articles on racial issues every Sunday during February in its "Ideas" section as part of its recognition of Black History Month. The first, written by the white director of a branch library in town, comments on the need for a civil rights museum in the city and uses his own family history to help argue his point. The second is a reprint of a speech given by an African American professor speaking at a celebration of Martin Luther King Day at Bennett College in Greensboro. Read the two articles, and pay attention to the persona of the writers, the way they use evidence, and how they appeal to their audiences.

WHY WHITE PEOPLE NEED A CIVIL RIGHTS MUSEUM IN GREENSBORO

I always had taken comfort in the fact that I was from a family too poor to own slaves. As far as I knew, our ancestors were all dirt-poor farmers, sharecroppers and mill workers. I felt sure that no one with a DNA link to me was guilty of the sin of slavery. In fact, my grandfather had told us that one of our South Carolina ancestors had been openly opposed to slavery and had taught slaves to read, even though it was illegal to do so. Needless to say, I liked that story and I wanted to go to my grave thinking that my ancestry was a combination of poor sharecroppers and good abolitionist stock.

But my brother is a scientist and he answered my question with the facts: One branch of our family did have enough money to own a small number of slaves.

In Dr. King's most famous speech, he cried out for a day of equality and harmony between the "sons of former slaves and sons of former slave owners." Before that day, I hadn't felt that I was kin to either of these groups, but suddenly I felt as if my DNA had rearranged itself and linked me, against my will, to the plantation owners of the Mississippi Delta. My working class heritage, of which I am proud, was now tainted by a bloodline connection to slave owners. I sat there, a few miles away from the levees and the plantations, feeling that I had gone deeper into the South and deeper into my own heritage than I had really wanted to go.

. . .

History is like family ancestry: We can't selectively decide whom we want to be related to, and we shouldn't selectively decide which parts of history we want to remember. History, like our DNA, continues to shape the present in ways we cannot recognize. . . . We will not be able to understand current issues such as racial profiling, achievement gaps, racial mistrust and school redistricting until we understand the full implication of what transpired between blacks and whites when the river rose over the levees in Greenville and when the demonstrators in Greensboro were abused.

IS RACISM STILL ALIVE? OR HAVE WE OVERCOME?

Racism is our shibboleth. It is the sign and symbol by which we are known and remembered around the world, for this civilization cursed itself long before it became a nation. The white men and women who founded it with such high purpose let that purpose be demeaned by the enslavement of those black men and women called to maintain and develop what they founded.

. . .

We turn again to the memory of Martin Luther King, whose life was itself the clearest expression of what America claimed to be but never was. We look again at the America he knew and the America he dreamed about, and because we share his dreams we wish that somehow he could be here now, alas! not to see those dreams fulfilled, for that is a long way off, but to bring us together again and to revive us in the continuing struggle toward the realization of what he dreamed about.

Activity

In a sentence or two, describe the argument that each of these writers is making about race. Now consider how each man is making his argument. What evidence do they offer? What support do they give for their positions? Are those positions more alike or different? What do these pieces assume about readers?

Using What You Read

If you were writing your own piece for the newspaper about race or giving a speech about it to your school, you would no doubt revise what the writers above have said to make use of your own context, to fit your own ideas and experience. And that's the essence of all revision: to rethink what you've read and heard—including what you've read and heard in your own draft—to get closer to what you're discovering to be the purpose of the writing. So, having read these two pieces, try the following activity.

Activity

Write a beginning discussion of race as you see it, from your own personal experience, your understanding of culture and history, and books you've read. Use the ideas presented by one or both of the writers above for your own emerging argument or speculation about race. You'll be revising your ideas based on the need to include one or both of these examples; you'll be revising the examples as you fit them into your own context. Once you have a short draft, read your work aloud to your group. See if they feel you've been fair to the writers as you've included them in your argument. See if you can describe your speaker's voice and your aim to them. Does your group agree with you? Your group will help you revise, too, to help you get closer to what you want to achieve, especially in having someone else understand what you're trying to say.

Revising Your First Effort

When you revise, you test your own truth as a writer. How do you conduct this test for truth? You look back to find out how you sound and to find when you hear your own voice speaking. It sounds different than it does when you first compose because now you're hearing the words on the page as a *reader* as well as a writer.

Suppose you began your draft this way: "Race is still a problem, but progress has been achieved." You might read back and cross out that sentence. "Race is still a problem, but we've made progress." What made you decide to change the first sentence? You can hear the difference in the two. The first sentence sounds more formal, distant. And why is that? The word *achieved* carries more precise definition somehow than *made* and so feels explanatory. And the passive construction *has been achieved* puts you, the writer, out of the message, making your voice sound far away from the subject and from your readers. In some cases, of course, you want to achieve that distance. You've written essays or reports in which you wanted to highlight findings rather than your part in discovering those findings. And taking the "person" out of the writing is one way to do that.

But suppose you make the change above. Why do you revise the sentence? Apparently, you've decided you don't want to be far removed from the subject; you want somehow to be involved in it. And you want your reader to be involved too. You use the word *we* to signal that you see yourself, and your readers, as part of something, such as a community or a culture. Revising with a notion of voice or persona, with a sense of readers, and with an idea of subject, you are making changes rhetorically. You're using the elements of Aristotle's triangle to achieve your purpose more effectively.

Whether you're conscious of it or not, you are thinking rhetorically as you make the change from the more to the less formal sentence. When you revise, you read back and make changes in part to "get it right with the self," as British language theorist James Britton said. You listen to yourself, ask questions of yourself, and try changes in words, punctuation, and paragraphing to see if the writing seems to "work" better, or "sound right." Sometimes when you revise, you're trying to make sure your text is correct or you're adding sentences to make it longer, but these are concerns with audience, not with your own ideas about the text you've written.

As you're getting your piece to sound right to you, you're also thinking about other rhetorical concerns that will make it sound right to others. Becoming conscious of these, you can become an even more effective reviser of your own work.

Revising for Persona

The writer's personality on the page, his or her voice, can be the most powerful tool a writer possesses. The best way to revise for voice, or persona, is to listen to that voice and test its sound. Like tuning a guitar, you'll get in the habit of hearing the note that's a little too high or too loud, and you'll adjust your word, sentence, or punctuation to make the chord harmonious.

You sometimes find your persona in the acts of writing and revising. You realize in the process of formulating your ideas and planning your approach that you sound informed or passionate or objective or distant. And developing your persona as you revise helps you to come up with new ideas, new illustrations, and new word choices.

But often your persona is implicitly given to you in an assignment. When you write your college admissions essay and the directions are to tell of an experience that has shaped you as a student, you understand that you need to write as a teenager, as a student, and, because it's an essay that will help get you admitted to a university, as someone who cares about education and learning. You want to show that you understand the conventions of academic and formal writing, so you avoid clichés, slang, and digressions. You check to make sure that you've spelled words correctly, that you haven't made punctuation errors. And you want to sound interested and appealing; you're asking readers to see you as a good candidate, a good student, and a reflective thinker. Understanding the persona your words create can make you a persuasive writer.

Activity

Here's a quick exercise: Make the voice in this sentence sound more angry.

"The mass of men live lives of quiet desperation."

Now make the voice sound more informal.

Do you see how quickly you can change the feeling you have about the writer and the subject by changing the words that give you a sense of the writer's persona?

Revising for Audience

The people your writing interacts with constantly influence your thinking. For much of the writing you accomplish in school, you know your audience well. It's a teacher, who has indicated to you in comments and evaluations of your work what he or she expects or hopes for from the writing. Think about what you know of your teacher's expectations: clarity, development of ideas, knowledge of subject, use of detail. There are probably lots of others. And for different courses, the teacher as audience has some varying expectations. In writing for a biology class, your audience wants to be able to repeat experiments and so expects no omissions of procedure. In asking you to write a paraphrase for a history class, your teacher expects no digressions or personal asides; he or she wants you to demonstrate your understanding of the texts. In some classes, originality is prized; in others, brevity. As a student, you learn, sometimes almost unconsciously, about audience through a teacher's conversation and responses.

When you write other pieces for which the teacher is not the main audience—the school newspaper, a journal, a group presentation—you take into account expectations too, even though sometimes you're not as sure about those expectations as you might be with teachers, since you don't get the same kind of direct feedback from newspaper readers or your fellow students. And when you write for distant audiences, as in the college admissions essay or an advanced-placement exam, you infer from the directions and from reading similar pieces what the audience believes, needs, or expects from you. In these cases, the Socratic maxim "Know thyself" can help you. You know what makes you interested or bored, convinced or doubtful, and you can use this knowledge as you revise your writing.

Revising Subject

The content, point, or subject matter of a piece of writing is a complex concern for a writer. Writers often believe that the main point in the rhetorical triangle is the subject point. "I just read about whatever topic they assigned and found out as much as I could about it. Then just wrote it up," one writer explained as she was describing her writing process in a composition class. For many assignments, knowing the subject does seem to be the most important thing. Writers need proof, they need evidence, and they need detail to be convincing.

Revising with subject in mind, a writer may go back to the library or to the Internet to find additional support for descriptions of the rain forest climate along the Amazon or for an explanation of chaos theory or for an argument about the value of the space program or for a claim that Huck Finn is not naïve. The subject or thesis about the subject can also be developed by talking to others and by jotting down ideas as they suggest themselves in reading the beginning of a draft. The more you think and talk about a subject, the more you know of it.

Revising Evidence

You need proof that helps persuade a reader, and evidence comes in many forms. Writers decide how much evidence and what kinds of evidence to use based on their growing understanding of the subject, of voice, and of the audience. They revise that evidence to make their writing increasingly convincing.

- **Narrative.** Stories, anecdotes, and examples all serve as evidence and as ways to develop subjects. Look back at your essay on race. Did you use a story? If so, why? The first article on race (page 111) uses narrative to explain the subject—the need for a civil rights museum—and to frame the argument. The advantage of narrative is clear: readers get to know the writer and understand his or her persona through a story, even when it's not a story about the writer. And readers like stories because they're usually easily understood and easily connected to the readers' own experiences. Of course, narrative is more appropriate for some writing tasks than for others. A narrative can be merely a distraction if you're writing to explore the rhetorical techniques in Frederick Douglass's prose. It might be clearly inappropriate in a reflection on an experiment. You might edit a story out of a final draft for these reasons. Or you might insert one as you revise.
- **Logic.** Writers use the logic of ideas—how one idea necessarily follows another, how one claim justifies another—constantly in their writing. As we explained in Chapter 2, Aristotle used two terms to define this logical

manipulation of ideas, the **syllogism** and the *enthymeme.* The syllogism suggests two premises, neither of which is arguable, and then draws the inescapable conclusion.

> Van is a politician.
>
> Politicians all have suspect motives.
>
> Van's motives are suspect.

Logical reasoning using either the syllogism or the enthymeme (syllogistic reasoning with one premise assumed rather than stated, as in "Van is a politician, and I'm suspicious") is often highly persuasive, and academic writing uses this kind of reasoning all the time. You should be ready to revise with an idea of logical order in mind. What are your unstated premises? Are they probable or useful? Do readers understand the progression of your ideas so that they follow your line of thinking and might be inclined to agree?

■ **Data.** Probably the kind of evidence you're most familiar with and use most consciously is data—research that supports the conclusions you're drawing. You locate this research in the books and articles you read on your subject, in reports and findings from researchers, and in newspaper articles, interviews, and case studies. Data help make your case, providing support outside your own experience or logic, that the position you take has merit. In your essay on race, your data may come from cultural criticism, biographies of civil rights figures, primary documents from the 1960s, or interviews and other sources. As you revise your work, you examine your data, testing to make sure that you have enough, that you've dealt with the data fairly, and that you haven't hidden data that present an opposite position.

How, and if, any kind of data gets used depends on all the rhetorical factors we've been discussing, but most especially on the context for your writing. The rhetorical situation—what purpose you're trying to accomplish, who your audience is, and what kind of assignment you have—determines the data you'll use as evidence. Knowing and acting on that rhetorical situation is perhaps the single most important element in learning to revise and invent throughout your writing process.

Interchapter

3

Overview of the Major Points in Chapter 3

- Writers develop substantial pieces of writing by following a complex, recursive process. All aspects of the writing process are influenced by the rhetorical situation in which the writer is working.

- As writers work through a process on a piece of writing, they develop a sense of intention, a belief that what they are writing is important to them, and a sense that they have a reason to write beyond fulfilling an assignment.

- The central acts of writing are invention and revision, both of which operate continually throughout a writer's process.

- Writers become more fluent and effective by tapping into many sources to discover material for their writing, by keeping journals, and by discussing their emerging work regularly with classmates and/or a writing group.

Activities and Discussion Questions for Chapter 3 Use these questions and comments to guide your own discussion and to guide your writing about these literary works.

Henry David Thoreau, "An Essay on Civil Disobedience" (published 1849)

The text appears on pages 210–225. Suppose that you decide to write on some aspect of a citizen's duty to either respect his or her government or resist it. Describe what such a composition would be—an essay, a letter, a Web site, an editorial, a speech? How would you develop a sense of intention? How would you go about writing it?

Eavan Boland, "It's a Woman's World" (published 1982)

The text appears on pages 226–227. You decide to write on some aspect of a woman's rights and roles in our society. Describe the form such a piece of writing might take—a **dialogue,** a researched essay, a journal entry, a poem? How would you develop a sense of intention? How would you proceed as you begin to write?

Alice Walker, "Everyday Use" (published 1973)

The text appears on pages 228–237. You decide to write on some aspect of either ethnic identity or family relationships. Describe the form your piece of writing might take—a story, an interview, a feature story for a newspaper, a history? How would you develop a sense of intention? How would you proceed as you begin to write?

Rhetoric and the Reader

4

" 'And'—what do you know?—'they all lived happily ever after.' "

One must be an inventor to read well.

Ralph Waldo Emerson, "The American Scholar"

Just as writers create a text so that it achieves an intention, readers likewise process a text so that it achieves an intention. Readers invent and revise ideas about what they read. They add details to texts; they agree or make arguments. They are above all actively involved with what they read; if they can't be active, they can't read very well. At that point, they stop listening to the text and just look at words. Aristotle knew that the audience who listened to a speech brought with them particular beliefs and experiences that shaped what they'd hear. It was up to the speaker to use those beliefs and experiences to help the audience understand or appreciate the message—or even change their minds—as they listened to the speech. Today, speakers and writers likewise expect listeners and readers to bring their beliefs and experiences to bear on texts and, in so doing, to make meaning from the texts they hear and read.

Predicting What's Next

Once upon a time . . . What's the next word? Most readers have no trouble predicting that the word that follows that phrase is *there*. How do readers know that word? It doesn't follow the ordinary English sentence pattern to put the word "there" next. If it were an ordinary English sentence, it would read something like "Once upon a time a wicked witch lived. . . . " But somehow that doesn't sound right—because readers know that *Once upon a time* begins a fairy tale, and fairy tales *always* have *there* after *Once upon a time:* "Once upon a time, *there* lived a wicked, frightening, hideous old witch. She lived in a cave all alone, so wicked and so frightening that even the bats hid from her in the farthest corners of the rock." What will happen next? You might not know the exact words (and there aren't any, since we're making this fairy tale up), but you could predict that sometime soon there'll be a sentence that will read something like *And then one day. . . .* In fairy tales, there's always a turn like that; somebody or something new comes into the forest and changes fairy tale life. Finish the sentence for yourself. Then ask your friends how they finished it. There will probably be some similarities because many of you will have the same expectations for the tale. Will there be a princess? A prince? A magic spell?

Readers predict like this all the time. In fact, in order to read, they *must* predict. How do they make predictions? They read in units, or "chunks" of meaning, not word by word. Readers are always reading for meaning, reading fast and moving ahead to find the next bit of meaning they can hold onto. In fact, if you were to get very close to someone reading intently, you could see that the eye moving across the page doesn't move in just one direction. It moves back and forth very quickly, reading ahead and then looking back to retrieve necessary bits of information not attended to at first.

The process is fast, this going back and forth, and unconscious for the most part. Lots of readers believe they read every word, for example. Or they believe they're much slower readers than they actually are. Readers become conscious of how they predict and revise predictions, make choices and remake them, only when they encounter a text that's too difficult for them, one where they must reread often, go back continually to check what they might have missed. If you've ever read a text too difficult for you because you didn't have enough information or experience to bring to the text or because the language was too difficult or specialized, and you've had to read word by word, you know how you lose interest fast. You can't read fast enough to predict, so you can't enjoy or understand what you're reading.

Readers make their predictions about what they read based on all kinds of factors. They predict based on what they know about the kind of text they're reading, as you did with the fairy tale. They predict based on their own experience with the subject of the text, the sound of the writer's voice, and their knowledge of grammar and sentence structure. Everything that readers know helps them to read a text and predict accurately. As readers read, they gather more and more data about the narrator, the genre, the tone, and the sentence structure, and understand more and more clearly which of their own experiences are most helpful to their reading. As a result, readers get better at predicting the further into a text they read.

Activity

Here's a test to illustrate how much, and how well, you predict when you read. It's called a **cloze test,** and it's based on the idea that readers read in chunks, rather than in words. The educational theorist George Herbert Mead determined that for most readers, a chunk includes seven or so words, so the cloze test leaves about every seventh word blank and asks the reader to figure out what word makes sense in the blank.

> They lived in a hamlet swept _____ by winds from the land and _____ from the sea.

The first sentence of this paragraph reads, "They lived in a hamlet swept *alternately* by winds from the land and *winds* from the sea."

If you had been reading along and had noted the word *alternately*, you would have likely predicted *winds* as the word for the second blank. If you had skipped over *alternately*, you'd have likely predicted another word like *waves*, perhaps, for the second blank. *Waves* would be a good choice, in fact, because of the alliterative balance with the *w* sound in *winds*.

Try the rest of the paragraph. In your mind, fill in the blanks as you read. Suggest only one word for each blank.

> A steep road _____ along by cliffs and wastelands, leading, it _____, to nothing human. And that was _____ it was called the deserted _____, L'Abandonée. At certain times everyone there _____ be filled with dread, like travelers _____ in a strange land. Still young _____ strong, always dressed in a worker's _____, Minerva had a glossy, light mahogany _____ and black eyes brimming over with _____. She had an unshakable faith in _____. When things went wrong she would _____ that nothing, no one, would ever _____ out the soul God had chosen _____ for her and put in her _____. All the year round she fertilized _____, picked coffee, hoed the banana groves, _____ weeded the rows of sweet potatoes. _____ her daughter Toussine was no more _____ to dreaming than she.

After you make guesses for as many blanks as you can (there may be blanks you can't figure out easily, so skip them), move into your small group, and try to come up with a word for every blank. You'll need to decide together about which word fits best in each blank. Think about how you make decisions about which word to choose.

In this activity, the paragraph in the cloze test is from the first chapter of the novel *The Bridge of Beyond* by Caribbean writer Simone Schwarz-Bart. As you go over the actual words from the novel (the words appear at the end of this chapter), you will probably discover that your guesses get more accurate the further into the paragraph you read. Why? You are building up information and making decisions about what kind of character Minerva might be, about where the story takes place, about what kinds of events might happen. You'll notice that some words—conjunctions, prepositions—are easy to figure out. Other words, adjectives especially, are more difficult to think of. But your understanding of narrative, of the forms stories take, might make you able to predict fairly smoothly. Many words you selected will be synonyms for the actual words in the text, showing how well you understand the conventions of sentences and of the genre of the story.

Activity

Cloze tests on nonfiction present more challenges sometimes, since nonfiction often uses more specialized vocabulary and is less dependent on a familiar story line. Try this piece of nonfiction. Guess which words belong in the blanks, as before, and then confer with your group to see if you can agree on most of the words.

> Chaos breaks across the lines that _____ scientific disciplines. Because it is a _____ of the global nature of systems, _____ has brought

together thinkers from fields _____ had been widely separated. "Fifteen years _____, science was heading for a _____ of increasing specialization," a Navy official _____ charge of scientific financing remarked to _____ audience of mathematicians, biologists, physicists, and _____ doctors. "Dramatically, that specialization has reversed _____ of chaos." Chaos poses problems that _____ accepted ways of working in science. _____ makes strong claims about the universal _____ of complexity. The first chaos theorists, _____ scientists who set the discipline in _____, shared certain sensibilities. They had an _____ for pattern, especially pattern that _____ on different scales at the same time. They had a taste for randomness and complexity, for jagged edges and sudden _____. _____ in chaos— and they sometimes call _____ believers, or converts, or evangelists—_____ about determinism and free will, _____ evolution, about the nature of conscious _____.

In this paragraph, from the beginning chapter of James Gleick's book *Chaos,* the discussion centers on how theory in physics has begun to redefine areas of thought and to forge links across disciplinary boundaries. Although it's about physics, this book is written for nonspecialists, as perhaps you can tell even in this little sample; the word choice is not overly specialized, and there are beginning definitions and a kind of story that weaves the information together. Still, it may be harder for you to make decisions about how to fill in the blanks best. See which words seem to be easiest for you and your group to agree upon. Look at the end of the chapter to find the missing words in this cloze test.

Understanding How Readers Predict

In these two activities, part of your decision as you predicted and changed your predictions based on rereading and on your group's discussion came about as you began to understand more about the rhetoric of the paragraphs you read. As you read, you made inferences about the speaker's or narrator's persona, about the subject, and about what you as a reader are expected to know or to want to learn. In the opening from *The Bridge of Beyond,* for example, the narrator chooses words that begin to tell the reader about important elements in the character of Minerva. She's strong, has an unshakable faith in *herself,* and works hard, dressed as always in a worker's *overall.* She is kind and beautiful, the emblem of the fairy tale heroine. In fact, *The Bridge of Beyond* is a kind of fairy tale, a myth with magic and danger and a happily-ever-after ending. Can you find places in the paragraph that suggest the faraway character of the novel or its mythical qualities? Think of the name of the village, for example.

In the paragraph from *Chaos,* the writer adopts an almost jovial tone (can you pick out words that indicate that tone?), although he's talking about difficult scientific issues. He uses a narrative—beginning with *fifteen years ago*—to help the reader. And he humanizes the scientists who first made the discoveries that were to lead to the development of chaos theory: "They had an *eye* for pattern," he tells us. Consider how different the tone might be if he had chosen instead to say, "The first chaos theorists were interested in pattern." You wouldn't be as interested. You might speculate about why the speaker creates this tone and uses narrative at the opening of this book on a new theory in physics.

A writer's choice of words reflects the depiction of character and the writer's intention, and you get better at predicting qualities of character and writer's intentions as you read further. Of course, you bring your own knowledge and beliefs to what you read as well. How you value your own experiences as a reader and writer, what you know about the kind of text you're beginning, how you feel about the subject—all of these will be factors in determining how you read the writer's intentions. Readers and writers work together to create meaning in texts.

Rosenblatt and Interaction: Two Kinds of Reading

Reading theorist Louise Rosenblatt explains the interaction between reader and writer's text this way.

Rosenblatt shows that it's in the combination between readers (and all they bring with them) and texts (and all they offer) that the **poem** happens. Notice: When Rosenblatt uses the term *poem*, she is not referring to a specific type of text, one that may have line divisions, meter, rhyme scheme, and so on. *Poem* is the term Rosenblatt uses for interpretation, for meaning making, and this process happens only in interaction between readers and texts. If readers can't, or won't, bring their own experiences and ideas to their reading of a text, then interpretation, or meaning, is lost. Readers might under-

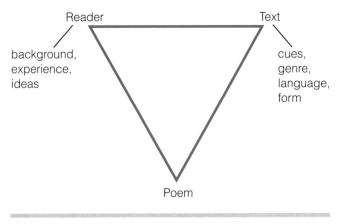

Rosenblatt's Triangle

stand words on the page but little about their importance or their context. Reading must in some sense always be made personal for it to be made meaningful.

Rosenblatt also discusses *kinds* of readers. As readers, we read with varying intentions—aims or purposes. Texts remain the same, but readers change, and their reasons for reading those texts vary. Rosenblatt defines two kinds of reading that you'll be familiar with from your own experience. **Efferent reading** is reading for information, for the facts or ideas that readers can *do* something with. The word *efferent* comes from the Latin word, *efferre,* which means "to carry away." Readers reading efferently hope to carry away from the text something they will put to use. Readers usually read textbooks efferently; they read recipes, manuals, handbooks, directions, musical scores, and lots of other texts for what those texts will allow them to do. Did you read the opening from *Chaos* efferently once you had all the words?

Aesthetic reading is reading for experience, for the chance to enter the world that the text presents, to become immersed in the words, ideas, images, and story within the text. Readers reading aesthetically are not so much interested in carrying away information for particular uses of their own as they are in carrying themselves into the text. Readers often read fiction and poetry aesthetically; they read drama, letters, and their own journals for how those texts let them feel, or to experience what's in the text. Look again at the opening to *The Bridge of Beyond.* Did you pay attention to its language? Did you try to imagine what the character looked like and who she was? If so, you responded aesthetically to the novel's opening.

But it's certainly possible to read a novel efferently or a science book aesthetically. If you are searching for metaphors in Schwarz-Bart's book (or filling in blanks), you're reading the novel efferently. When you read a novel looking only for what you can carry away with you to use in an essay or to answer a question on an exam, you miss the aesthetic response. And readers who hear music in their heads when they read a musical score read the sheet music aesthetically, appreciating the chord changes and ingenious repetitions, perhaps not even trying to play the piece themselves. Even a textbook could be read aesthetically for its design or its voice.

Activity

Imagine that you were instructed to begin reading a text that someone had told you was written by a paleontologist about a perspective on evolutionary history as it has been located in a group of ancient fossils. Before beginning this reading, discuss with your group members your expectations about tone, word choice, and level of interest and engagement. Talk openly about how these expectations would affect your reading.

Now, read a segment of that book:

FROM CHAPTER 1 OF *WONDERFUL LIFE*

A Prologue in Pictures

by Stephen Jay Gould

And I will lay sinews upon you, and will bring up flesh upon you, and cover you
with skin, and put breath in you, and ye shall live.

—Ezekiel 37:6

Not since the Lord himself showed his stuff to Ezekiel in the valley of dry bones
had anyone shown such grace and skill in the reconstruction of animals from disar-
ticulated skeletons. Charles R. Knight, the most celebrated of artists in the reanima-
tion of fossils, painted all the canonical figures of dinosaurs that fire our fear and
imagination to this day. In February 1942, Knight designed a chronological series of
panoramas, depicting the history of life from the advent of multicellular animals to
the triumph of *Homo sapiens,* for the *National Geographic.* (This is the one issue that's
always saved and therefore always missing when you see a "complete" run of the
magazine on sale for two bits an issue on the back shelves of the general store in
Bucolia, Maine.) He based his first painting in the series—shown on the jacket of
this book—on the animals of the Burgess Shale.

Without hesitation or ambiguity, and fully mindful of such paleontological
wonders as large dinosaurs and African ape-men, I state that the invertebrates of
the Burgess Shale, found high in the Canadian Rockies in Yoho National Park, on
the eastern border of British Columbia, are the world's most important animal fossils. Modern multicellular animals make their first uncontested appearance in the
fossil record some 570 million years ago—and with a bang, not a protracted
crescendo. This "Cambrian explosion" marks the advent (at least into direct evidence) of virtually all major groups of modern animals—and all within the minus-
cule span, geologically speaking, of a few million years. The Burgess Shale
represents a period just after this explosion, a time when the full range of its products inhabited our seas. These Canadian fossils are precious because they preserve
in exquisite detail, down to the last filament of a trilobite's gill, or the components
of a last meal in a worm's gut, the soft anatomy of organisms. Our fossil record is
almost exclusively the story of hard parts. But most animals have none, and those
that do often reveal very little about their anatomies in their outer coverings (what
could you infer about a clam from its shell alone?). Hence, the rare soft-bodied fau-
nas of the fossil record are precious windows into the true range and diversity of
ancient life. The Burgess Shale is our only extensive, well-documented window
upon that most crucial event in the history of animal life, the first flowering of the
Cambrian explosion.

The story of the Burgess Shale is also fascinating in human terms. The fauna
was discovered in 1909 by America's greatest paleontologist and scientific adminis-
trator, Charles Doolittle Walcott, secretary (their name for boss) of the Smithsonian
Institution. Walcott proceeded to misinterpret these fossils in a comprehensive and
thoroughly consistent manner arising directly from his conventional view of life: In
short, he shoehorned every last Burgess animal into a modern group, viewing the
fauna collectively as a set of primitive or ancestral versions of later, improved
forms. Walcott's work was not consistently challenged for more than fifty years. In
1971, Professor Harry Whittington of Cambridge University published the first

monograph in a comprehensive reexamination that began with Walcott's assumptions and ended with a radical interpretation not only for the Burgess Shale, but (by implication) for the entire history of life, including our own evolution.

Once you have finished the reading, discuss with your group members how the voice and **stance** of the author (the late Stephen Jay Gould) influenced your reading. Did the voice and stance lead you to alter your expectations that the text might be dry or difficult, too specialized or only concerned with reporting on findings? Did you find yourself reading the text not only for information about the fossils and what they might mean to the study of evolution but also for the excitement of the discovery and for the sense of shared engagement with the paleontologist's perspective?

Rosenblatt, Reading, and Rhetoric

Rosenblatt's primary goal in identifying efferent and aesthetic readings is to help readers respond appropriately to the texts they read. If you attend a poetry reading, the experience of the "reading"—that is, listening to the poet read—is meant to be aesthetic, designed to have you experience emotions and ideas through the interesting turns of its language. On the other hand, if you're in a computer lab listening to a speaker describing how to create a Web page, you're meant to "read" the talk efferently, by taking notes or following instructions on your own machine. Should you consider only the way the speaker phrases sentences or repeats a metaphor, you might miss the overall point and fail to learn much about Web pages. To understand your efferent and aesthetic possibilities as a reader is to begin the process of reading well. Rosenblatt's discussion also shows readers just how powerful they are in the act of reading, and how much their own disposition affects how they'll read and understand the texts they encounter.

You probably can see the rhetorical implications of Rosenblatt's work. The writer producing the text has to know how to create possibilities for readers to engage with the words on the page, to bring what they know to bear on what they read. The writer uses those "cues" to help guide readers' responses and to attempt to persuade readers to the position the writer wants them to adopt. Sometimes that persuasion is as simple as "You're really going to like this piece, I promise, so keep reading." Fiction often has that as a persuasive message. James Gleick's *Chaos* might be saying something like, "You may think this is tough stuff, but chaos theory is all around you, and you ought to read this because it is so exciting." Both messages say, "Keep reading." Gleick is also persuading his readers that chaos theory makes sense and offers new areas of study and cooperation to science and philosophy. Simone Schwarz-Bart may be persuading her readers of the value of oral culture, of dialect, and of the beauty of the island myths. Both writers use words and the forms they choose to make connections with readers strong enough to convey their persuasive intentions.

As a reader, then, you analyze and respond to the intention of the author and to the text itself. You pick up on the writer's cues—the indications given about aim through words and punctuation and sentence structure, as well as through the tropes and figures you worked with in Chapter 2. You understand the role you're being asked to play as the reader, and you decide whether your primary response is to enter the text or to take something from it, to become an aesthetic or an efferent reader. And in doing this kind of response and analysis, you predict. As you predict your role as a reader, you decide whether and how you'll play it. As you predict the writer's intention, you decide whether you believe it or agree with it. When you respond in this way, you are engaging in the process of rhetorical analysis, of looking at the elements of rhetoric and how they combine to produce their effects on you as a reader.

Rhetorical Analysis of Chaos

To illustrate how the principles of rhetoric work in a text—that is, to show how a rhetorical analysis might be accomplished—let's look at the excerpt from *Chaos* in detail. It's important to remember that what we'll analyze is just a small fragment, but even a paragraph or two can reveal intention and effect.

> James Gleick wants to introduce readers to chaos theory and establish that it has beneficial possibilities for science. He makes his argument by creating a writer's voice that's both readable and knowledgeable. And he invites readers to share the chaos theorists' belief that looking everywhere for knowledge rather than in just one specialized area leads to new and better knowledge.

Notice that this first paragraph of the rhetorical analysis touches on all the points in Aristotle's triangle. It mentions purpose—"the beneficial possibilities" of chaos theory. It describes Gleick's persona—"readable and knowledgeable." It acknowledges audience—"invites readers to share" in understanding the chaos theorists' position. The subject, chaos theory, is mentioned in the first sentence.

What should happen next? As the writer analyzing Gleick, you might want to illustrate your claims about the rhetoric of the piece by demonstrating, through examples from the paragraph, how they work.

> Gleick begins with a definition of chaos as a science of "the global nature of systems." He quickly moves to claim that the connection of areas of science that have been traditionally separated has been the result of chaos theory and that it's a useful benefit for science. Quoting a Navy official who speaks approvingly of chaos having begun to reverse the dangers of "increasing specialization" in science, Gleick demonstrates his own position: that posing new problems in science might lead to new breakthroughs in scientific knowledge.
>
> Throughout the paragraph, Gleick's voice is conversational, even easygoing. "They had an eye for pattern," he says, speaking of the first chaos researchers. "They had a taste for randomness." The personal qualities of the scientists themselves makes even readers who might be leery of reading such a scientific book

relax. Gleick clearly wants to introduce readers to a theory he believes has possibilities for changing the way we all think.

The reader analyzing Gleick could, and should, go on to speak of other rhetorical moves in the text—for example, the statements of definition, the non-specialized language, and Gleick's mostly unstated belief in the importance of new ways of thinking that gets inserted into the paragraph in several places. But the three beginning paragraphs are enough for you to see how you might proceed to analyze a piece rhetorically, looking at its elements and making claims about its intent. A reader who analyzes a piece of writing rhetorically could also at some point talk about its effect—how a reader might or does react to the piece. Of course, whether you choose to emphasize effect or not, a rhetorical analysis always assumes that the reader's response is key and always explains that response, since the reader is a point on the rhetorical triangle.

Matching Experience and Intention

Writers consciously and unconsciously use readers' experiences and beliefs to guide their own decisions in the texts they write. The formats they employ, the narrators they choose, the level of language they use, and the evidence they provide are all in great measure based on the predictions they make about how their audiences will read their work. And they are able to make these predictions because they are readers themselves.

"Form is the appeal," philosopher Kenneth Burke says, and form—length, paragraph breaks, dialogue, chapter headings, and so on—guides readers in their expectations and predictions. We pick up a novel. Before we read the title or author, we already begin to make predictions and develop expectations. The book will have characters, conflicts, messages. It will have chapters. If the novel is long, we wonder about its complexity and its scope. We consider how much time might elapse from first to last chapter, and how much time we'll devote to reading it. If we pick up a short story instead, we'll expect less time to elapse, perhaps; we won't expect chapters.

Burke uses a scene from *Hamlet* to talk about the importance of readers' sense of form. In the scene, Hamlet speaks about the ghost of his father appearing to him. The scene is set up to make the audience anticipate the ghost. When, instead, the soldiers at watch begin a playful conversation, readers are momentarily frustrated and then lulled into their conversation, for the moment forgetting the ghost. When he does appear, the moment is all the more striking for its delay, and Burke shows how the audience finds pleasure in having their expectations for form gratified.

Whatever readers read, they use what they know about forms to make interpretive decisions about the text and to guide themselves in making meaning. Readers are asked to fill in a lot of information from their experience and ideas. The first chapter of *David Copperfield* by Charles Dickens begins with the chapter title "I Am Born." We immediately assume that the title of the book refers to the "I" in the chapter heading. This is to be the story of David Copperfield, then, and it will begin at the beginning, with his birth. We might already have questions about why Dickens should begin there. Is the birth particularly significant? Will the novel spend a lot of time with Copperfield as an infant or young child? And how old is David when he's writing?

The first chapter ends with infant David lying in his basket, his mother in her bed, and his aunt leaving the scene, disappointed that he is born a boy. The second chapter begins this way:

> The first objects that assume a distinct presence before me, as I look far back into the blank of my infancy, are my mother—with her pretty hair and youthful shape— and Peggotty, with no shape at all, and eyes so dark that they seemed to darken their whole neighborhood in her face, and cheeks and arms so hard and red that I wondered the birds didn't peck at her in preference to apples.

When a chapter ends and another begins, readers provide the transition. Notice that as a reader, you had to move forward in time from the baby in the basket to the narrator as an older person remembering his mother and his nurse. You filled in the gap between the chapters with your understanding that the novel would flash back and forth in time.

These gaps in the text are the places where readers are most active in using their expectations to make decisions about the meaning of the text and the writer's intention. In fact, writers often make gaps part of their rhetorical strategy to keep readers active and engaged as they read. The space between one character's speech and another's is a gap that readers are invited to fill in with ideas about expression, gesture, or movement. Sometimes gestures are written in without speech. "After he finished his tirade, she quietly refilled her cup." Readers fill in the gap with speculations about what "she" might be thinking and not saying. When a writer begins a new chapter with a line like "The next year was a blur" or ends a chapter with that line, readers move through time quickly, filling in the gap of time with their own speculations and settling quickly into the next moment. Readers are able to add information, create dialogue, and understand what happens between one moment and the next because of their experiences in the world outside the text and because, as they read, they become increasingly part of the world inside the text. By a few chapters into *The Scarlet Letter*, readers can predict how Hester will respond to a question from the townspeople because they've heard her respond before and have seen her in similar situations in earlier sections of the novel.

In nonfiction reading and writing, gaps occur as writers invite readers to fill in parts of arguments or explanations. Readers predict the kinds of evidence that might be offered, the type of opinion the writer might develop, and the organizational strategy the writer might follow. If the writer makes an argument or takes a position, readers will expect to fill in the premises that the writer leaves out.

Here is the opening from Toni Morrison's Nobel Prize speech, delivered to the members of the Swedish Academy in 1993. As you read, consider where you are invited to fill in gaps in the text.

> Members of the Swedish Academy, Ladies and Gentlemen:
> Narrative has never been merely entertainment for me. It is, I believe, one of the principal ways in which we absorb knowledge. I hope you will understand, then, why I begin these remarks with the opening phrase of what must be the oldest sentence in the world, and the earliest one we remember from childhood: "Once upon a time. . . ."
> "Once upon a time there was an old woman. Blind but wise." Or was it an old man? A guru, perhaps. Or a *griot* soothing restless children. I have heard this story, or one exactly like it, in the lore of several cultures.
> "Once upon a time there was an old woman. Blind. Wise."
> In the version I know the woman is the daughter of slaves, black, American, and lives alone in a small house outside of town. Her reputation for wisdom is without peer and without question. Among her people she is both the law and its transgression. The honor she is paid and the awe in which she is held reach beyond her neighborhood to places far away; to the city where the intelligence of rural prophets is the source of much amusement.

You, the reader reading the speech, begin with the idea of the text *as* a speech, so the first gap you must fill in has to do with context, or **setting.** Toni Morrison is standing before an audience of Nobel Prize judges and officials and invited guests. She is there to receive literature's highest honor. Once she begins to speak, readers fill in other gaps about her intention for that audience, about her own persona as writer and speaker, about what they know about fairy tales and old women. They might puzzle over the word *griot*, filling in the possible gap of definition by connecting it to the wise village elder that Morrison describes. They consider associations between wisdom and age, between power and race and gender. They predict that soon in the speech will come the line "And then one day. . . ."
And it does.

> One day the woman is visited by some young people who seem to be bent on disproving her clairvoyance and showing her up for the fraud they believe she is.

Readers understand that the fairy tale Morrison offers will serve as an example of an argument she will make in the speech, and they already predict that the argument will have something to do with the power of narrative.

> Be it grand or slender, burrowing, blasting or refusing to sanctify; whether it laughs out loud or is a cry without an alphabet, the choice word or the chosen silence, unmolested language surges toward knowledge, not its destruction. But who does not know of literature banned because it is interrogative; discredited because it is critical? Erased because alternate? And how many are outraged by the thought of a self-ravaged tongue?

> Word-work is sublime, she thinks, because it is generative; it makes meaning that secures our difference, our human difference—the way in which we are like no other life.
>
> We die. That may be the meaning of life. But we *do* language. That may be the measure of our lives.

Notice that the questions are ways of asking readers to fill in gaps, as they invite readers to reflect on censorship and freedom in writing as well as on the power of language.

In conversation, too, speakers and listeners use gaps all the time. "I'm a Quaker," a college student might say to explain a decision to take part in a peace demonstration. Listeners would easily fill in the missing part of the explanation—that part of the Quaker religion is its belief in pacifism. Therefore, identifying himself as a Quaker is enough information for the speaker to give about his reasons for his action. These reading/listening gaps are a kind of enthymeme, just as we explained in Chapter 2. The logic of syllogistic reasoning moves in a cause-effect pattern. *If* one premise is so, *and* a second premise is also true, *then* a conclusion about the second premise can be made.

The enthymeme "John is a Quaker; *therefore,* John is a pacifist" omits the premise that all Quakers are pacifists. Like literary moments where the reader fills in missing information, the enthymeme is structured as a gap in the text, and it forces readers to become active meaning makers as they read. The use of syllogistic reasoning and of gaps in texts not only fosters logical meaning making and the logical persona of the writer but also assures that readers become part of the transaction in making sense of the texts they read.

Much of the time, premises omitted by speakers and writers are obvious ones, as in the Quaker example above. But writers can also assume agreement by ignoring a premise that all readers might not believe or understand or by jumping to a conclusion without stating the premises for it. Readers might be led to a conclusion and accept it without understanding all the premises the conclusion is based upon. A writer who says, "We should give to charity. We're Americans," omits a premise that might be stated as "Americans are generous and always help those less fortunate." Perhaps not everyone would agree if the major premise were stated, and that is one reason why it's important to recognize how writers use gaps and enthymemes to structure their ideas. Recognizing the underlying reasons for a claim, readers fill in gaps that make them analyze arguments effectively and make them active cocreators of what they read.

Activity

Read this segment of an essay by Amy Tan on her mother's heavily Chinese-inflected English dialect and language differences in general. With your group, create an enthymeme that expresses what you believe Tan's position to be. Remember that there should be a premise and a conclusion stated and one premise left implicit so that the reader fills it in.

Lately, I've been giving more thought to the kind of English my mother speaks. Like others, I have described it to people as "broken" or "fractured" English. But I wince when I say that. It has always bothered me that I can think of no way to describe it other than "broken," as if it were damaged and needed to be fixed, as if it lacked a certain wholeness and soundness. I've heard other terms used, "limited English," for example. But they seem just as bad, as if everything is limited, including people's perception of the limited English speaker.

I know this for a fact, because when I was growing up, my mother's "limited" English limited *my* perception of her. I was ashamed of her English. I believed that her English reflected the quality of what she had to say. That is, because she expressed them imperfectly her thoughts were imperfect. And I had plenty of empirical evidence to support me: the fact that people in department stores, at banks, at restaurants did not take her seriously, did not give her good service, pretended not to understand her, or even acted as if they did not hear her.

You will find more than one line of reasoning in these two paragraphs, more than one set of premises and conclusions. See what you come up with as your group shares its findings with other groups in the class.

Activity

Tan gives some background and experience to begin to develop an argument about language and thought, and as a reader you likely can sense the direction she will head in the essay. Now read the opening to another essay, this one by William Zinsser. The essay begins in a more deductive way, with a group of letters from students.

COLLEGE PRESSURES

Dear Carlos: I desperately need a dean's excuse for my chem midterm which will begin in about 1 hour. All I can say is that I totally blew it this week. I've fallen incredibly, inconceivably behind.

Carlos: Help! I'm anxious to hear from you. I'll be in my room and won't leave it until I hear from you. Tomorrow is the last day for . . .

Carlos: I left town because I started bugging out again. I stayed up all night to finish a take-home make-up exam & am typing it to hand in on the 10th. It was due on the 5th. P.S. I'm going to the dentist. Pain is pretty bad.

Carlos: Probably by Friday I'll be able to get back to my studies. Right now I'm going to take a long walk. This whole thing has taken a lot out of me.

Carlos: I'm really up the proverbial creek. The problem is that I really *bombed* the history final. Since I need that course for my major I . . .

Carlos: Here follows a tale of woe. I went home this weekend, had to help Mom, and caught a fever so didn't have much time to study. My professor . . .

Carlos: Aargh! Trouble. Nothing original but everything's piling up at once. To be brief, my job interview . . .

Hey Carlos, good news! I've got mononucleosis.

In your group, consider these questions:

- What do you deduce the aim of Zinsser's essay might be?
- What's the rhetorical effect of beginning with the group of notes from students to their counselor?
- What line of syllogistic reasoning might follow from what you assume the aim of Zinsser's piece to be?

Rhetorical Analysis: You Try It

Now that you have read brief rhetorical analyses of the opening to *Chaos* and of a portion of Toni Morrison's Nobel Prize speech, you have some idea of the kinds of approaches you might use as you analyze a piece rhetorically and examine the underlying patterns of argument and the gaps you're invited to fill in. The next step is for you to try a short rhetorical analysis of your own with the opening paragraph of Toni Morrison's novel *Sula*.

First, a little background on Morrison and her work is helpful to set the rhetorical context for your analysis. As you might have concluded from reading the excerpt from her Nobel Prize speech, Morrison is overtly a rhetorician, often speaking directly of her aim and her intended effect on readers with the language she chooses and the perspective on events she takes. She doesn't diminish her craft or her desire to affect an audience, her need to communicate a point or an argument most powerfully and effectively. In an interview on PBS several years ago, Morrison talked about her novel *Beloved,* which had just won the Pulitzer Prize for fiction. Asked her reason for writing about the horrific events the novel describes, the murder of a child by its mother to prevent the child from being taken into slavery, Morrison said, "I wanted to bring to slavery a personal face." She stated clearly her *rhetorical* intent, her desire to have readers understand in a human and narrative way what slavery had meant to the millions who suffered under it.

This clarity about her own aim with regard to her subject matter and her audience is evident in all her work. Several years ago, in a talk at the University of North Carolina, where she explored her writing process, Morrison discussed how she deliberately chose the plants *nightshade* and *blackberry* in the opening line to her novel *Sula*. She understood both the effect she wanted and the likely connections her readers would make to the words, their sound, and their meaning.

Sula is a novel about African American families living in a small segregated hilltop neighborhood in southern Ohio called, ironically, the Bottom. It's a story of pride and self-doubt, of racism and tragedy, of love and forgiveness. The main character is Sula herself, a woman who escapes the Bottom and then returns to unsettle the lives of everybody who lives in the Bottom.

Activity

Here is the opening paragraph of *Sula*. You will write a rhetorical analysis of it. Think about what you've just read about Morrison and her work. Read the excerpt quickly, and then go back and read it again, noting words or phrases that seem especially evocative to you as you read. You want to read *aesthetically* at first, drawing yourself into the world that Morrison presents. When you look back at individual elements in the passage, you'll be searching for information to help you explain your response. That more *efferent* activity will be enriched by reading first to enjoy and speculate.

> In that place, where they tore the nightshade and blackberry patches from their roots to make room for the Medallion City Golf Course, there was once a neighborhood. It stood in the hills above the valley town of Medallion and spread all the way to the river. It is called the suburbs now, but when black people lived there it was called the Bottom. One road, shaded by beeches, oaks, maples and chestnuts, connected it to the valley. The beeches are gone now, and so are the pear trees where children sat and yelled down through the blossoms to the passersby. Generous funds have been allotted to level the stripped and faded buildings that clutter the road from Medallion up to the golf course. They are going to raze the Time and a Half Pool Hall, where feet in long tan shoes once pointed down from chair rungs. A steel ball will knock to dust Irene's Palace of Cosmetology, where women used to lean their heads back on sink trays and doze while Irene lathered Nu Nile into their hair. Men in khaki work clothes will pry loose the slats of Reba's Grill, where the owner cooked in her hat because she couldn't remember the ingredients without it.

Here are some questions to help your thinking about the passage:

- How do details contribute to the rhetoric?
- What is the tone? How do you decide?
- How does Morrison make the place itself seem significant?
- Where do you detect irony in the voice of the speaker or in the situation the speaker describes?

You might begin your rhetorical analysis by working in your group to think through the elements of rhetoric as they appear in the passage. In your group, choose one of the following questions to respond to. Share your responses with the other groups in your class.

- Who's speaking, and how do you characterize the speaker?
- What is the subject?
- Who is the audience? What do they know and need to know?
- What is the writer's aim as it appears so far?

After talking with your group and listening to other groups, write your analysis. Rhetorical analysis begins with readers' recognition of their own experience with a text, the reaction they get from the writer's words, images, and structures. Remember to pay special attention to the language of the passage itself—its word choice, its use of imagery, and the length and variety of its sentences. And use your reactions (and those of your group members) to help you decide what's most significant in the paragraph.

- Read and describe the feeling you get from the passage. As you consider words that describe your feeling, you begin to name the *tone* of the passage.
- Read back to account for the words you've chosen to describe your feeling. You'll discover that the diction, the particular word choices Morrison makes, affects your choice of words. Identify some of Morrison's word choices that connect with the words you've used to describe your reaction.
- Notice phrases or images that seem especially vivid. Accounting for these images will allow you to expand your first reactions.
- Examine how Morrison uses sentences, looking at their length and complexity. Her construction of sentences and sentence patterns (or **syntax**) affects your reading. Notice how sentences balance one another, or how repetition of sentence patterns contributes to your response to the passage.

You could go on with the passage from *Sula* by talking about another element that is definitely a part of your reading process and related to your ability to fill in gaps: prediction. As a reader, you are always guessing about matters of character, plot, theme, and conflict, as well as sentence and word meanings. The cloze test showed you how prediction works to make sense of the sentences and words in a passage. Readers build up more effective predicting skills the longer they read because they begin to use what has come before to make sense of what's coming next. Readers always travel back and forth in time this way—for example, remembering what David Copperfield said about his nurse Peggotty in that book's Chapter 2 as they read about her engagement and marriage in Chapter 30.

This ability to move forward and backward with the eye and the brain is essential for good reading to take place, for the *poem* to happen, as Rosenblatt would say. Taking what you've said about *Sula* as a starting place and using your *repertoire* of information about Morrison, what might you predict will happen next, or even finally, in the novel? It's interesting how much gets established early on in the reading of any text and how often readers predict accurately even after the first few pages.

Activity

As you begin to read the next book or play you're working on in class, keep a journal of predictions and revisions. Read the first chapter or so, and then make some guesses about character, argument, or outcome. Write again when you begin to revise some of your ideas; at that point, explain what makes you change your mind. Engaging in this running commentary about your reading will allow you to see how active and creative a reader actually is in the process of reading.

Activity

The following excerpt from Leslie Marmon Silko's "Yellow Woman and a Beauty of the Spirit" grapples with differences between "old time" and "modern" ways of looking at people and the world. Silko grew up on the Laguna Pueblo reservation in New Mexico and spent a great deal of time as a child with her great-grandmother, listening to stories of the old days.

> Grandma A'mooh would tell about the old days, family stories about relatives who had been killed by Apache raiders who stole the sheep our relatives had been herding near Swahnee. Sometimes she read Bible stories that we kids liked because of the illustrations of Jonah in the mouth of a whale and Daniel surrounded by lions. Grandma A'mooh would send me home when she took her nap, but when the sun got low and the afternoon began to cool off, I would be back on the porch swing, waiting for her to come out to water the plants and to haul in firewood for the evening. When Grandma was eighty-five, she still chopped her own kindling. She used to let me carry in the coal bucket for her, but she would not allow me to use the ax. I carried armloads of kindling too, and I learned to be proud of my strength.
>
> I was allowed to listen quietly when Aunt Susie or Aunt Alice came to visit Grandma. When I got old enough to cross the road alone, I went and visited them almost daily. They were vigorous women who valued books and writing. They were usually busy chopping wood or cooking but never hesitated to take time to answer my questions. Best of all they told me the *hummah-hah* stories, about an earlier time when animals and humans shared a common language. In the old days, the Pueblo people had educated their children in this manner; adults took time out to talk to and teach young people. Everyone was a teacher, and every activity had the potential to teach the child.

Make some predictions about this text based on the introduction to Silko and the excerpt itself. What do you expect the argument to be? Why does the writer begin with the description of Pueblo ways of educating? How might she develop her argument?

Building the Reader's Repertoire

Readers use all their experiences to make sense of what they read. They remember their own pasts. They test their own knowledge. They use what they know about the writer. They call upon their own beliefs and opinions. They compare forms and genres they're familiar with to the ones they're reading. Reading theorist Wolfgang Iser calls this wealth of information and experience within the reader the **repertoire.** Other reading researchers call it nonvisual information or, simply, experience. The idea is that readers can call upon what they need in order to interpret and re-create the text as they're reading. It follows, then, that the more readers know—about reading, authors, life, ideas, history— the richer the repertoires they can draw upon. The broader and deeper the repertoire, the more engaging and satisfying the reading experience.

How might readers go about building their repertoire? Of course, much of that building happens in school with the kinds of experiences and information gathering that school provides. But outside school, reading and generally living in the world build information, experience, and ideas that readers use when they read. Becoming conscious of what you learn by reflecting on it in a journal (either written by hand or on the computer) is a good way of consciously building your repertoire. Taking careful stock, at the beginning of reading, of what you know and what you think you need to know is another way. Reading related texts, investigating Internet sources, talking to other people—all are ways of adding to your own fund of experiences that will deepen and enrich your reading experience.

With *David Copperfield*, consider what you know. You know about children and young boys, about what a mother means to a child. That's important in this novel since David's mother dies early in his life. What might you not know? Details of rural England in the nineteenth century? Child labor laws? These elements might be important in the story, and the story itself might reveal the information. But even if the novel doesn't tell a reader everything about rural life in England over a century ago, readers can use what they *already* know to make sense of what they're learning. Readers may not know much about England or the nineteenth century, but they may know a good deal about small towns in this country or about feeling isolated. The point is that even when you don't know everything you need to know to read most efficiently, you know *something* of what you need to know, and knowing something allows you to read more. As you read, you begin to know more and more of what you need to know.

Reading nonfiction or nonnarrative texts, you use similar strategies, building on what you know already to learn more as you read. In Silko's essay, while you might be unfamiliar with the cultural practices of the Pueblo in New Mexico, you know about generational differences and about how children learn and are taught. You know how people use examples to create arguments and to state positions. You use these understandings as you learn about Silko's own experience and you compare them with yours.

Sometimes readers are asked to read texts that they don't have enough of a repertoire to read effectively. That's why it often happens that a book a reader has read in tenth grade and disliked becomes a favorite if the reader reads it again in college. The book hasn't changed; the reader has. The repertoire has broadened.

As a reader, you are both a consumer and a producer; you respond to the texts you read, and you help create them by using your own experience, opinions, and ideas to make sense of the text and to respond to it appropriately. When you open a textbook, you begin with a certain mind set that predisposes you to read in special ways, and you read with expectations about the author's tone and voice and the textbook's format—expectations that help you read efficiently and meaningfully. Expectations about style, form, and meaning guide you in reading all kinds of work from textbooks to speeches to poetry. Understanding your role as a reader helps complete the rhetorical transaction among writer, reader, and text and lets you communicate with the texts you read, even when you sometimes don't know everything about the subject or the context of what you read as you begin.

Activity

In your group, discuss any times in which you've read a book more than once and found the second reading experience radically different from the first one. Consider how your repertoire affected your changed response to the book. Discuss the same process using a film you've seen more than once.

Activity

Read the following excerpt, the beginning of the essay "One Moment on Top of the Earth" by Naomi Shihab Nye. Then, in your group, discuss what you already know about her subject or the details she presents and what you still need to know to predict and to understand her position. The entire essay is included at the end of this chapter.

One Moment on Top of the Earth
For Palestine and for Israel

In February she was dying again, so he flew across the sea to be with her. Doctors came to the village. They listened and tapped and shook their heads. She's a hundred and five, they said. What can we do? She's leaving now. This is how some act when they're leaving. She would take no food or drink in her mouth. The family swabbed her dry lips with water night and day, and the time between. Nothing else. And the rooster next-door still marked each morning though everything else was changing. Her son wrote three letters saying, Surely she will die tonight. She is so weak. Sometimes she knows who I am and sometimes she calls me by the name of her dead sister. She dreams of the dead ones and shakes her head. Fahima said, Don't you want to go be with them? And she said, I don't want to have anything to do with them. You go be with them if you like. Be my guest. We don't know what is best. We sit by her side all the time because she cries if we walk away. She feels it, even with her eyes shut. Her sight is gone. Surely she will die tonight.

Reading Your Own Writing

We've talked in earlier chapters about the importance of revision in the writing process and about the way that creating and altering ideas intertwines for writers as they look ahead and read back. One of your most important tasks as a reader is to know how to read your own writing most helpfully and efficiently. As discussions of writing processes suggest, you read your own writing unconsciously in large measure; with every phrase your eye quickly travels back to check on what you have said and how it sounds. Reading back in this way actually allows you to continue to write. Some research shows that writers who are kept from looking back at their writing as they are producing a draft fairly quickly become hesitant or even stymied at how to proceed. They lose the ability to write because they aren't able to read.

This quick and nearly unconscious reading is, as the writer Eudora Welty put it, your "test for the truth" of your idea. You listen to how you sound, to the words you've chosen; you think about the argument you're trying to develop or the details you're describing or the mood you're capturing. And as you read back, you "write" ahead, considering what you might place next and how you'll move from one point to another. This reading activity is one of the primary tools for all writers.

When you read your own work after you have completed a draft, you're looking at how the end product meets the expectations you've assigned to it as you've been reading back during the process. As a reader of your own text, make sure you can answer the following questions:

- What does the first sentence or first paragraph allow readers to predict?
- What does the vocabulary, your use of examples, or the way you make your argument suggest about the repertoire a reader needs in order to interpret your text effectively?
- What tone do you attempt to carry throughout your text? Point to some words that suggest that tone.
- How clearly do you make connections among the points or ideas you've written about?
- As a reader, do you have to fill in lots of gaps in order to keep reading?
- As a writer, have you paid attention to your reader? As a reader, do you feel that attention has been paid to you?

These questions can be useful when you read drafts by your friends and members of your group. One reason why writers often like to get comments from another reader is that they need to validate their own reading of the text, to see if the way they have read their own text matches another reader's experience. Thinking about your role as a reader of your text allows you to make helpful comments and useful suggestions for writers, including yourself, to follow in the revision of essays. What you do as a reader—gather ideas, predict, revise—is in so many ways what you do as a writer, and you can rely on this similarity to guide your reading as well as shape your writing.

Activity

Choose a draft of an essay that you're working on, and consciously make yourself into a reader of your piece by considering what you're learning, feeling, and thinking as you read the draft. Make notes to yourself; read portions aloud; listen for your voice as you read and write. Point out one place where you use prediction, revision, gaps, and background repertoire.

Here are the two selections from the cloze tests (pages 124 and 125), this time reprinted with all their words in place.

FROM *THE BRIDGE OF BEYOND*

by Simone Schwarz-Bart

They lived in a hamlet swept <u>alternately</u> by winds from the land and <u>winds</u> from the sea. A steep road <u>ran</u> along by cliffs and wastelands, leading, it <u>seemed</u>, to nothing human. And that was <u>why</u> it was called the deserted <u>village</u>, L'Abandonnée. At certain times everyone there *would* be filled with dread, like travellers <u>lost</u> in a strange land. Still young <u>and</u> strong, always dressed in a worker's <u>overall</u>, Minerva had a glossy, light mahogany <u>skin</u> and black eyes brimming over with <u>kindness</u>. She had an unshakable faith in <u>life</u>. When things went wrong she would <u>say</u> that nothing, no one, would ever <u>wear</u> out the soul God had chosen <u>out</u> for her and put in her <u>body</u>. All the year round she fertilized <u>vanilla</u>, picked coffee, hoed the banana groves, <u>and</u> weeded the rows of sweet potatoes. <u>And</u> her daughter Toussine was no more <u>given</u> to dreaming than she.

FROM *CHAOS*

by James Gleick

Chaos breaks across the lines that <u>separate</u> scientific disciplines. Because it is a <u>science</u> of the global nature of systems, <u>it</u> has brought together thinkers from fields <u>that</u> had been widely separated. "Fifteen years <u>ago</u>, science was heading for a <u>crisis</u> of increasing specialization," a Navy official <u>in</u> charge of scientific financing remarked to <u>an</u> audience of mathematicians, biologists, physicists, and <u>medical</u>

doctors. "Dramatically, that specialization has reversed <u>because</u> of chaos." Chaos poses problems that defy accepted ways of working in science. <u>It</u> makes strong claims about the universal <u>behavior</u> of complexity. The first chaos theorists, <u>the</u> scientists who set the discipline in <u>motion</u>, shared certain sensibilities. They had an <u>eye</u> for pattern, especially pattern that appeared on different scales at the same time. They had a taste for randomness and complexity, for jagged edges and sudden <u>leaps</u>. <u>Believers</u> in chaos—and they sometimes call themselves believers, or converts, or evangelists—<u>speculate</u> about determinism and free will, <u>about</u> evolution, about the nature of conscious <u>intelligence</u>.

Here is the complete essay, the first paragraph of which appears on pages 141–142.

ONE MOMENT ON TOP OF THE EARTH

by Naomi Shihab Nye

For Palestine and for Israel

In February she was dying again, so he flew across the sea to be with her. Doctors came to the village. They listened and tapped and shook their heads. She's a hundred and five, they said. What can we do? She's leaving now. This is how some act when they're leaving. She would take no food or drink in her mouth. The family swabbed her dry lips with water night and day, and the time between. Nothing else. And the rooster next-door still marked each morning though everything else was changing. Her son wrote three letters saying, Surely she will die tonight. She is so weak. Sometimes she knows who I am and sometimes she calls me by the name of her dead sister. She dreams of the dead ones and shakes her head. Fahima said, Don't you want to go be with them? and she said, I don't want to have anything to do with them. You go be with them if you like. Be my guest. We don't know what is best. We sit by her side all the time because she cries if we walk away. She feels it, even with her eyes shut. Her sight is gone. Surely she will die tonight.

Then someone else who loved her got on an airplane and flew across the sea. When she heard he was landing, she said, Bring me soup. The kind that is broth with nothing in it. They lit the flame. He came and sat behind her on the bed, where she wanted him to sit, so she could lean on him and soak him up. It was cold and they huddled together, everyone in one room, telling any story five times and stretching it. Laughing in places besides ones which had seemed funny before. Laughing more because they were in that time of sadness that is fluid and soft. She who had almost been gone after no eating and drinking for twenty days was even laughing. And then she took the bread that was torn into small triangles, and the pressed oil, and the soft egg. She took the tiny glass of tea between her lips. She took the match and held it, pressing its tiny sulfuric head between her fingers so she could feel the roughness. Something shifted inside her eyes, so the shapes of people's faces came alive again. Who's that? she said about a woman from another village who had entered her room very quietly with someone else. She's lovely, but who is she? I never saw her before. And they were hiding inside themselves a tenderness about someone being so close to gone and then returning.

She wanted her hair to be washed and combed. She wanted no one arguing in her room or the courtyard outside. She wanted a piece of lamb meat grilled with fat dripping crispily out of it. She wanted a blue velvet dress and a black sweater. And they could see how part of being alive was wanting things again. And they sent someone to the store in the next town, which was a difficult thing since you had to pass by many soldiers. And in all these years not one had ever smiled at them yet.

Then the two men from across the sea had to decide what to do next, which was fly away again, as usual. They wished they could take her with them but she, who had not even entered the Holy City for so long though it was less than an hour away, said yes and no so much about going they knew she meant no. After a hundred and five years. You could not blame her. Even though she wasn't walking anymore, this was definitely her floor. This voice calling from the tower of the little village mosque. This rich damp smell of the stones in the walls.

So they left and I came, on the very next day. We were keeping her busy. She said to me, *Marhabtein*—Hello twice—which is what she always says instead of just Hello and our hands locked tightly together. Her back was still covered with sores, so she did not want to lie down. She wanted to eat whatever I had with me. Pralines studded with pecans, and chocolate cake. They said, Don't give her too much of that. If it's sweet, she'll just keep eating. She wanted cola, water and tea. She wanted the juice of an orange. She said to me, So how is everybody? Tell me about all of them. And I was stumbling in the tongue again, but somehow she has always understood me. They were laughing at how badly I stumbled and they were helping me. It was the day which has no seams in it at the end of a long chain of days, the golden charm. They were coming in to welcome me, Abu Ahmad with his black cloak and his cane and his son still in Australia, and my oldest cousin Fowzl the king of smiling, and Ribhia with her flock of children, and the children's children carrying sacks of chips now, it was the first year I ever saw them carrying chips, and my cousin's husband the teller of jokes who was put in prison for nothing like everybody else, and the ones who always came whose names I pretended to know. We were eating and drinking and telling the stories. My grandmother told of a woman who was so delicate you could see the water trickling down her throat as she drank. I had brought her two new headscarves, but of course she only wanted the one that was around my neck. And I wouldn't give it to her. There was energy in teasing. I still smelled like an airplane and we held hands the whole time except when she was picking up crumbs from her blanket or holding something else to eat.

And then it was late and time for sleep. We would sleep in a room together, my grandmother, my aunt Fahima, my cousin Janan of the rosy cheeks, a strange woman, and I. It reminded me of a slumber party. They were putting on their long nightgowns and rewrapping their heads. I asked about the strange woman and they said she came to sleep here every night. Because sometimes in such an upsetting country when you have no man to sleep in the room with you, it feels safer to have an extra woman. She had a bad cold and was sleeping on the bed next to me. I covered my head against her hundred sneezes. I covered my head as my father covered his head when he was a young man and the bombs were blowing up the houses of his friends. I thought about my father and my husband here in this same room just a few days ago and could still feel them warming the corners. I listened to the women's bedtime talking and laughing from far away, as if it were rushing water, the two sleeping on the floor, my grandmother still sitting up in her bed— Lie down, they said to her, and she said, I'm not ready—and then I remembered how at ten o'clock the evening news comes on in English from Jordan and I asked if

Interchapter

4

Overview of the Major Points in Chapter 4

- Reading depends on being able to make predictions and revise those predictions.
- Readers carry with them a repertoire of information and experience that helps them read effectively.
- Readers develop hypotheses about what they read and, based on their own repertoires of information, fill in gaps in the text.
- Readers respond to and use rhetorical considerations—of subject, speaker, audience, and purpose—as they read and interpret.
- Readers are like writers.

Activities and Discussion Questions for Chapter 4 Use these questions and comments as guides for your own discussion and writing about these works.

Henry David Thoreau, "On the Duty of Civil Disobedience" (published 1849)

The text appears on pages 210–225. Discuss the following questions with your small group, or write a well-organized essay that you share with your group.

1. How does Thoreau's opening statement, where he describes the best government, help you predict the way in which Thoreau is going to make his argument? By reading only the first paragraph of his essay, what might a reader predict about other arguments Thoreau might make?

2. What knowledge do you have about Thoreau as a writer or person that influences the way you read this text? What do you know about civil-rights protests in the twentieth century that help you connect to Thoreau's position?

3. Where in the allusions Thoreau makes do you fill in gaps in the reading? How do you fill them? (Did you find the allusion he makes to his famous piece *Walden?*)

4. How do you respond to Thoreau's argument? Which of his strategies do you find effective? Consider his use of evidence, his persona, and his use of appeals.

5. How does Thoreau use language, especially metaphor, to make his argument clear and strong?

Eavan Boland, "It's A Woman's World" (published 1982)

The text appears on pages 226–227. Use these questions for small-group work or as the basis for an essay on this poem.

1. What associations do you bring with you to the title "It's a Woman's World"?

2. How do you read the tone of the poem? What words signal the tone for you as you read?

3. Rewrite this poem in prose, trying to maintain the same tone. Read your piece to your group, and discuss the effect of the change.

4. How does Boland use history to help make her aim clear? How do you use what you know about history and women to help you connect with her aim?

Alice Walker, "Everyday Use" (published 1981)

The text appears on pages 228–237. Use these questions to help you begin a draft of an essay or as discussion questions with your small group.

1. How do the first words—a dedication—help you predict the events that might take place in the story? How does the dedication help you read the ending?

2. How do you use that dedication to connect with your own experience?

3. What's the rhetorical effect of Walker's use of the second person, "you," in the story?

4. What events or motivations are left out of the plot of the story? How do you fill in those places that the narrator remains silent about?

Readers as Writers, Writers as Readers

Making Connections

PEANUTS *reprinted by permission of United Feature Syndicate, Inc.*

> Ever since I was first read to, then started reading to myself, there has never been a line read that I didn't *hear.* As my eyes followed the sentence, a voice was saying it silently to me. It isn't my mother's voice, or the voice of any person I can identify, certainly not my own. It is human, but inward, and it is inwardly that I listen to it. It is to me the voice of the story or the poem itself. The cadence, whatever it is that asks you to believe, the feeling that resides in the printed word, reaches me through the reader-voice. I have supposed, but never found out, that this is the case with all readers—to read as listeners—and with all writers, to write as listeners. It may be part of the desire to write.
>
> *Eudora Welty,* One Writer's Beginnings

Eudora Welty, who died in 2001 at age 92, wrote *One Writer's Beginnings* in 1982. It is a memoir, a look back at her life as a novelist and short story writer, and it evocatively explores the influences on her writing, especially the importance of her small-town southern upbringing and her storytelling family. Like many memoirs of writers, Welty's book also considers *how* she became a writer. Reading the lines above, you can see Welty emphasizing how the voice she heard as a reader and as a writer guided her. For Welty, voice was the element that brought readers and writers together.

In earlier chapters, we discuss voice as we consider how a writer creates a persona on the page and as we describe how a reader comes to understand tone in a written text. In both the lines above and in the following passage from her memoir, Welty suggests something else about voice: how important it is to *hear* when you read and to *listen* when you write.

> The sound of what falls on the page begins the process of testing it for truth, for me. Whether or not I am right to trust so far I don't know. By now I don't know whether I could do either one, reading or writing, without the other.
>
> My own words, when I'm at work on a story, I hear too as they go, in the same voice that I hear when I read in books. When I write and the sound of it comes back to my ears, then I act to make my changes. I have always trusted this voice.

Do Welty's words strike a familiar chord with you? When you read, do you hear what Welty calls the "reader-voice"? When you write, do you listen for that voice to help you decide what word to choose, where to put a comma, how long to make a sentence? In this chapter, we explore how writers improve their skill and confidence by using what they know as readers and how readers expand their critical and interpretive ability by using what they know as writers. In particular, we consider what reading and writing teach us about voice.

Reading and Writing: Different? Similar?

Despite Welty's comment, and our own encouragement to see reading and writing as mutually reinforcing and complementary in this book, it may seem to you that the acts of reading and writing are more different than they are similar. For one thing, while most people identify themselves as readers, far fewer consider themselves writers. Reading seems to be an activity that anyone can do, statistics about the continuing literacy problem in this country notwithstanding. Writing seems to be a more specialized skill. To identify yourself as a reader simply says that you're literate; to say you're a writer is to claim a vocation.

If you were making a list of differences between reading and writing, you might come up with some of these words to describe how the two acts seem different:

Reading	Writing
Receives	Creates
Interprets	Produces
Internalizes	Externalizes
Passive	Active

As we'll see, reading and writing are much more alike than they are different, and once you begin thinking about them together, the separate lists above begin to blend. Reading is as active, as creative, and as productive as writing. And writing is as interpretive, as receptive, and as internalized as reading. Reading and writing are sometimes taught as separate, only tangentially related, activities: a student reads first and then writes to demonstrate that he or she has read, for example, or a student writes so that someone else can read and evaluate the writing. But seeing reading and writing as simultaneous strengthens mightily the skill of interpretation, and the ability to interpret is a rhetorical skill.

Activity

Many people don't remember learning to read. Students will sometimes say that it seems like they always knew how to read, or that one day they just could read, and they don't recall how it happened. They often have vivid memories of learning to write, maybe because writing—taking the big pencil and the wide-lined paper and forming letters—is so much more a physical act than reading.

This activity is designed to help you think about reading and writing connections. Go back to your early childhood or an early time in your schooling—third grade, maybe, or first grade, or even before—and write about a memory of reading or writing. Do you remember something about your first-grade reading group? Having to read aloud? Writing a story that was put on the bulletin board? Being corrected for misspelling? Being read to at night? Pick a memory that stands out for you. Write to evoke the scene—the classroom, the other children around you, yourself. You might speculate about why the scene stands out for you, what it means in terms of how you see yourself now as a reader or writer.

After you write your memory, share it with your group. See if there are similarities in your responses. Describe the voice you hear as you read the memories from each of your group members.

The Literacy Memory

Students who've written about their literacy memories often have a lot to say. They remember being read to—how they knew exactly when to turn the page even before they could read words because they had listened to the story so often. They write about composing poems with great confidence at home and then going to school and being shocked that their teachers didn't find their creations as wonderful as they had thought they were. They write of being afraid to turn in a paper because it would get corrected. They remember being in a slow reading group or a fast one and how they knew without being told whether they were "good" or "bad" readers.

One student writing her literacy memory writes, "I remember being so proud when I could 'read' the sign for McDonald's. I was little, maybe two or three, but I knew that yellow *M*. And I would say McDonald's! My mom would sometimes stop and get me French fries. Maybe that's why I wanted to read. I thought I'd get something."

How does a child *read* before she knows her letters? How does she write before she can spell? People learn to read and write in the same way that they learn to negotiate the world around them; they learn how to understand signs and how to respond to them. They *interpret* words on the page in the same way that they interpret the world and their own experience. And it's this activity of interpretation—understanding and acting on meaning—that links reading and writing and makes them both part of the larger activity of *composing,* or of the imagination.

Children "read" the big *M* on the McDonald's sign and know what it means to them. French fries! It isn't long before the same children read other signs—their own names, the title of a favorite cartoon, the first line of a story. When they go to school, they will learn to read texts as they learned to read *McDonald's,* by understanding what the symbols they see on the page stand for. But in order to read words, they use what they already know about how to read signs—not only the McDonald's sign, but also their mothers' expressions, the cat's meow, and the wind before a rainstorm.

As with reading, children learn to write by using what they already know about how meaningful symbols are. Do you remember writing your name when you were very young? Those letters that made up a word stood for *you*, so they were especially meaningful. When writers begin to compose whole sentences and whole stories, they do so with a sense that the words they write carry meaning. Sometimes youngsters *write* scribbles on the page and then "translate" those marks aloud for listeners. The marks carry meaning that the children will willingly explain if readers can't interpret them on their own.

So both reading and writing carry with them the idea of making meaning. And both reading and writing are special instances of making meaning, since we make meaning all the time, from the time we wake up until we dream at night.

Where does rhetoric fit into this scheme that brings together reading and writing? Rhetoric, as we've discovered, is about intention and effect. A writer uses particular words and images, claims and evidence, with an aim in mind. A reader has purposes for reading, and the way those purposes match the writer's purposes constitutes the effect of the piece. Later, we'll have more to say about how writers and readers link their intentions and decide on effects. For now, it's important to remember that readers and writers are always linked by rhetoric, by their desire to communicate and to interpret ideas.

Activity

Reread your literacy memory piece, and then write a paragraph in which you explain your intention. Identify some of the signals you used to get that intention across. Next, in your group, read one another's literacy memories, and ask group members to write for each other person a short paragraph that explores the voice of the speaker, the attitude toward reading or writing it expresses, the choice of details and images, the use of figurative language, or the argument it creates. See how your intention statement matches the responses from other members of the group.

The Process of Making Meaning: Readers as Writers

There is, then, creative reading as well as creative writing.

Ralph Waldo Emerson, "The American Scholar"

How does a reader read "creatively"? How important is reading creatively to understanding, interpreting, and analyzing texts well? A significant part of your work as a student is to read skillfully enough to be able to explore texts precisely and analytically. When you take standardized tests for college entrance or write analytical essays for courses in college, you are expected to read closely, with attention to how words and ideas work in the text. Does that view of reading fit with reading creatively?

When readers use a repertoire of experiences and ideas and information as they read, they read creatively. And, as we saw in Chapter 4, readers *must* use their repertoire in order to read at all because they're always reading for meaning, expecting it, and lining up what they already know with what they're learning. Readers, then, are creating the text as they respond to it, just as writers create the text as they write it.

When Frank Smith, a prominent reading theorist and teacher, talks about the process of reading, he uses many of the same words that teachers and students use to describe what happens when they write. Using cognitive theory—ideas about how the brain works—Smith shows that the brain processes information in chunks; it can't record everything it sees. Readers don't read every word on a page; if they did, they couldn't read fast enough to make meaning. You might have listened to struggling young readers pronouncing every word of stories they are reading. They read haltingly, often pointing to each individual word as they say it. If someone stops these readers to ask what the sentence means, they can't answer. They have to work so hard to identify individual words that they can't make sense of the text as a whole, or even of the meaning of the sentence. Think about difficult texts you've encountered as a reader. Have you noticed that you can read a line or a paragraph and not know what you've read after you finish? You're being forced to read too slowly to make meaning. And making meaning is the key to reading.

Because readers can't read every word, because they need to read relatively quickly to get information to the brain, readers *predict*, decide what they *expect* the next word, the next phrase, the next chapter to be about. For young readers, or readers who read texts that are too far beyond their own repertoires, the ability to predict is hampered so much that they can't interpret. They can't read creatively enough to make meaning. Prediction, or creatively deciding on meaning, is crucial to reading, therefore, and the skill of prediction is one that writers use as well.

Activity

1. Complete the word at the end of this sentence:

   The captain ordered the mate to drop the an_____.

2. Make a prediction about the following words:

   Love in the Time of Cholera

Think of the questions you need to answer before you can predict anything about the two groups of words above. Write some of your questions, and then make a prediction about what the sentence in #1 might be about.

You probably predicted easily the end of the word in the sentence above. You were able to predict because of what you know about the words *captain* and *mate*. The context of the sentence allowed you to make meaning easily. If you were actually reading the sentence in an essay, you wouldn't even be conscious that you had predicted and would read on without actually seeing the word *anchor*.

In fact, the only way you'd know that you had predicted would be if your prediction turned out to be wrong. Read the rest of the sentence.

> The captain ordered the mate to drop the an_____, and the furry, long-nosed animal scurried across the deck.

Once you complete the sentence, you have to go back to the word you've predicted and revise your guess. You find the word *anteater,* and then you move on; you probably wonder why an anteater is aboard ship, so you make another prediction—that you'll find out more about the anteater in the next sentence.

As readers, we predict, create hypotheses, test them as we read, and revise our guesses. Throughout a story or an essay or a chapter, we continue the process; we acquire more skill and confidence in predicting and revising as we build up more and more information from what we've already read.

Now, return to *Love in the Time of Cholera,* the second group of words at the beginning of this activity. What sort of predictions did you make about that group of words? Someone in your group, or you yourself, might have known this phrase already. It's the title of a novel by Gabriel García Márquez, a Colombian author. But even if you didn't know it beforehand, you might have predicted it was a title anyway. It sounds like one. It's not a complete sentence, for one thing, and several words in the phrase begin with a capital letter. Furthermore, the title sounds as if it belongs to a novel rather than a history book; after all, how many history books have *love* in the title? The reason the phrase sounds like a title, the reason you predict that it's a novel, is that you know about stories, about how writers try to engage your interest in them. And if you think about it, you can predict even more. For one thing, you can predict that disease will present complications for the main characters, who, you predict, love one another. The setting for this story is probably removed from the present day or is a place where cholera epidemics still occur. Once you begin to ask questions of yourself, you discover how much you already know and how much you can predict even before you begin to read.

When you read quickly—for example, on a multiple-choice test that asks you to comprehend bits of text quickly and accurately—your skills of prediction become acute.

Activity

To test the role of prediction on a multiple-choice test, read the following passage, and then, with your group, answer the questions that follow it. As you make decisions, talk together about how and why you decide on one answer rather than another. (The passage and questions, by the way, are from a past advanced-placement English language and composition examination, released by the Educational Testing Service.)

> It is the fate of those who toil at the lower employments of life, to be rather driven by the fear of evil, than attracted by the prospect of good; to be exposed to censure, without hope of praise; to be disgraced by miscarriage, or punished for neglect, where success would have been without applause, and diligence without reward.
>
> Among these unhappy mortals is the writer of dictionaries; whom mankind have considered, not as the pupil, but the slave of science, the pioneer of literature, doomed only to remove rubbish and clear obstructions from the paths of Learning and Genius, who press forward to conquest and glory, without bestowing a smile on the humble drudge that facilitates their progress. Every other author may aspire to praise; the lexicographer can only hope to escape reproach, and even this negative recompense has been yet granted to very few.
>
> —*Samuel Johnson, Preface,* A Dictionary of the English Language, *1755*

1. Which of the following best describes the passage?
   a. an appeal for the readers' sympathy and admiration
   b. a brief overview of the methods that the author used
   c. a summary of the principles according to which the author worked
   d. a warning to the reader about the complexity of the ensuing work
   e. a challenge to those who would doubt the accuracy of the author's work

2. One prominent stylistic characteristic of the first paragraph is the use of
   a. metaphor
   b. understatement
   c. parallel syntax
   d. personification
   e. **euphemism**

3. Which of the following best describes Johnson's use of the terms "slave of science" and "pioneer of literature" (lines 7–8)?
   a. The contrast between the two terms emphasizes the variety of possible responses to the dictionary.
   b. Both sensationalize the difficulty of the lexicographer's research.
   c. The difference between the two terms illustrates the range of the lexicographer's experience.
   d. Both exaggerate the public's lack of admiration for lexicographers.
   e. Each illustrates what is meant later in the sentence about "Learning and Genius."

4. In line 9, "who" refers to
   a. "unhappy mortals" (line 6)
   b. "mankind" (line 7)

  c. "pupil" (line 7)

  d. "the slave" (line 7) and "the pionier" (line 8)

  e. "Learning and Genius" (line 9)

In some ways, the first question *should* be the hardest—though, for reasons we'll explain below, it probably wasn't. To answer the first question, you had only the first two paragraphs of the passage to consult. In other words, you had less information than you needed to predict with complete confidence, although you might have predicted well enough to answer *a*. See if you can find words or phrases in the first paragraph that make an appeal to a reader's sympathy or admiration.

The other three questions guide you directly to the appropriate lines, asking you to recognize terms (Question 2), understand tone (Question 3), and comprehend sentence structure (Question 4). All these questions, as most multiple-choice questions do, require that you read both attentively and creatively. Question 2 is the most dependent on your prior knowledge, since you have to choose from a list of literary terms not defined in the text. Students of rhetoric and of sentence of structure will recognize *c*, parallel syntax, as the correct term. But you might come up with the correct response simply by eliminating the others. Question 3 depends on your understanding of the nuance of words and the voice of the speaker, whose description of himself as an "unhappy mortal" and a "humble drudge" sounds exaggerated and therefore slightly tongue in cheek. (The answer to Question 3 is *d*, by the way.) And Question 4 asks you to check your prediction and your reading by assuring that you understand the antecedent for the pronoun "who," so that you know what's being talked about in the sentence: the "Learning and Genius" (*e*), who "press forward to conquest and glory."

More About Prediction and Revision in Reading

The preceding sample of multiple-choice questions illustrates making predictions and revising them. It's a skill that improves with practice, but it essentially mirrors what readers do all the time, in all kinds of reading. They make decisions, formulate ideas, and revise them. The first question in the series, the one for which you had the least information, may have been the easiest to answer in fact because it required the most in terms of prediction and the least in terms of factual knowledge.

Often, a timed set of questions gives you little time to exercise revision, at least directly, and that's why when you answer questions or read for information that you need immediately, you often read the whole piece quickly to get the main idea and to set your predictions most accurately. One question often helps you answer the next with more skill, and so even in a timed reading, you revise as you go along, just as you do when you read more deliberately or when you write.

Here's one more example of reading and prediction, from Beryl Markham's memoir *West with the Night*, about her adventures in Africa.

> How is it possible to bring order out of memory? I should like to begin at the beginning, patiently, like a weaver at his loom. I should like to say, "This is the place to start; there can be no other."
>
> But there are a hundred places to start for there are a hundred names—Mwanza, Serengetti, Nungwe, Molo, Nakuru. There are easily a hundred names, and I can begin best by choosing one of them—not because it is first nor of any importance in a wildly adventurous sense, but because here it happens to be, turned uppermost in my logbook. After all, I am no weaver. Weavers create. This is remembrance—revisitation; and names are keys that open corridors no longer fresh in the mind, but nonetheless familiar in the heart.
>
> So the name shall be Nungwe—as good as any other—entered like this in the log, lending reality, if not order, to memory:
>
> DATE—16/6/35
>
> TYPE AIRCRAFT—Avro Avian
>
> MARKINGS—VP—KAN
>
> JOURNEY—Nairobi to Nungwe
>
> TIME—3 hrs. 40 mins.
>
> After that comes, PILOT: Self; and REMARKS—of which there were none. But there might have been.

The writer gives us readers lots to make guesses about in her opening. We come up with questions as we read: What is this memoir about? Why are the names so significant? What kind of person is she? What are the remarks left blank in her log? Will the memoir fill them in? Does she die in a plane crash? Our questions help propel us into the reading, help us read for meaning, and allow us to guess and revise those guesses as we read.

We're also thinking, consciously or not, about the writer's rhetoric. How does she engage us in the piece we're about to read? What does she want us to feel or to believe? What is she really writing about—planes or Africa or adventure or something else? We begin to consider, in other words, how Markham attempts to create her effects and how we respond to them.

A few examples from the opening illustrate how readers might take note of Markham's rhetoric. She begins with a rhetorical question. You may be familiar with that term (it came up in Chapter 2). It describes a question where no real answer is expected because it's a question either to which the speaker believes there is no real answer or to which the answer is implied in the question itself. It's a question designed for effect, to get the reader's attention, to heighten the moment. This question in particular does make readers stop for a minute to consider an answer. How *does* the mind impose order on all the memories it stores? Even though it is a rhetorical question, we sort of expect a response from the writer—maybe because it's the first line of the text—and she gives it to us in a fashion in the next line by telling us first what she can't do. She can't order her memory by beginning at the beginning.

Markham uses the metaphor of the weaver to make a comparison between the act of weaving and the act of writing about memories. She'd like to begin like the weaver, she tells us, because then she'd know exactly where and how to start. But, as she points out, remembrance is different from weaving. Weaving has order; memory must create it. The weaving metaphor helps readers think about how Markham does decide to begin her story, not by beginning at the beginning, as the weaver must, but by picking up the loose thread of a name, and proceeding from there.

The **format** within the third paragraph—its typeface, sentence structure, paragraphing—is written to look like the actual entry from her pilot's logbook, and its effect is to give a feeling of actuality, of **verisimilitude,** to the memoir. It feels as though Markham has stopped to consult her log, where she had recorded the bare details of the trip from Nairobi to the name she has picked to begin her story with, Nungwe. She establishes her point about memory, which we pick from the wealth of data in our brains more or less randomly, beginning with Nungwe because it's a name "as good as any other." And she ends this section with the one-line paragraph "But there might have been," leading us as readers to anticipate what comes next, the details her log omitted. She draws us in with that line, builds our curiosity and our beginning involvement.

As readers, we've done quite a bit of predicting before we turn the first page of the memoir. We predict adventure and perhaps danger, we predict many names and places of the exotic locales in Africa in the early part of the twentieth century, and we guess about Markham's background and personality. Our predicting leads us to read on. It allows us to begin to make meaning.

Whatever kind of reading you do, whether to complete an exam, acquire information, or be entertained, you write the text you read as you predict and revise in the process of interpretation.

Prediction and Revision in Writing: Writers as Readers

Like reading, writing involves the skills of predicting, working out hypotheses, and revising ideas. You already know a lot about how a piece of writing proceeds in a series of steps or stages. You have an idea or an assignment or maybe just a good opening line—and even that much material can amount to a hypothesis. You predict for yourself what kinds of detail you'll need to include, where you'll add a bit of dialogue, when you'll establish your argument.

"Sometimes I just begin," says a first-year college writing student. "I'm not sure where I'm headed, but writing a sentence or two kind of leads me on." When you begin to write, your predictions about where you're headed may not be formulated completely; you may simply have an assignment to write an argument about a topic or to analyze a character. You may have collected information about a topic and have at hand statistics or quotations from published sources but little idea of what you'll do with the data in front of you. If you let yourself begin to write without a definite thesis sentence or outlined plan, you often will find what composition theorist Peter Elbow calls the "center of gravity," the place where you begin to locate what you want to say and how you'll say it. From that center, you begin to predict what you'll use, where you'll include information, what your voice should sound like on the page. In the final, finished composition, you may end up using very little of what you produce in the "free write," but the very process of doing it is very productive—it's a great way to start the processes of predicting and revising that are so much a part of successful writing. As productive as "free writing" is, however, it can also take time for a center to emerge or for a draft to take shape. Taking quick notes as you read an essay you'll be writing about—copying phrases, asking questions—is another way to begin the vital processes of predicting and revising.

Activity

In the last chapter, you read the opening paragraphs of Toni Morrison's novel *Sula.* Look back at that opening (pages 136–137), and then write a few lines of your own about a place you know of that no longer exists or exists only in your memory. A park where you used to play that's now a mall? A neighborhood that's changed? A store you used to walk to? Call up the place in your memory, and then write as quickly as you can for five or so minutes.

Now look back at what you've written. How does it sound to you? As you answer that question for yourself, as you read the text you've written, begin thinking about what you'd write next. Then write one more line.

The last line you write shows your prediction and revision. It might be a beginning center of gravity for your piece. Writers use what they've already written—and already read—to proceed to the next line or next chunk. Reading aloud helps, and hearing feedback from someone else helps too. Have your group read one another's paragraphs, asking group members to speculate on where they think the writing might go next.

You might choose to continue with this piece after hearing from your group. One thing you might discover in writing about the place that's disappeared is that you have more of an understanding of what Morrison is suggesting in her opening to *Sula* after having written about the issue yourself. You're a better reader because you've written.

More About Prediction and Revision in Writing

In writing and in discussing your writing with others, you exercise both the skills of prediction and revision. Writers typically think of revision in terms of whole texts, but just as with reading, revising writing is ongoing, occurring as soon as you write a word or a line. You make a revision so quickly that it's nearly unconscious. "I don't want to sound too mad," says a writer to herself. "I better not say the word *bitter*." "Go on with that quote," another writer says to himself. "Then you can use the last line to get you to the next point." Writers say things like this all the time to themselves, but they're seldom aware of it because it's almost always below the level of conscious thought. As you write, you can try to slow yourself down enough to hear yourself planning and revising. It's interesting to do, but eventually it will be too slow a process. We predict and revise far too quickly as readers and writers to be conscious all the time of what we're doing.

When you revise whole texts, or whole sections of a paper, you begin to be more conscious of how and why you're making changes. For some writers, this process is the most difficult part of writing. But it begins to seem easier once writers think of themselves as readers. As a reader, you might ask yourself the following: What do I like the best in my piece? What's the best line? Where does the piece come alive? Instead of revising by looking for what's wrong or missing in your draft, look for what's best, what you like. Begin to revise outward from the place you liked when you read it. That place is usually where you, the writer, hear your voice most clearly. Next time you're revising a draft of a paper you're working on, practice revision by beginning as we've suggested, with the sentence or section that feels the most accomplished. You'll be revising using what Welty calls your "reader-voice."

Here are some other suggestions for revising:

- If you have time, let the draft "rest" for a while—a day or a couple of hours—before you look at it again.
- Listen for your voice as you read to yourself a section of your draft. Places where you don't like the voice are usually spots where you've been vague, repetitious, or overly general.
- Get a friend or group member to read a part of your draft to you. Take note of what works and what doesn't as you listen.

Voice and Rhetoric

Writers who hear the reader-voice—in other words, writers who are able to become readers of the texts they write—are paying attention to the rhetoric of their writing. These writers think about how they sound to themselves, how they might sound to others, and how clearly they have communicated their point and their subject. They probably do not consider all these elements at once; in fact, they could stymie themselves if they attempted to think of them all at once; but during the process of writing a piece, all these rhetorical concerns emerge. When writers ask themselves or their writing group questions such as "How do I sound?" and "Does this sentence sound okay?" they are using voice to guide rhetorical choices. And voice is a good guide.

Peter Elbow talks about voice often in his discussions about writers and writing. In teaching writing, he realized that he and his students always liked best the writing that somehow sounded the most real. It had voice. Elbow suggests that writers begin to look for the places—the words, the lines, the paragraphs—where they hear the quality of voice that somehow makes the writing seem real to them. One way to do that is to ask others to tell you where they hear voice most clearly in your work. Another way is to read aloud or to simply listen hard as you read to yourself. "Writing with voice is writing into which someone has breathed."

Some writing, Elbow says, has no voice: "Writing with no voice is dead, mechanical, faceless. It lacks any sound. Writing with no voice *may* be saying something important, or new; it may be logically organized; it may even be a work of genius. But it is as though the words came through some kind of mixer rather than being uttered by a person." You know this kind of writing; you've read it. Perhaps even written it. One of our students describes her own writing with no voice as "writing just to do the assignment. I don't feel like I own it because I don't care enough except to get it done."

What Elbow doesn't say is that writing with no voice is writing that doesn't pay attention to rhetoric. The reader of a piece of no-voice writing doesn't sense a person behind the words or anybody interesting. The writer hasn't created a relationship with the reader or the subject, or hasn't considered the context of the writing. In some writing, the voice may be fake rather than absent. And having a fake voice—too intimate, too academic, too arch—is the result of not understanding how to use rhetoric to illuminate ideas by creating relationships between reader and writer.

Most of the excerpts in this book have voice, we think, and that's why as readers we appreciate them. Some excerpts use personal examples as well as direct address to readers. Frank DeFord's column in Chapter 1 does those things. Others, like Gleick's *Chaos* excerpt, use no personal examples but establish a relationship of engagement with the subject and with the reader that feels authentic. It feels like writing that's been "breathed into." A piece with voice invites the reader to understand, to participate, to be convinced.

What We Hear When We Read and Write

Writers and readers respond to words, ideas, and arguments in a host of ways that depend on their own contexts—their education, their mood, their personality, their beliefs, their experience. Knowing that words were always tied to meaning for both the speaker and the hearer, Aristotle developed three categories to describe the tools a speaker might use in the process of inventing ideas and making choices. The categories, the three appeals that we introduce in Chapter 1 and explain further in Chapters 2 and 3, apply to the listener as well; they describe the ways that listeners are persuaded to the speaker's **point of view.** Aristotle described them this way:

There are then these three means of effecting persuasion. The man who is to be in command of them must, it is clear, be able (1) to reason logically, (2) to understand human character and goodness in their various forms, and (3) to understand the emotions—that is, to name them and describe them, to know their causes and the way in which they are excited.

The Logical Appeal: Logos

A speaker can use logical reasoning—logos—to appeal to the reasoning function of an audience. Speakers who back up their claims with factual evidence and support from sources and who can lead listeners through a logical chain of events toward a conclusion emphasize logos. "Nine out of ten doctors agree," claims an advertisement for a painkiller, and readers are invited to conclude that since the percentage of experts who concur about the value of the product is overwhelming, they should agree on its value as well. Statistics, charts, graphs—all are used often to appeal to readers' sense of objectivity and reason.

Logical reasoning is the simplest way to persuade. A writer states a claim and then supports it, logically or empirically. In a deductive claim, or **deductive reasoning,** the statement comes before the support (even though logically it follows the proof) because the writer wants readers to evaluate the claim as they're reading along. The proof itself may be deductive or the result of **inductive reasoning;** it may begin with general principles and proceed with particulars that follow from those principles, or it may begin with examples (or experiments or cases) and generalize logically from them.

Here's another brief example from James Gleick's book, *Chaos.* (An excerpt from his book appears in Chapter 4.) This example demonstrates how deductive reasoning works in a logical argument.

> In fluid systems and mechanical systems, the nonlinear terms tend to be the features that people want to leave out when they try to get a good, simple understanding. Friction, for example. Without friction, a simple linear equation expresses the amount of energy you need to accelerate a hockey puck. With friction the relationship gets complicated, because the amount of energy changes depending on how fast the puck is already moving. Nonlinearity means that the act of playing the game has a way of changing the rules. You cannot assign a constant importance to friction, because its importance depends on speed. Speed, in turn, depends on friction. That changeability makes nonlinearity hard to calculate, but it also creates rich kinds of that twisted behavior that never occur in linear systems.

Stated as a syllogism, the premises and conclusion of this small paragraph might look something like this:

> The world is complex.
> Nonlinear systems in physics account for complexity.
> Nonlinear systems render a fuller account of the world.

Gleick proves his point with the example of friction and the illustration of friction with the hockey puck. Gleick doesn't state the first premise directly but, instead, assumes the audience already believes it. Gleick does, however, support the first premise with the proof that the friction example offers. The conclusion—that nonlinear systems create a fuller account of the way the world works—is stated directly and reinforces his statement that nonlinear systems in physics account for complexity. When we analyze Gleick's argument as a syllogism, we state the premises explicitly, even though Gleick himself doesn't, and we show how he moves logically from premise to statement to conclusion in order to bring readers to agreement.

The syllogism is an effective form of logical reasoning when the writer can't count on his readers to fill in any missing premises because the ideas are too complex, perhaps or because a premise might be overlooked. Gleick's specialized subject matter and his desire to keep readers involved in that subject lead him to make his statements directly. Often in syllogisms, the premises are stated rather than implied to provide emphasis. For example, in the famous "Socrates is mortal" syllogism described in Chapter 2, Plato wanted to highlight Socrates's mortality, so he reinforced it by reminding his listeners that Socrates was a man. Writers have to be careful if they state all the premises, however; you've heard people dismiss arguments by saying that the speaker just "stated the obvious." Readers sometimes feel that they are being treated condescendingly to if all premises, especially ones that are obvious or universally accepted, are stated.

The enthymeme, introduced in Chapter 2, is a kind of syllogism that writers use continually when they're using logical reasoning, in part to avoid stating the obvious. As writers, we assume certain premises to be common knowledge, such as the fact that Socrates was a man or that *The Scarlet Letter* is a nineteenth-century novel. We use enthymemes as well to be more persuasive than we might be with the syllogism, omitting premises that might be rejected too quickly as obvious if they were stated directly. We invite readers into the argument by allowing them to fill in premises and to reach conclusions through logical progressions of ideas.

In analyzing something you've read, let's say a character in a novel, you use logical appeals when you quote the text and cite scenes from the novel or from secondary sources to support your ideas about the character. For example:

> Hester Prynne only seems to be a victim in *The Scarlet Letter*. In truth, she refuses the role of victim time and again as she acts on her own behalf and on behalf of her child. "Look you to it," she warns Dimmesdale when the town threatens to remove Pearl from her care. She becomes a valued member of her small community by making herself invaluable, at sick beds and in the rooms of the dying as well as in her skill at needlework, so much so that her letter of shame eventually seems to many to stand for "Able" or even "Angel." In his study of the novel, *The Office of the Scarlet Letter,* Sacvan Bercovitch describes Hester in just that way.

You can see in this excerpt the writer's use of logical support—quotations, scenes, and support from a book of literary criticism by Bercovitch—to aid the writer in making a claim about Hester's role in the novel. Readers are convinced by the reasoning behind the claim, reasoning that comes from the writer's careful, close reading of the work. Notice, too, the voice of the piece. The writer doesn't waffle: the reader knows exactly what the writer thinks about Hester's role in the novel and why.

When writers write academic prose, like Gleick's study of nonlinear physics or essays of literary analysis, they typically use logical reasoning. Readers anticipate facts, data, examples, and logic when they read writing meant to inform and convince them. Readers expect the voices of writers using logic to be reasoned as well, not too emotional, and not too intimate. (Of course, much nonfiction writing makes use of all the appeals, just as fiction does). But other writing—fiction and literary memoir, for example—uses logos as well. Here's an example from Beryl Markham's memoir:

> "We fixed the runway," he said, "as well as we could."
>
> I nodded, looking into a lean-boned, sun-beaten face.
>
> "It's a good job," I assured him—"better than I had hoped for."
>
> "And we rigged up a windsock." He swung his arm in the direction of a slender pole whose base was surrounded by half a dozen flares. At the top of the pole hung a limp cylinder of cheap, white "Americani" cloth looking a bit like an amputated pajama leg.
>
> In such a breeze the cylinder ought to have been fully extended, but instead, and in defiance of the simplest laws of physics, it only dangled in shameless indifference to both the strength of the wind and its direction.
>
> Moving closer, I saw the lower end had been sewn as tightly shut as needle and thread could make it, so that, as an instrument intended to indicate wind tendency, it was rather less efficient than a pair of whole pajamas might have been.
>
> I explained this technical error of design to Ebert and, in the half-light of the oil torches, had the satisfaction of seeing his face relax into what I suspected was his first smile in a long, long time.

Markham explains her own logical reasoning here to demonstrate her competence and expertise. She's a pilot who knows both what a windsock does and how one must be rigged. Logically, the way the amateurs on the ground have put the windsock together won't work. Readers realize it, see its humor, and respond both to her knowledge and the good will of the people trying to help her as she lands her plane in the field.

Activity

Create a syllogism or enthymeme from the paragraph on *The Scarlet Letter*.

The Ethical Appeal: Ethos

When writers create a voice, the persona of their piece, they also create a relationship with readers that is based on a kind of trust. Writers ask readers to believe them, to bear with them, to listen to them because, they imply, they're trustworthy and believable, and they have good intentions. They use what Aristotle called the ethical appeal, ethos, by establishing their own account-ability in the communicative act of speaking or writing. In any writing, then, ethos finds a place. Readers believe that James Gleick knows what he's talking about as he describes the history of chaos theory; he's established his back-ground and knowledge early in the book, and his careful, reasoned tone and well-documented sources lead readers to accept his authority as a speaker. In the Beryl Markham excerpt just above, readers trust Markham's expertise as well the goodwill she feels toward the men who've tried to help her.

But writers often highlight the ethical appeal in more direct ways than by creating a credible voice in their writing. If the issue to be discussed is highly contentious, if opinions on the best course of action vary widely, if facts them-selves are hard to come by or misleading, writers often use their own sense of ethics and their readers' sense of ethics to persuade. The sentence "Ninety-nine percent of doctors agree" might be logical, but it depends for its effect on the fact that *doctors,* not random population groups or other professional people, agree on the brand of painkiller to use. Readers trust doctors to know about painkillers, and if doctors say a medical product is worthwhile, it's not only logical proof but ethical proof as well. In fact, the medical profession is regarded highly in a general way by many readers. If a doctor speaks, listeners might be more inclined to feel trust than if a person from some less highly regarded profession spoke.

The ethical appeal highlights the character of the speaker. Remember Quintilian's dictum about the "good man speaking well" (page 4). The "good" speaker is good because he or she is ethical, and readers depend on that good-ness as they evaluate the argument.

Here's another excerpt from Markham's story that highlights the ethical appeal. She has visited the room of a man dying from blackwater fever, and this is a part of her conversation with him:

> The man on the bed was dying like that. He wanted to talk because it is possible to forget yourself if you talk, but not if you only lie and think.
>
> "Hastings," he said. "You must know Carl Hastings. He was a White Hunter for a while and then he settled down on a coffee plantation west of Ngong. I won-der if he ever married? He used to say he never would, but nobody believed him."
>
> "He did, though," I said. It was a name I had never heard, but it seemed a small enough gesture to lie about a nebulous Carl Hastings—even, if necessary, to give him a wife.
>
> In the four years Bergner had been away, the town of Nairobi had swelled and burst like a ripe seedpod. It was no longer so comfortably small that every inhabi-tant was a neighbor, or every name that of a friend.
>
> "I thought you knew him," Bergner said; "everybody knows Carl. And when you see him you can tell him he owes me five pounds. It's on a bet we made one Christmas in Mombasa. He bet he'd never get married—not in Africa, anyway. He said you could boast about living in a man's country, but you couldn't expect to find a marriageable woman in it!"

"I'll tell him about it," I said; "he can send it by way of Kisumu."
"That's right, by way of Kisumu."

Here, Markham tells a lie to comfort a dying man she doesn't even know, and readers respond to her kindness. We characterize her as a good person, and our trust in her as a speaker and a person increases as she describes her "small enough" gesture. Writers using the ethical appeal ask a reader to examine their character, to infer from their words the ideals or morals they hold dear. Writers using the ethical appeal make a strong link to their readers, as they suggest that the ideals they believe in are the same ones as, or are similar ones to, those values the readers hold themselves. "I would tell a lie like that," we say to ourselves, "if it could give a dying man a little pleasure or peace in his last moments." We like Markham's character because it responds to something in our own.

The Emotional Appeal: Pathos

The strongest, most direct, and thus most dramatic appeal writers make when they try to persuade their readers is the emotional appeal, or pathos. Aristotle calls on speakers to understand the emotions, to name them and describe them, "to know their causes and the way in which they are excited." Knowing about human emotions and understanding how those emotions are created within a person allow a speaker to find the words and the forms that appeal to the emotions the speaker wants to evoke.

We've heard and read many examples of the emotional appeal in our daily lives, in advertisements, in movies and on television, in political speeches, in sermons, and in editorials. Emotions are more immediate and sensory than logic or ethics, so we respond more readily when our emotions are involved. That's why, of course, appeals to the emotions, while dramatic, can also be dangerous. Groups have been incited to perform violent actions under the influence of a speaker who has moved them to anger or desperation. The emotions work quickly, and if speakers want an audience to act, not just think, they often make appeals to the emotions.

Think of advertisements you've seen recently on television or in magazines. One typical advertisement for automobiles shows a car with a backdrop of a beautiful sunset and a beautiful woman leaning on the hood. There's not much logical appeal in such an advertisement; neither the scenery nor the woman accompanies the car when a person buys it. But the emotional connection is clear. "If I drive such a car, might I not be able to go to places like the one shown in the picture? And if I'm the driver, might I not find someone who'd admire my choice enough to travel with me?" Love, lust, pride, excitement, and other emotions can all be provoked in the viewer captivated by the ad.

Here, from Markham's book, is one more example that highlights the emotional appeal. As you read, think of the emotions that the author feels and that she attempts to transmit to her readers.

I patted Buller and he wagged his lump of a tail to say he understood the need for silence. Buller was my accomplice in everything. He was a past master at stealth and at more other things than any dog I ever owned or knew.

His loyalty to me was undeviating, but I could never think of him as being a sentimental dog, a dog fit for a pretty story of the kind that tears the heartstrings off their pegs; he was too rough, too tough, and too aggressive.

He was cynical toward life, and his black-and-white hide bore, in a cryptology of long, short, and semicircular scars, the history of his fighting career. He fought anything that needed to be fought, and when there was nothing immediately available in this category, he killed cats.

One night a leopard, no doubt the chosen avenger of his species, crept through the open door of my hut and abducted Buller from the foot of my bed. Buller weighed something over sixty-five pounds and most of it was nicely coordinated offensive equipment. The sound and the fury of the first round of that battle sometimes still ring in my ears. But the advantage was with the attacker. Before I could do much more than scramble out of bed, dog and leopard disappeared in the moonless night.

Markham begins this scene with a description of her dog, Buller, and her description is overtly unsentimental. She even notes that Buller himself is not a "sentimental dog" but a ferocious, though loyal, one. The scene that follows, where Buller is pulled from Markham's bed and dragged away by a leopard, is emotionally powerful because readers recognize in her description her love for the dog, her constant companion. Because she writes without exclamation points, in a matter-of-fact style, and with some humor—the leopard she imagines singled out to exact revenge on Buller—our emotional response is even stronger. We feel her terror and then sadness when she realizes Buller has been taken. If readers are animal lovers themselves, their response is even more emotional perhaps than for other readers. Markham uses understatement to heighten our reaction as we are left to imagine for a moment what might have happened to this independent, brave, and beloved animal.

One other example of emotional appeal and emotional response before we leave this section. You no doubt recall your own experience with September 2001, during the days after the attacks on the World Trade Center and the Pentagon. Our emotions during those weeks were intense. You probably remember where you were when you first heard the news and remember as well your first feelings, initially of shock and disbelief, then horror and sadness as all of us began to learn the toll of human life these attacks exacted.

We've talked about how rhetoric operates in all kinds of communication, in images and pictures, in symbols and graphics as well as in words. And images often evoke intense emotional response. The American flag—so evident in those days flying at half-mast on public buildings, stuck in the coat pockets and car windows of millions of citizens, waving in the rubble of what was the World Trade Center, draping coffins of the victims—called up strong emotions: determination, pride, and belief. Lots of other images were used rhetorically in those days to express the writers' or artists' attitude and to connect emotionally with an audience numbed and saddened by the tragedy.

The *New Yorker* cover for the week of September 24, 2001, was one such powerful and emotional rhetorical statement. The cover was completely black, with just the *New Yorker* logo in white lettering at the top. Its blackness suggested tragedy and death, expressed the darkness and fear that many, especially in New York, felt after the planes crashed into the Twin Towers. The cover was so dark that readers might have missed the underlying image, but when they held the magazine at an angle or in strong light and looked at it intently, they realized that the cover was not black but dark gray. Beneath the gray was a darker image, the silhouette of the towers. The image was all the more chilling because viewers discovered it on their own, and the emotions that discovery provokes are extremely powerful.

Readers experience a variety of emotions in response to writers' use of images and other verbal techniques. The variety depends on the readers' personal beliefs, desires, or fears. But writers count on readers to feel at least somewhat similar to the way they feel. That's why Socrates's advice to the thinker to "know thyself" has long been the surest means that writers have for understanding how to appeal to readers and that readers have for understanding how to negotiate and respond to those appeals.

Activity

Look at some recent advertisements to see if you can find examples of emotional appeals. Share them with your group. See if together you can figure out how appeals to logic or to ethics might also be part of the ads you've brought in.

Activity

Recall a stirring speech from a movie you've seen, and analyze it for its emotional appeal. *Braveheart* has such a scene; *Titanic* does, too. Think about the effect of the speech on you as a viewer. Do you respond positively to it? Are you critical of it? (If you find yourself critiquing the scene rather than responding positively to it, something in the words or the ideas behind the words might contradict your own sense of logic or ethics.)

The Appeals Combined

Probably no piece of discourse exhibits only one of the three kinds of appeals, for writers and readers bring a complex set of understandings, experiences, and kinds of knowledge to bear on what they write and read. We've isolated bits of discourse in the pieces above to demonstrate how one appeal might be highlighted for readers and promoted by writers, but it's also true that you may have responded in emotional ways to our example of ethos or ethically to our illustration of pathos. To demonstrate how all the appeals might combine for you as a reader, we've chosen an example of a famous speech, one many of you have read or have heard at least the first few lines of. It's Mark Antony's speech in Shakespeare's play *Julius Caesar*. Antony is speaking at Caesar's funeral, as his friend and follower, and the speech Shakespeare creates for him becomes an elegy to Antony's sovereign and friend.

But it's more than that. Caesar has been assassinated by Brutus and other compatriots who believed that Caesar had become a tyrant and a danger to Rome. The people of Rome have agreed, and they are at first hostile to Antony, whom they see as an **apologist** for Caesar's ambitious, imperious rule. Antony wants to change their minds, but he has to operate subtly and carefully. As you read, notice how Antony uses the rhetorical device of **repetition,** as well as irony, to turn the crowd from its belief in Brutus and the rightness of his cause to anger against him.

> ANTONY.   Friends, Romans, countrymen, lend me your ears;
>
> I come to bury Caesar, not to praise him.
>
> The evil that men do lives after them;
>
> The good is oft interred with their bones;
>
> So let it be with Caesar. The noble Brutus
>
> Hath told you Caesar was ambitious;
>
> If it were so, it was a grievous fault,
>
> And grievously hath Caesar answer'd it.
>
> Here, under leave of Brutus and the rest—
>
> For Brutus is an honorable man;
>
> So are they all, all honorable men—
>
> Come I to speak in Caesar's funeral.
>
> He was my friend, faithful and just to me;
>
> But Brutus says he was ambitious;
>
> And Brutus is an honorable man.
>
> He hath brought many captives home to Rome,
>
> Whose ransoms did the general coffers fill:
>
> Did this in Caesar seem ambitious?
>
> When that the poor have cried, Caesar hath wept:
>
> Ambition should be made of sterner stuff:
>
> Yet Brutus says he was ambitious;
>
> And Brutus is an honorable man.

You all did see that on the Lupercal

I thrice presented him a kingly crown,

Which he did thrice refuse: was this ambitious?

Yet Brutus says he was ambitious;

And, sure, he is an honorable man.

I speak not to disprove what Brutus spoke,

But here I am to speak what I do know.

You all did love him once, not without cause:

What cause withholds you then, to mourn for him?

O judgment! Thou art fled to brutish beasts,

And men have lost their reason. Bear with me;

My heart is in the coffin there with Caesar,

And I must pause till it come back to me.

FIRST CITIZEN.   Methinks there is much reason in his sayings.

SECOND CITIZEN.   If thou consider rightly of the matter, Caesar has had great wrong.

THIRD CITIZEN.   Has he, masters? I fear there will be a worse come in his place.

FOURTH CITIZEN.   Mark'd ye his words? He would not take the crown;

Therefore 'tis certain he was not ambitious.

FIRST CITIZEN.   If it be found so, some will dear abide it.

SECOND CITIZEN.   Poor soul: his eyes are red as fire with weeping.

THIRD CITIZEN.   There's not a nobler man in Rome than Antony.

FOURTH CITIZEN.   Now mark him, he begins again to speak.

Act III, scene 2

Antony is successful in changing the minds of Roman citizens about the character both of Caesar and of Brutus and his companions. By the end of his oration, which continues for several more pages, the crowd is inflamed with the desire to find and kill Brutus—"We'll burn the house of Brutus!" "We'll mutiny!"—before the speech a hero and after a traitorous villain. In those remaining lines, Antony stops to gather his emotions, mentions Caesar's will but delays until the end of the speech revealing its contents, asks the listeners to examine Caesar's wounds with him, and finally reads the will, which leaves money to each citizen and bequeaths Caesar's private gardens to the public. "I am no orator, as Brutus is," Antony tells them, but the crowd's reaction and the response of readers and audiences suggest how powerful a speaker Antony is, how much he has understood and used voice.

Mark Antony's manipulation of the audience through rhetorical appeals shows how speakers who understand their listeners can move them to belief and action. Antony understands his audience, perhaps because he understands himself. By the end of the scene, his voice and the voice of the people become one.

Here's one more example of a speech using the appeals in complex and interesting ways. It's from Sojourner Truth's speech to the Women's Rights Convention in Cleveland, Ohio, in 1851. Sojourner Truth, a former slave, was speaking to a group of men and women about the need for women's suffrage. Many men in the audience had jeered at earlier speakers and called out counterarguments as Sojourner Truth began speaking herself. In some versions of this speech, the recorder of the speech (Truth herself could not read or write) intersperses her own commentary about Truth's actions and gestures as well as crowd reaction in much the same way that Shakespeare writes of the crowd's reaction to Antony's plea. Both Antony and Truth are speaking to a crowd at least partially and initially hostile. As you read, see if you discover other similar patterns in the speeches.

AND AIN'T I A WOMAN?

Well children, where there is so much racket there must be somethin' out o'kilter. I think that 'twixt the Negroes of the North and the South and the women at the North, all talkin' 'bout rights, the white men will be in a fix pretty soon. But what's all this here talkin' 'bout?

That man over there say that women needs to be helped into carriages, and lifted over ditches, and to have the best place everywhere. Nobody ever helps me into carriages, or over mud-puddles, or give me any best place! And ain't I a woman? Look at me! Look at my arm! I have ploughed, and planted, and gathered into barns, and no man could head me! And ain't I a woman? I could work as much and eat as much as a man—when I could get it—and bear the lash as well! And ain't I a woman? I have borne thirteen children, and seen 'em mos' all sold off to slavery, and when I cried out with my mother's grief, none but Jesus heard me! And ain't I a woman?

Then they talk about this thing in the head; what's this they call it? ["Intellect," whispered some one near.] That's it honey. What's that got to do with women's rights or Negro's rights? If my cup won't hold but a pint and yours holds a quart, wouldn't you be mean not to let me have my little measure full?

Then that little man in black there, he says women can't have as much rights as men, 'cause Christ wasn't a woman! Where did your Christ come from? Where did your Christ come from? From God and a woman! Man had nothin' to do with Him.

If the first woman God ever made was strong enough to turn the world upside down all alone, these women together ought to be able to turn it back and get it right side up again; and now they is asking to do it, they better let 'em. 'Bliged to you for hearin' me, and now ole Sojourner hasn't got nothin' more to say.

Activity

Examine the excerpt of Mark Antony's speech for the three appeals. Note spots where you find those appeals, and talk together in your group about your reasons for the selection. Notice when in the speech Antony uses which appeals. Consider the responses of the citizens to what they have heard.

Activity

Examine one of your own compositions for the three appeals. Consider your format and organization, your diction, and your examples. Analyze your rhetoric. Or trade compositions with a classmate to locate the appeals and their effect on you as a reader.

Interchapter

5

Overview of the Major Points in Chapter 5

- Both readers and writers listen for the voice of a text in order to interpret and to make decisions about what might come next in the text. Listening for the "reader-voice" helps readers and writers test the effectiveness of their texts.
- Words are signs.
- Freewriting helps readers create meanings for texts they read.
- Writers read their own texts as they emerge and use what they've written to guide subsequent writing decisions.
- Active readers co-create the texts they read.
- To complete the transaction between reader and writer, both make use of and respond to rhetorical appeals.

Activities and Discussion Questions for Chapter 5   Use these questions and comments as guides for your own discussion and writing about these works.

Henry David Thoreau, "On the Duty of Civil Disobedience" (published 1849)

The text appears on pages 210–225. In your group, discuss the following questions. You might use some of these questions as the basis for a well-organized essay or journal entry.

1. Identify a section of Thoreau's essay that you find especially dramatic or effective. Read it aloud to your group. How does your voice reading the section change or enrich the meaning of the passage?

2. After rereading the first few paragraphs of the essay, stop to write a response to what you've read, concentrating on the phrases or the

positions you hear emerging in Thoreau's argument. How does your piece of writing reinforce or challenge Thoreau's points?

3. Freewrite about Thoreau's essay. Read back over your freewriting, and then write one more sentence. Make that sentence the beginning point for your group's discussion of "Civil Disobedience."

4. How would you define Thoreau's primary appeal to you as a reader? Find examples where Thoreau's use of logic, ethics, or emotion strikes you as effective or where it seems ineffective. Discuss in your group how the appeals work differently for different readers.

5. What are some unstated premises that Thoreau implies in making his argument? Create a syllogism or an enthymeme from one of the points Thoreau makes. Do you agree with the conclusion?

Eavan Boland, "It's a Woman's World" (published 1982)

The text appears on pages 226–227. In your group, discuss the following questions. You might use some of these questions as the basis for a well-organized essay or journal entry.

1. How do you react to the use of *we* and *our,* first-person plural, in the poem? Where does it place you as a reader?

2. Write a short essay that explains how individual word choices in the poem affect your emotions or opinions as you read.

3. How do you feel about the word *outrage* in stanza 11? Write a response that explains Boland's use of the term and your reaction to it.

4. Create an enthymeme to explain Boland's argument in the poem. Discuss these enthymemes in your group as beginning points for an essay on the rhetoric Boland chooses as she writes the poem.

Alice Walker, "Everyday Use" (published 1973)

The text appears on pages 228–237. In your group, discuss the following questions. You might use some of these questions as the basis for a well-organized essay or journal entry.

1. Freewrite briefly about the very general issue of family relationships or sibling relationships. Read at least a few sentences of your response aloud to your group, and discuss how the writing helps you think about the issues of family present in Walker's story.

2. Read aloud a passage where the "I" narrator seems to be an especially strong character and the "you" being addressed seems especially present. What does the reading suggest to you about the relationship between the reader and the speaker?

3. Ask some questions that you don't think this text completely answers. See if you can answer some of those questions with your group or in a journal entry.

4. Consider the ending of the story, looking back to see how the ending is prepared for in earlier sections. If you can come up with a different ending for the story, rewrite the ending, trying to achieve Walker's tone and using Walker's narrator.

Rhetoric in Narrative

6

PEANUTS *reprinted by permission of United Feature Synidcate, Inc.*

> Narrative has never been merely entertainment for me. It is, I believe, one of the principal ways we absorb knowledge.
>
> Toni Morrison, *Nobel Prize lecture*

In her Nobel Prize lecture in 1990, Toni Morrison asks her audience to think about the way readers use narrative to understand ideas and to gather knowledge, about the way a story gets told, and about the uses of language to communicate ideas, argue claims, and persuade to action. Morrison is interested in the *rhetoric* of the story—its aim and its effect. As Morrison says in her speech, "The vitality of language lies in its ability to limn the actual, imagined and possible lives of its speakers, readers, writers."

Morrison emphasizes language as the connecting medium between writer and reader. Not just the subject of the tale but also the art of its telling will determine how readers "absorb knowledge." Morrison underscores the importance of rhetoric as a tool for writers and readers of all kinds of narratives, both fictional and nonfictional. The language of a crafted story, a narrative, is heightened, designed to express, explain, persuade, entertain. Even lyric poetry, though typically without a story line, carries persuasive intent to a reader and uses the same rhetorical tools—arrangement, word choice, persona—to build its message, make its moves, explore its moment.

In this chapter, we discuss the uses of rhetoric in three genres of literature sometimes called belles lettres—fiction, drama, and poetry. We've used fiction in other chapters; in this chapter, we concentrate on these three familiar literary genres, looking at the reading of literature through a rhetorical lens by using terms you already know as tools to analyze literature. *Character, setting, plot, theme, narrator,* and *imagery* are terms you no doubt use often as you talk and write about the novels, plays, and poems you read in and out of class. We'll use these same terms to talk about intent, method, and effect—the rhetorical decisions made by the writer and reader. Examining literature rhetorically enriches your reading of literary texts and can help you see more deeply into the work as well as into your response to it.

> The author cannot choose to use rhetorical heightening. His only choice is of the kind of rhetoric he will use.
>
> Wayne Booth, *The Rhetoric of Fiction*

Wayne Booth's *The Rhetoric of Fiction* was first published in 1961 and quickly became an important resource for critics and teachers interested in how fiction works to achieve its effects on readers. The central premise of the book is that fiction (in a later edition, Booth expanded his ideas to include all narrative, fiction and nonfiction alike) is *inescapably* rhetorical; that is, authors work to achieve effects based on their understanding of the interrelationships among reader, speaker, and subject. As Booth claims in the passage above, writers *must* use rhetoric. Their only decision is *how* they will use it. As a result, fiction carries persuasive intent just as speeches and letters to the editor do. The message in fiction or drama or poetry may be less direct than the message in other genres; the text may carry many messages rather than just one, or the writer may be persuading the reader only to enter the world of the text. But the communication between reader and writer exists in poetry, fiction, and drama just as in pieces of nonfiction, and understanding how that communication works enriches the experience of reading all kinds of literature.

Rhetoric insists on bringing the reader into text, on making the reader a part of the transaction as characters speak and act, and as the textual world takes shape. The writer, as well as the narrator, depends on the reader to help complete the transaction to make sense and find resonance in the story—by using what the reader knows about plots and people and life.

One of Booth's insights is how deeply embedded in the story the *author* must be, how much the author directs matters by placing characters in a setting and situation and by reporting the action as it unfolds. Many young writers are familiar with "show, don't tell," a maxim that directs authors to stay behind the scenes, to refuse to manipulate or to refuse to talk directly to the reader about the fact that they are manipulating for effect. In realistic fiction and drama, writers are presumed to be invisible so that audiences might "suspend their disbelief," a phrase the nineteenth-century poet and critic Samuel Taylor Coleridge used to talk about how an audience allow themselves to see the stage as a world. Some authors do attempt invisibility; they let a narrator or a central character "tell" the reader about what might be going on, and they suggest how a reader might be expected to feel. Other writers more overtly make themselves a part of the action by commenting on events and guiding the reader's reactions to those events. In either case, as Booth shows, writers are never really invisible; they use words and create movements among their characters to persuade an audience to believe. So, when writers show, Booth suggests, they also inescapably tell.

To make his point, Booth uses lots of examples from classic literature like the *Odyssey* to realistic twentieth-century fiction. Booth takes the opening scene from the *Odyssey*, for example, to illustrate how Homer conveys his persuasive intent. At the beginning of the poem in the translation Booth uses, the goddess Athena speaks to Zeus:

> "It is for Odysseus that my heart is wrung—the wise but unlucky Odysseus, who has been parted so long from all his friends and is pining on a lonely island far away in the middle of the seas."

And Zeus replies:

> "How could I ever forget the admirable Odysseus? He is not only the wisest man alive but has been the most generous in his offerings. . . . It is Poseidon . . . who is so implacable towards him."

Readers discover in the opening not just the facts of Odysseus's plight but also how we are supposed to feel about his condition. It's true that readers never learn much about the actual Homer writing the epic, but readers learn quickly how Homer feels about his main character and how he would like us to feel. Homer has Athena use the words _wise_ and _unlucky._ He describes Athena's sympathetic reaction by telling readers that her "heart is wrung."

In the rest of this chapter, you'll find examples of writers who intrude themselves deliberately into their stories, writers who hide behind a narrator (sometimes one who they appear to dislike), and writers who move into the consciousness of many characters or none or one. The way in which writers place themselves in or out of their fictional worlds is itself a rhetorical decision, in part shaped by how writers assume that readers will read and understand the story.

Character

Characters are the actors in a fictional world. They interact in that world in ways that readers recognize or are surprised by based on what readers know of the real world of their own experience. To a great extent, we care about the world of the fictional text because we are engaged by the characters we read about and come to know. We may feel sympathy, dislike, amusement, or horror toward them, but we feel something. Authors present their characters in deliberate ways; they choose language, gesture, action, and appearance that make the clearest, most persuasive description of the character, to help readers respond appropriately and effectively.

If you look back at the bit of dialogue from the _Odyssey,_ above, you'll see that Homer has told us almost nothing about the characters who are speaking and much about the character they speak about, Odysseus. To figure out why Homer chose to reveal character in this indirect way, consider that Homer's epic was originally heard rather than read, and the story of the _Odyssey_ was a story, like other Greek myths, that the audience of his day already knew well. The early Greeks who first heard the _Odyssey_ knew the functions and personalities of all the gods in the myths. They knew Athena as the goddess of war and wisdom, and so recognized the compliment she paid Odysseus when she called him wise. They knew that Zeus, her father, was the supreme god and therefore most powerful in determining the fortunes of men.

Homer, in other words, didn't need to explain the personalities of the two speakers because he could count on his audience using what they knew and believed of the gods to make sense of the gods' dialogue and determine how to feel about the fortunes of Odysseus. Homer places Athena and Zeus at the beginning to show audiences that they should feel sympathy for the hero, just as the gods do. Zeus and Athena are reliable speakers, immortal and wise, and their judgment is meant to be trusted. Homer communicates to his audience—

his immediate one in ancient Greece, and his more distant one in the twenty-first century—his own admiration and sympathy for Odysseus through the gods' conversation at the beginning of his poem. We are prepared to admire and like him even before he appears on the scene and speaks.

Activity

Write a small scene (just a few lines or a paragraph) where Odysseus reveals his character through speech or action. You might show Odysseus as wise, brave, unlucky, or by any other characteristic that you glean by reading the lines spoken by Athena and Zeus, above. Then share your paragraph with your groupage Notice the variety of approaches group members take as they suggest to their readers how to feel about Odysseus.

Rhetorical Choices for Character

As you wrote your scene for the preceding activity, you gave Odysseus words that demonstrate something about his personality and gave him actions that express something of his character. You made these rhetorical choices deliberately because you counted on your reader's understanding of how those words and actions suggest personal attributes. Knowing how you use rhetoric as a creator of characters will help you to understand the effect of rhetoric on you as a reader of characters.

Here's an example of a character introduced in another way. As you read, listen for the writer's voice underneath the description.

> Thomas Gradgrind, sir. A man of realities. A man of facts and calculations. A man who proceeds upon the principle that two and two are four, and nothing over, and who is not to be talked into allowing for anything over. Thomas Gradgrind, sir—peremptorily Thomas—Thomas Gradgrind. With a rule and a pair of scales, and the multiplication table always in his pocket, sir, ready to weigh and measure any parcel of human nature, and tell you exactly what it comes to. It is a mere question of figures, a case of simple arithmetic. You might hope to get some other nonsensical belief into the head of George Gradgrind, or Augustus Gradgrind, or John Gradgrind, or Joseph Gradgrind (all supposititious, non-existent persons), but into the head of Thomas Gradgrind—no, sir!

This passage comes from Charles Dickens's novel *Hard Times,* which is about education and the working classes, among other things. Dickens's novels often teach lessons—think of the case of Ebenezer Scrooge in *A Christmas Carol*—and Dickens created relationships with his readers that allow them to see readily which of his characters are most sorely in need of a lesson. Scrooge, you remember, needed to learn a lesson about charity, and the three Christmas ghosts taught him. Based on the choices Dickens makes as he describes Grad-grind in *Hard Times,* readers understand quickly that he is not a character to be admired.

Activity

Examine Dickens's description, looking for the signals Dickens gives about Gradgrind's character. Pay special attention to vocabulary and to the syntax, or sentence structure, that the writer uses. Share your responses with your group, and you'll see how many examples you've found together.

Flat and Round, Static and Dynamic

Like many writers, Dickens creates vivid characters by identifying them with a few, memorable character traits or physical features. The characters always act *in character;* that is, they never surprise us or confuse us by their complexity or indecision or transformation. Scrooge is transformed, but readers are unsur-prised by the change. The entire story, from Scrooge's comment that deaths of the poor would "decrease the surplus population" to the final "God bless us, everyone!" has led us to expect transformation. We know almost from the beginning that Scrooge is a character who can, and will, be rehabilitated. And we're gratified when the transformation happens.

Characters who are less complex, who are readily identifiable by gestures, speech, and actions, are useful for writers as they communicate their ideas to readers. E. M. Forster, literary critic and novelist, called these kinds of charac-ters **flat characters.** It's an unfortunate word in a way because flat characters are not dull, or poorly depicted, as the word itself might suggest. Flat charac-ters simply act as we expect them to and become memorable because they're made identifiable through speech, appearance, or gesture. Mr. Gradgrind is a flat character. His name gives him away, the *grind* suggesting something unre-lenting and merciless. Dickens presents another character in *Hard Times,* a school principal, whose name is even clearer: Mr. McChoakumchild. His name tells what he's like and—because Dickens gives him that name and not some other—what Dickens thinks of him.

Characters who are more complex, who change their minds, attitudes, and actions, or who take readers through a process of conflict along with them, are in Forster's terminology **round characters.** Forster defined round characters as ones who "can surprise convincingly." Readers might not expect particular characters to change their minds or move to a new spot or struggle with a deci-sion, but if readers feel that characters' actions make sense, even when they're unexpected, the writer has depicted characters' complexity well.

It's harder to capture a character's roundness in only a paragraph or two because the complexity of the character usually emerges slowly over the course of time and pages in a story, but here's an example of how the round character is employed and depicted by the writer of a contemporary novel.

> At thirty six, bereft, brimming with grief and thwarted love, Quoyle steered away to Newfoundland, the rock that had generated his ancestors, a place he had never been nor thought to go.
>
> A watery place. And Quoyle feared water, could not swim. Again and again the father had broken his clenched grip and thrown him into pools, brooks, lakes and surf. Quoyle knew the flavor of brack and waterweed.
>
> From this youngest son's failure to dogpaddle the father saw other failures multiply like an explosion of virulent cells—failure to speak clearly; failure to sit up straight; failure to get up in the morning; failure in attitude; failure in ambition and ability; indeed, in everything. His own failure.
>
> Quoyle shambled, a head taller than any child around him, was soft. He knew it.
>
> Annie Proulx, *The Shipping News*

What makes us label Quoyle "round" and not "flat"? For one thing, the physical description doesn't tell us everything about the character, nor does the psychological one. That is, Quoyle doesn't seem to be a character who can be summed up quickly or easily like Mr. Gradgrind can be. Quoyle might be a large, lumbering, awkward, and odd-looking fellow, but he is also painfully conscious of himself. Notice the last line of the passage: "He knew it." Quoyle is sad about his failure and disheartened by his family's reaction to him. He "shambled," a word that suggests head-down embarrassment at his difference. He was "soft," and we're left to imagine if that softness is more than physical, if he is perhaps gentle. We don't know what will become of him; we wonder how he will manage. The careful way that Proulx has described him makes us feel his longing, loneliness, and fear. In sum, we understand that Quoyle is complex, not simple. And we're already prepared, on the first page, to sympathize.

How does Proulx manage to evoke all these reactions in a reader? She places the description as the opening to the novel to let readers know Quoyle's significance; she brings in Quoyle's family background in just a few sentences to suggest the psychological conflicts that haunt Quoyle into adulthood; she selects words that allow for both revulsion and sympathy; she looks unsympathetically at Quoyle's failings, which in a paradoxical way heightens readers' sympathetic reaction. Looking at these techniques, a reader begins to understand Proulx's decisions as rhetorical.

As readers move through the novel, they find Quoyle in a variety of situations, confronting dilemmas, engaging in activities, and considering strategies. Our responses to Quoyle develop and deepen over the course of the novel, and that change in *our* response to Quoyle is another reason that he can be characterized as a round rather than flat character. Readers feel more about him at the end of the story than at the beginning, whereas flat characters usually provoke the same feeling from beginning to end.

Another way to contrast characters is to see them as static or dynamic. The difference between these two types of characters is fairly self-explanatory. **Static characters** don't change or move much; we know everything about them that we need to know from their first introduction. The author uses them in various ways—as foils to other, more complex characters; for humor or ridicule; and/or to establish tone or theme more decisively in the minds of readers. **Dynamic characters** do change, and they are harder for readers to get a handle on. Often, writers make complex or round characters dynamic and simple or flat characters static, but not always. Mr. Gradgrind is a static character who is also flat, while Scrooge is a flat character who is dynamic. Odysseus is a relatively complex character, with difficult decisions to make and conflicting emotions, but he is also static: his bravery, intelligence, and leadership ability never waver during the course of the story. You might look back at the description of Quoyle to see if you can decide whether he will be static or dynamic and consider why you think so.

Character and the Pentad

A way of considering character and other literary elements rhetorically is to use Kenneth Burke's pentad, mentioned in Chapter 2, to explore characters' actions and motives, and to understand the structure of narratives. The pentad includes the act, which names what took place in thought or action; the scene, the background or situation where the act occurred; the agent, or person performing the act; the agency, how and with what means the act is performed; and the purpose, why the act is done.

The pentad is useful for seeing situations, or plots, in their complexity and for uncovering rhetorical motives in all kinds of narratives and all kinds of acts. It's especially useful in figuring out human motivation and so provides a helpful tool to analyze narratives.

The five points of the pentad operate cooperatively, in ratios, as Burke called them. For example, the *scene-act* connection, or ratio, describes how a background—cultural, historical, familial—affects an act, such as a murder, the building of a highway, a marriage, or the passing of a law. The *scene-agent* ratio tells how a background connects to a person; how ideals, personality characteristics, or individual choices are affected by that background; or how the actor uses a background. Let's say two people meet, fall in love despite their families' objections, and commit double suicide. That's the story of *Romeo and Juliet*. The scene-act ratio would examine how family (or society or culture) contributes to the deaths. The scene-agent ratio would describe how society (or family or culture) contributes to the character of Juliet or Romeo. The other elements in the pentad contribute additional perspectives on a situation by exposing additional choices that writers make. Consider, for instance, how agency is important in *Romeo and Juliet*. Because they mislay messages and bungle their attempts to help, both the nurse and the priest become agencies in the deaths of the young lovers.

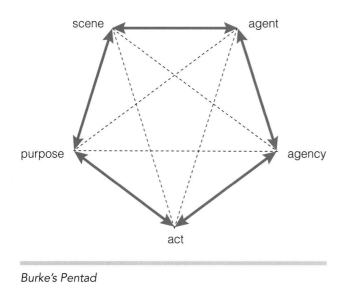

Burke's Pentad

Say the writer of an analysis of *Romeo and Juliet* begins with the question, "Why did Romeo and Juliet die?" How might the writer use the pentad to help answer the question—that is, explain the act?

- **act-agency:** They died because their plans for escape went awry.
- **act-scene:** Their families' opposition and mutual hatred drove them to commit double suicide.
- **act-purpose:** They wanted to be together so desperately that they chose to die rather than live in a world without one another.
- **act-agent:** They died when one took poison and the other stabbed herself.

All these explanations are accurate, but some explain more fully the reasons for the deaths than others. A writer might choose to highlight one pair rather than another to guide readers in understanding the motivations that are most appropriate to the writer's own purposes. The way Shakespeare chooses to end the play, as well as his use of the flat characters of the nurse and the priest as agencies for the deaths, might be clues to help readers locate the ratios that most fully explain the tragic outcome of Romeo and Juliet's story.

The pentad is useful for examining all the elements in narrative and their relationship to others. *Setting* is another term for Burke's *scene*; *theme* can be connected to *purpose*; *conflict*, to *act*. What Burke's discussion adds is an insistence on seeing each of these elements in combination rather than in isolation so that the complexities of narrative get revealed and the rhetorical possibilities that emerge from highlighting one connection and submerging another get exposed. In the discussion of literary elements that follows, think about how the pentad's combinations might be applied to your reading.

Activity

Choose a novel or a short story your class has read together, and write a brief analysis of one character. Focus on one ratio to explain the actions of that character. You might have each member of your group concentrate on a different ratio, which will add depth and perspective to the text you're analyzing.

Setting

When speakers step to a podium, they use and are affected by the context that surrounds them. The auditorium, the stagelights, the time of day and year, the local and national news stories that people have been talking about that day—all contribute to speakers' decisions about how to arrange and deliver the speech. Likewise, events in the world, past and present, can become significant factors in how speakers and writers compose their work and how effective their product is. In fictional narratives, the context, or setting, becomes the stage on which characters act out their lives, and writers of fictional narratives must decide how to use this stage to its best rhetorical effect.

As readers and movie audiences, we're quite familiar with the rhetorical effects of setting on the theme, or purpose, of a story, and on the way setting reinforces tone and characters' preoccupations. Stereotypical settings tell us about genre, plot, and theme early on in a narrative. We're prepared to predict that if it's a dark and stormy night, the story must be a mystery and something dangerous, maybe even deadly, is about to happen. You can imagine other stereotypical settings easily by thinking of *genres* of narratives. The fairy tale, the Western, the science fiction story, and the detective thriller often are set in locales that audiences immediately recognize as typical of their genre, and audiences experience the story with that genre in mind. As they present the story, writers make use of an audience's expectations about setting. Sometimes they use audience's expectations to surprise us rather than confirm what we already expect. In some recent films, for example, "It was a dark and stormy night" begins a comedy rather than a horror story.

Stereotypical settings, also called **stock settings,** function as a kind of shorthand method for letting readers know how to engage with the story. More often in the narratives you read and analyze, writers use particular, rather than stock, settings for their plots and characters. But in all kinds of settings, time and place become rhetorical elements in the story, and writers use them to provoke understanding and reaction from the audience and to affect and motivate characters in the story as they respond to what surrounds them.

One way to recognize the rhetorical importance of setting is to notice where writers position descriptions of time and place. The passage from *Sula* you read in Chapter 4 describes the Bottom, the section of a small town in Ohio that is the setting for the novel. Morrison begins the book with the description, "In that place . . . " Only later do readers get introduced to the characters who live in the Bottom. Morrison makes her setting influence characters' actions—their isolation, their sense of community and belonging—and become part of a message about the continuing effects of slavery and oppression. The name *the Bottom,* placed at the top of the hill, suggests the ironic twist of fate that gives the poor African American population of the town what will become the most prized land. The importance that Morrison places on setting and its relationship to characters (in Burke's terms, the scene-agent ratio) is made clear by her decision to open the novel as she does.

Here's the opening passage of *The Scarlet Letter.* Consider how Nathaniel Hawthorne is using setting as he begins the story:

> A throng of bearded men, in sad-coloured garments and gray, steeple-crowned hats, intermixed with women, some wearing hoods, and others bareheaded, was assembled in front of a wooden edifice, the door of which was heavily timbered with oak, and studded with iron spikes.
>
> The founders of a new colony, whatever Utopia of human virtue and happiness might originally project, have invariably recognized it among their earliest practical necessities to allot a portion of the virgin soil as a cemetery, and another portion as the site of a prison. . . . Certain it is, that, some fifteen or twenty years after the settlement of the town, the wooden jail was already marked with weather-stains and other indications of age, which gave a yet darker aspect to its beetle-browed and gloomy front. The rust on the ponderous iron-work of its oaken door looked more antique than anything else in the new world. Like all that pertains to crime, it seemed never to have known a youthful era. Before this ugly edifice, and between it and the wheel-track of the street, was a grass-plot, much overgrown with burdock, pig-weed, apple-peru, and such unsightly vegetation, which evidently found something congenial in the soil that had so early borne the black flower of civilized society, a prison. But, on one side of the portal, and rooted almost at the threshold, was a wild rose-bush, covered, in this month of June, with its delicate gems, which might be imagined to offer their fragrance and fragile beauty to the prisoner as he went in, and to the condemned criminal as he came forth to his doom, in token that the deep heart of Nature could pity and be kind to him.

Notice how the setting gets established first by a quick generalization about the building of civilization and then a close-in observation of the prison door and the rose. Hawthorne emphasizes the conflict between prison door and rose—symbolically between punishment and forgiveness, ugliness and beauty—that will continue through his tale. The imagery used to describe prison and rose provides readers with a direct contrast: the prison is the grotesque "black flower" of civilization, and the rose the "deep heart of Nature" that will pity and be kind.

Hawthorne makes setting an active force in his plot by pitting civilization against nature in the form of the prison/scaffold/town on one side and the rose/forest/wilderness on the other. The characters in the drama move between these two scenes, the two opposing forces that affect all their actions and decisions.

In other works, setting is not as overtly symbolic and rhetorical as in Hawthorne's stories and novels. In plays, for example, the details of setting are often left up to the director to fill in, and writers may provide only bare outlines of place or time. Or playwrights may specify props, the portable and detailed elements of setting, rather than specify time and place.

The details of setting in a play are often spare, leaving the director and the audience to imagine the larger contexts for the room, the street, or the forest where the action of the play might take place. Because few details are provided—*Oliver's house, Duke Frederick's court, the forest of Arden* (the setting descriptions for Shakespeare's *As You Like It*)—stage directors and set designers locate the elements and details that will convey most effectively time, place, mood, and aim. Those set elements become suggestive or symbolic, especially since the limitations of the stage make it impossible to re-create completely the actual details of a place. Looking at Tom Stoppard's setting directions, below, you might consider how some of the details suggest that time and place will be significant in the play.

Activity

Read the stage directions for Tom Stoppard's play *The Real Thing*. Then write a paragraph speculating about how the details of setting might become important. Notice that readers aren't provided details of time or place beyond "living room." Can you infer period? Culture?

> *Living-room. Architect's drawing board, perhaps. A partly open door leads to an unseen hall and an unseen front door. One or two other doors to other rooms.*
>
> MAX *is alone, sitting in a comfortable chair, with a glass of wine and an open bottle to hand. He is using a pack of playing cards to build a pyramidical, tiered viaduct on the coffee table in front of him. He is about to add a pair of playing cards (leaning against each other to hold each other up), and the pyramid is going well. Beyond the door to the hall, the front door is heard being opened with a key. The light from there changes as the unseen front door is opened.*
>
> MAX *does not react to the opening of the door, which is more behind him than in front of him.*

Activity

Think about how you'd stage a production of a play you know well. Write directions for, or draw, a set for *Romeo and Juliet* or another play you know well. Compare your set with ones created by others in your group to see what each set has highlighted.

Summary and Scenic Narration

Setting, of course, has to do with time. The time period of the story might be used to suggest customary behaviors or attitudes that will prove to be important to the plot. The time period of *The Scarlet Letter*—seventeenth century—is significant because of what we associate with Puritan behavior in New England. We're predisposed to discover repression, judgment, humorlessness, and so on in characters' attitudes, even if those beliefs are stereotypical and prove false in the working out of the plot. Time is used for rhetorical effect in other ways, too. Time of day or year can be rhetorically significant; think of Tennessee Williams's plays, where the heat of summer becomes part of the mood of the story as well as a parallel to the characters' desires and anger.

Just as important in thinking about time is the way a writer stretches out and collapses time for effect. **Summary narration** has the narrator of the story briefly relate or sum up events so that the plot can move ahead quickly to another point: "Henry served ten years in the Army before he saw her again." **Scenic narration,** on the other hand, lets the narrator stretch out the description of a moment, sometimes for longer than it would take to accomplish in real time. Let's say the sentence above is the last sentence in a chapter. A new chapter begins, and it will use scenic narration, with one scene, one moment, dramatized for the reader.

Like all the details of setting, scenic narration and summary narration provoke different reactions in readers; they carry different rhetorical effects. Summary narration, which generalizes and summarizes events, distances the reader from the characters and from the events. Writers use summary when they want to move ahead quickly and when they want to tell readers what events mean. Scenic narration—more vivid, more playlike—allows readers to participate more directly in the moment and make more judgments about meaning for themselves.

Setting, as we've suggested, provides cultural clues that help readers understand conflicts and characters. In *The Scarlet Letter,* the prison door, the scaffold, and the forest are all setting details that suggest what this Puritan culture values and fears. One of the pleasures of reading fiction is that a reader enters another world and another culture. Entering a new world through the details of cultural setting presents one of the difficulties in reading, too, if that setting is a place or time far removed from our own.

Setting, because it's atmospheric, evokes emotional and intellectual reactions from readers. Setting helps carry thematic messages and character motivations and rationales for actions. Think about the ratio between scene and each of the other points on the pentad as you examine a piece of literature, and you'll find new perspectives from which to analyze and respond to the work you're reading.

Here are some questions to guide your consideration of setting in literary works:

1. What are the details of physical setting? How, if at all, does setting change?
2. How are time and the passage of time used by the writer? How do they affect characters' actions and your response to them?
3. What details of culture (and time period) are reflected in setting details and in characters' actions or attitudes?
4. How does setting affect your feeling about the mood of the narrative? Does the atmosphere shift, and, if so, why might the writer make that shift?
5. What association do the physical objects or other setting details carry for characters or for you as a reader?

Activity

Write a paragraph or so of scenic narration that would come after the line, "Henry served ten years in the Army before he saw her again." Remember to include enough details so that your reader sees the scene rather than merely hears about it.

Activity

This landscape painting on page 193 is titled *Westward the Star of Empire Takes Its Way—Near Council Bluffs, Iowa.* Painted about 1865 by Andrew Melrose, it illuminates the setting for the westward expansion of this country. Examine the painting, and then write with your group a scene of conflict that this setting might serve as a backdrop for. Include characters if you wish, and be conscious of making them flat or round, static or dynamic.

Conflict and Plot

When listeners hear a story, they're always silently, and sometimes vocally, asking the question, "And then what happened?" As readers, we ask that question too as we read: "What's going to happen?" "What will she do?" We're propelled by the **plot,** the arrangement of events in the story. Good plots carry us along, highlighting the most important or exciting events by describing them in meaningful detail and by quickly relating in summary narration other, less significant or exciting events. Writers arrange narratives, or plot them, to keep readers asking questions. A good plot designs the particulars of the narrative to suggest attributes and motivations of characters, to

convey symbolic truths and themes, and, most important, to secure readers' involvement.

The **pace** of the plot—how quickly it moves from one event or action to another—gives writers a method for showing readers what's most significant to the characters in the story or to the message. The writer speeds up discussion or description to move to a scene of significance, where the action might slow for effect. The pace of a plot can emphasize character attitude or can create mood. "He turned the knob quietly, the tips of his fingers feeling the split in the cold metal. He closed his eyes, waiting for the sound that he was sure would follow—bare feet hitting the floor, a crash perhaps, cursing. He waited for a long time, standing there, eyes still closed. No sound." You can hear in that scene a deliberate slowing down that adds to the sense of danger or fear in the mind of the character. Careful pacing is essential for a good plot, and writers vary their pace to keep readers interested.

Writers move action forward and backward through time as well. **Flashbacks** and **flashforwards** allow writers to give past history and suggest how past events influence current actions, or how future actions will proceed from a present moment. In *A Christmas Carol,* Dickens uses both flashforwards and flashbacks in presenting the ghosts who come to call on Scrooge. The Ghost of Christmas Past is a flashback device; he shows Scrooge the scenes of his youth where he made the decisions that brought him to his miserly, and miserable, state. The Ghost of Christmas Future, a frightening emblem of death, takes Scrooge to the graveyard to gaze with horror on his own tombstone and to hear how little his acquaintances bemoan his passing.

Activity

In a novel or play you've read, find a place in the narrative where the pace changes. Write a paragraph about how the change reflects characters' attitudes or state of mind or how the change affects the meaning of the work.

Tragedy Versus Comedy

It's impossible to tell a story or to plot it without conflict. A character begins happy; then something happens, and he is no longer happy; maybe he dies. Or a character begins depressed; then something happens, and he becomes happy; maybe he gets married. These two scenarios represent, in their simplest forms, the way that tragedy and comedy work. And the *something* that happens between the stages of happiness and sadness, between connection and isolation, is the conflict.

In *A Christmas Carol,* Scrooge begins as a mean-spirited, rich, and lonely old bachelor with no friends and nothing good to say of anybody, but he ends as second father to Tiny Tim, reunited with his family, and a friend to all because he knows how to keep "Christmas in his heart." What has happened to change him? Dickens manipulates his story so that Scrooge faces a conflict within himself that changes the course of his actions and his life. The **plot devices,** or the elements of the plot that operate to cause the conflict and the change, that Dickens uses are the three ghosts, who remind Scrooge of his past, force him to face his present, and foretell his gloomy future.

Romeo and Juliet carries the opposite plot line. Romeo and Juliet begin in innocence and longing. Their first encounter, at the Capulet party, is blissful. But they end in sorrow and in death. Shakespeare's plot devices include the families' feud, the bumbling priest and nurse, and the main characters' own impetuous natures and youth.

Writers use rhetoric—the decisions they make to convey their intentions most effectively and to move a reader most completely—as they determine the plot elements and the kinds of conflicts they'll pose to their characters and in their plots. The final aim of a plot—is the writer's intention to create a tragedy? comedy? lesson in humanity? lesson in injustice?—will determine the outcome of the conflicts the writer's characters engage in. You're likely familiar with the kinds of conflicts that writers use as they tell stories.

Decisions: characters' psychology
Relationships: characters' social interactions
The elements: characters' interactions with culture and nature

Conflict in Decision Making

In this kind of conflict, a character faces his or her own fears, flaws, and desires, and then, after a time of competing thoughts or behaviors, acts for good or ill. Psychological conflict often has characters speaking to themselves in **soliloquy** or talking to others as if they're talking to themselves. Or a narrator might enter the consciousness of the character to explain the inner conflict the character faces. The famous soliloquy that begins, "To be or not to be. That is the question," voices the psychological conflict faced by Hamlet. Should he act to avenge his father, or should he suffer in silence? If you look back at the opening passage of *The Shipping News,* you can see how the narrator describes the psychology of Quoyle, the main character, and the conflict his past presents him with.

Conflict in Relationships

Conflict is most obvious among people or groups of people whose competing interests or beliefs drive their differences to the point of war, murder, estrangement, or disagreement. **Dialogue** is a typical way to show conflict between or among people, of course, where each person takes a competing position, and the reader makes decisions not only about who might be right but also about the reasons behind the disagreement. Descriptive scenes of battles where the narrator shows how one side outmaneuvers the other or makes tactical mistakes are useful ways of showing interpersonal or international conflict. Odysseus's many battles in the *Odyssey* with monsters, witches, gods, and men are clear examples of interpersonal conflict.

Conflict with the Elements

When characters build cities from forests, fight dragons, rescue others from flooding rivers, or face ruined harvests, they find themselves in conflict with the natural world. In some early novels and plays, characters addressed the elements directly, crying aloud to the heavens or shaking their fists and talking to the storm. They use **apostrophe,** language that addresses the natural world as if it were human. Characters can be in conflict with the heavens, marked by fate as Odysseus is, or marked by the society that surrounds them. Hester Prynne finds herself in conflict with her Puritan village in *The Scarlet Letter.* And for much of the novel she is isolated in that conflict, a lone figure whose very presence excites dismay and rebuke from the society she lives in.

Activity

Choose a novel or play your class has read, and describe its plot line by drawing a picture of it and then explaining the picture you've drawn. *A Christmas Carol,* for example, might be drawn as on page 196 and explained by the text below the graphic.

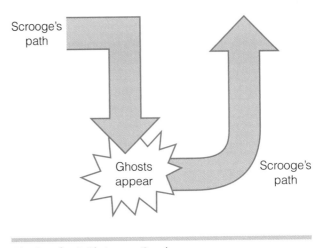

Plot line for A Christmas Carol

The character is headed toward a bad end; his views on humanity are pessimistic, and he has not met his responsibility to others. The ghosts arrive to change his mind, and he is in torment as he tries to make sense of their coming and their message. As he figures out their intention, he is persuaded to change his ways, and he sees a new path, where he develops attitudes precisely the opposite of those he began with.

Conflict and the Pentad

Burke's pentad reveals how a reader might examine the way that conflict works in a narrative. If you think of conflict as agency, the method or means for understanding actions, you can see how conflict affects the character, the action the character might take, the scene around the character, and the rationale for the character's decisions.

The following scene is from Henrik Ibsen's play *A Doll's House* (written in 1879). The scene comes at the end of the first act, where Nora Helmer has just had a conversation with Krogstad, who has helped her forge a document to save her father and has come to her in a thinly veiled blackmail attempt. This scene reveals something about Nora's husband, Torvald, and her relationship with him:

TORVALD: . . . Has anyone been here?

NORA: Here? No.

TORVALD: That is strange. I saw Krogstad going out the gate.

NORA: Did you? Oh yes, I forgot, Krogstad was here for a moment.

TORVALD: Nora, I can see from your manner that he has been here begging you to say a good word for him.

NORA: Yes

TORVALD: And you were to appear to do it of your own accord; you were to conceal from me the fact of his having been here; didn't he beg that of you too?

NORA: Yes, Torvald, but—

TORVALD: Nora, Nora, and you would be a party to that sort of thing? To have any talk with a man like that and give him any sort of promise? And to tell me a lie into the bargain?

NORA: A lie?

TORVALD: Didn't you tell me no one had been here? [*Shakes his finger at her.*] My little songbird must never do that again. A songbird must have a clean beak to chirp with—no false notes! [*Puts his arm around her waist.*] That is so, isn't it? Yes, I am sure it is. [*Lets her go.*] We will say no more about it. How warm and snug it is here!

. . .

TORVALD: Just think how a guilty man like that has to lie and play the hypocrite with everyone, how he has to wear a mask in the presence of those near and dear to him, even before his own wife and children. And about the children— that is the most terrible part of it all, Nora.

NORA: How?

TORVALD: Because such an atmosphere of lies infects and poisons the whole life of a home. Each breath the children take in such a house is full of the germs of evil.

NORA: [*coming nearer him.*] Are you sure of that?

TORVALD: My dear, I have often seen it in the course of my life as a lawyer. Almost everyone who has gone to the bad early in life has a deceitful mother.

NORA: Why do you only say—mother?

TORVALD: It seems most commonly to be the mother's influence, though naturally a bad father's would have the same result. Every lawyer is familiar with the fact. This Krogstad, now, has been persistently poisoning his own children with lies and dissimulation; that is why I say he has lost all moral character. [*Holds out his hands to her.*] That is why my sweet little Nora must promise me not to plead his cause. Give me your hand on it. Come, come, what is this? Give me your hand. There now, that's settled. I assure you it would be quite impossible for me to work with him; I literally feel physically ill when I am in the company of such people.

NORA: [*takes her hand out his and goes to the opposite side of the Christmas tree.*] How hot it is in here, and I have such a lot to do.

Activity

It's clear that there's a conflict between Nora and her husband. Consider the conflict as the agency in Burke's terms, and write a paragraph that explores how the conflict reveals something about the personalities of each of the characters (agency-agent), about the social and cultural scene around them (agency-scene), or about the message that either of the characters might be trying to convey through the conversation (agency-purpose).

Protagonist, Antagonist

In Ibsen's play, Nora and Torvald are the main characters, the **protagonist** and the **antagonist.** Nora, the protagonist, is the figure in the narrative whose interests the reader is most concerned about and sympathetic toward, and the author positions the protagonist in the plot so that readers understand her struggles most clearly. When she faces conflict, readers more or less side with her because we know her motivations. Nora's silliness, her hopes, and her terror at the prospect of losing everything strike a sympathetic chord in readers and viewers of the play. Torvald Helmer, the husband who misunderstands and condescends to Nora, is the antagonist because he encourages the silliness, blunts the hopes, and increases the terror. In other words, he opposes what readers (and the author) want for Nora and what she learns to want for herself.

But Torvald is also a representative of his time and place, and he plays a role assigned to him by the culture he lives in. Nora fights an antagonist greater than her husband; she's in conflict with her culture and its institutions.

Narrator: Point of View

When writers choose a narrator—the person who will tell their story—they make a rhetorical decision. Writers decide on a narrator based on how they envision the story and on how they envision readers experiencing the story. As readers, we develop emotional and intellectual relationships to events, places, and characters in the story because we view those events, places, and characters from a particular perspective. Our reaction to reading about an automobile accident—narrated, for example, by the driver of the car—will be different from our reaction to reading about it from the point of view of a witness standing on the corner.

First-Person Narration

Writers reveal elements of plot and character to their readers—and conceal them—by choosing to tell the story through the mind of a character *in* the story or through someone *outside* of it. The first-person narrator, most often someone inside the novel, may be the main character in the story, as Huckleberry Finn is in Mark Twain's novel.

> You don't know about me without you have read a book by the name of *The Adventures of Tom Sawyer;* but that ain't no matter. That book was made by Mr. Mark Twain, and he told the truth, mainly. There was things which he stretched, but mainly he told the truth. That is nothing. I never seen anybody but lied one time or another, without it was Aunt Polly, or the widow, or maybe Mary. Aunt Polly—Tom's Aunt Polly, she is—and Mary, and the Widow Douglas is all told about in that book, which is mostly a true book, with some stretchers, as I said before.

The first-person storyteller might also be a less central character who acts as an observer of the action and of the main character, as is Jack Burden in *All the King's Men,* by Robert Penn Warren.

> "My god, folks, it's Willie!"
> The remark was superfluous. One look at the faces rallied around and you knew that if any citizen over the age of three didn't know that the strong-set man standing there in the Palm Beach suit was Willie Stark, that citizen was a half-wit. In the first place, all he would have to do would be to lift his eyes to the big picture high up there above the soda fountain, a picture about six times life size, which showed the same face, the big eyes, which in the picture had the suggestion of a sleepy and inward look (the eyes of the man in the Palm Beach suit didn't have that look now, but I've seen it), the pouches under the eyes and jowls beginning to sag off, and the meaty lips, which didn't sag but if you looked close were laid one on top of the other like a couple of bricks, and the tousle of hair hanging down on the not very high squarish forehead. Under the picture was the legend: *My study is the heart of the people.* In quotation marks, and signed, *Willie Stark.* I had seen that picture in a thousand places, pool halls to palaces.

Here, from Maxine Hong Kingston's *Woman Warrior,* is a final example of a first-person narrator who is a group as well as an individual character in the story. The first-person plural pronoun establishes the individual as part of a larger group identity and thus makes a rhetorical point about the narrator's position.

> When we Chinese girls listened to the adults talk-story, we learned that we failed if we grew up to be but wives or slaves. We could be heroines, swordswomen. Even if she had to rage across all China, a swordswoman got even with anybody who hurt her family. Perhaps women were once so dangerous that they had to have their feet bound. It was a woman who invented white crane boxing only two hundred years ago. She was already an expert pole fighter, daughter of a teacher trained at the Shao-lin temple, where there lived an order of fighting monks. She was combing her hair one morning when a white crane alighted outside her window. She teased it with her pole, which it pushed aside with a soft brush of its wing. Amazed, she dashed outside and tried to knock the crane off its perch. It snapped her pole in two. Recognizing the presence of great power,

she asked the spirit of the white crane if it would teach her to fight. It answered with a cry that white crane boxers imitate today. Later the bird returned as an old man, and he guided her boxing for many years. Thus she gave the world a new martial art.

This was one of the tamer, more modern stories, mere introduction. My mother told others that followed swordswomen through woods and palaces for years. Night after night my mother would talk-story until we fell asleepage I couldn't tell where the stories left off and the dreams began, her voice the voice of the heroines in my sleepage And on Sundays, from noon to midnight, we went to the movies at the Confucius Church. We saw swordswomen jump over houses from a standstill; they didn't even need a running start.

As you can tell from all these examples, the first-person narrator reflects only what he or she sees or feels; readers get the "inside" view of events and of other characters from the narrator who observes and comments. With a first-person speaker, readers learn about the story from one side, and their view is therefore both subjective and intimate.

Third-Person Narration

Unlike the first-person storyteller, the third-person narrator gives readers a kind of distance on the events taking place in the story. The third-person narrator may be inside the mind of all the characters (**omniscient narration**), of one of the characters (**limited narration**) *or* of none of the characters (**dramatic narration**). Readers may get inside the head of one of the characters through a limited perspective or inside the head of all characters through an omniscient one, but the third-person pronoun—*he* or *she*—creates less intimacy and more seeming objectivity than does the first-person pronoun. The third-person narration suggests some outside figure observing the characters and describing their actions, even when the narration is from one of the characters' point of view. If you look back at the opening passage to *The Shipping News* (page 185), you'll see a third-person narrator who gives the main character's thoughts and also comments on that character. Here's a passage from the opening of *Emma*, by Jane Austen.

> The real evils indeed of Emma's situation were the power of having rather too much her own way and a disposition to think a little too well of herself; these were the disadvantages which threatened to alloy her many enjoyments. The danger, however, was at present so unperceived that they did not by any means rank as misfortunes with her.

In the preceding passage, it's easy to hear a narrator who is outside and beyond the mind of any one character, who sees into the motives and flaws of those being described. The narrator is omniscient because nothing is hidden from her, and thus nothing is hidden from readers.

Activity

The five passages from novels quoted in this chapter have different kinds of narrators, three in the first person (Hong Kingston, Penn Warren, and Twain) and two in the third person (Austen and Proulx). Read the passages again, and then decide in your group what your reactions to the characters are and what you think the narrator wants readers to think or believe as he or she tells the story.

Second-Person Narration

A note on second person: Second-person narration is unusual, in part because it's hard to sustain. (Try writing a story using "you" for a page or so). If you do find second-person narration, you will often sense tension or a feeling of immediacy as you read. Listen to this passage from John Hawkes's novel *The Lime Twig:*

> Have you ever let lodgings in the winter? Was there a bed kept waiting, a corner room kept waiting for a gentleman? And have you ever hung a cardboard in the window and, just out of view yourself, watched to see which man would stop and read the lettering on your sign, glance at the premises from roof to little sign—an awkward piece of work—then step up suddenly and hold his finger on your bell? What was it you saw from the window that made you let the bell continue ringing and the bed go empty another night? Something about the eyes? The smooth white skin between the brim of the bowler hat and the eyes?

Second-person narration is almost always connected to first-person telling. Hawkes's gothic-feeling, dreamy horror tale quickly moves into an "I-you" dialogue:

> I wouldn't advise Violet Lane—there is no telling about the beds in Violet Lane—but perhaps in Dreary Station you have already found a lodging good as mine, if you were once the gentleman or if you ever took a tea kettle from a lady's hands.

The conversation between writer and reader is made explicit in works that use the "you" overtly. You might look for that conversation in other works you read: *Catcher in the Rye,* by J. D. Salinger, uses "I-you,"and you can see it in the excerpt from *Huckleberry Finn,* above. Here's one more example, from the novel *Barchester Towers* by Victorian novelist Anthony Trollope. In this passage, Trollope stops the plot to assure his readers about the eventual fate of his heroine and to comment on the "I-you" relationship between writer and reader that he sees at the heart of reading:

> And here, perhaps, it may be allowed to the novelist to explain his views on a very important point in the art of telling tales. He ventures to reprobate that system

which goes so far to violate all proper confidence between the author and his readers, by maintaining nearly to the end of the third volume a mystery as to the fate of their favorite personage. . . . Have not often the profoundest efforts of genius been used to baffle the aspirations of the reader, to raise false hopes and false fears, and to give rise to expectations which are never to be realized?

. . .

Our doctrine is, that the author and the reader should move along together in full confidence with each other. Let the personages of the drama undergo ever so complete a comedy of errors among themselves, but let the spectator never mistake the Syracusan for the Ephesian; otherwise he is one of the dupes, and the part of a dupe is never dignified.

Trollope's interruption, his **narrative intrusion,** establishes a clear rhetorical relationship between writer and reader—and an ethical one. Readers should have "full confidence" in writers' honor not to trick or to surprise unfairly. The real relationship, Trollope seems to indicate, is not the one between reader and character but between reader and writer. It's a bold suggestion and one that Trollope was criticized for but one that has become increasingly popular in contemporary writing. Trollope suggests that it's not plot that's the most important, and not character, but the writer-reader connection, the rhetoric of the text. Trollope's narrator is a **reliable narrator;** that is, he tells his readers as much as he knows of the characters and their actions and doesn't mislead with false clues about them or about himself. We can trust his reactions, even if they are limited.

Reliable and Unreliable Narrators

Sometimes writers choose to tell their stories through the words of an **unreliable narrator,** one who deliberately holds back information or whose judgments are unsound so that readers suspect the information the narrator gives us. Edgar Allan Poe's narrators are sometimes unreliable because they're unbalanced. In Poe's short story "The Black Cat," the narrator's first words are about his sanity and rationality; his description of his morbid hatred for a cat with a strange eye that later gets transferred to his wife belies the assertion.

Narrators in Poems

We haven't talked much about poetry in this discussion of narrators, although the perspective from which poets describe the moments they evoke is often crucial to a reader's understanding and appreciation of the poem, especially, of course, in narrative poetry. Robert Browning's famous dramatic poems, where the narrator is a clearly defined character, show how much the teller of the tale in the poem matters. "Porphyria's Lover" describes a moment of possession, when the speaker, who has been morbidly unsure of his lover's true affection, realizes it:

> Happy and proud; at last I knew
> Porphyria worshiped me; surprise
>   Made my heart swell, and still it grew
> While I debated what to do.
> That moment she was mine, mine, fair,
>   Perfectly pure and good; I found
> A thing to do, and all her hair
>   In one long yellow string I wound
> Three times her little throat around,
> And strangled her. No pain felt she;
>   I am quite sure she felt no pain.

The poem's chilling vision is heightened by the first-person narrator, who is also the murderer. The tone of his voice might call to mind Poe, who, as just noted, also used insane but analytically insightful first-person narrators in both his poetry and fiction.

Lyric poetry, which by definition does not tell a story, or much of one, often makes use of a first-person speaker who explores a moment or a feeling memorable for the realization it evoked or the change it signaled. Although in lyric poetry, speakers may not make connections with other characters or even overt connections with readers, the perspective of the person telling about the experience is always important to the reader's ability and interest in experiencing the poem.

Here are some questions to guide your thinking about point of view in literary work:

1. Is there more than one point of view in the piece? How does the shift affect your reading?

2. How does the narrator feel about the characters in the story? What signals does the narrator give to suggest this feeling?

3. If the narrator doesn't comment much on the characters or situations or is indeed absent (as in drama), what details provide insight into the characters and their thoughts?

4. Is the narrator trustworthy or unreliable? How might you become aware of the unreliability of a narrator?

Activity

Read the following poem, by recent poet laureate Rita Dove. Then with your group decide how the speaker uses setting, character, or conflict to evoke a mood and connect with readers. It's important to know that the title refers to Rosa Parks, the southern woman who helped begin the civil-rights movement with her refusal to move to the back of the bus.

Rosa

How she sat there,
the time right inside a place
so wrong it was ready.

That trim name with
its dream of a bench
to rest on. Her sensible coat.

Doing nothing was the doing:
the clean flame of her gaze
carved by a camera flash.

How she stood up
when they bent down to retrieve
her purse. That courtesy.

Theme

The theme, or purpose or message, of a piece of literature is built from the combination of all the elements we've discussed so far. The kinds of characters and their positions in the story, the setting and atmosphere evoked by it, the conflicts described, the point of view of the story's telling—all work to give readers a sense of not just what the story is about but also what it's for. Writers and readers together create themes for the work; one reason that great literature provokes so much critical commentary is that many themes can emerge depending on who is reading, and when. Writers persuade us that they are telling some truth or giving us some insight about the real world outside the text.

Theme and the Pentad

Using Burke's pentad, you can see the relationship of theme to the individual elements in narrative. Consider, for example, the purpose-scene (theme-to-setting) ratio. Many stories, especially those with a significant conflict with the natural or social world, explore themes where setting, or scene, affects characters and meanings. In Herman Melville's novel *Moby Dick,* setting—the ocean and the whaling ship searching for the mysterious white whale—becomes almost a character. How the sailors confront the challenge of the ocean's power and changeable nature as well as the fearsome challenge of the great white whale is an important theme for Melville's work. Other ratios—purpose-act (theme to actions), purpose-agent (theme to character), or purpose-agency (theme to methods)—can each give you as a reader a way of seeing how theme develops in relationship to the individual elements in a text. Of course, it's possible to link purpose or theme to any of those elements, and that's one reason that readers find more than one theme in literary work.

Symbols

Writers use symbolic elements in their texts to help convey thematic ideas. A pot of geraniums on the windowsill can tell readers how much the characters want to establish roots and to have a home without their ever saying so. A sudden vision of people sitting together intimately can tell readers about relationships that have up to that moment been hidden from them. Character names like Mr. Gradgrind can carry a symbolic message, just as places like the poor fishing village in *The Shipping News* or the forest in *The Scarlet Letter* might.

Images

One of the most significant ways in which writers convey theme is through their use of language. The **imagery** they choose to describe characters, settings, and conflicts allows readers to experience the story in ways that suggest larger meanings for the work. The comparisons embedded in metaphors can establish tone and suggest theme through their comparisons. If you look at many of the examples above, you'll see how writers use metaphors to suggest more than literal description might. Quoyle has "a great loaf of a body" in *The Shipping News,* and readers become ready to expect that there may be a message about how such a "loaf" might rise.

Diction

Diction, or word choice, tells readers about time, place, and character and about theme. The dialect speech Twain uses in *Huckleberry Finn* differentiates characters—white from black, educated from uneducated, rich from poor. The fact that two of the dialect speakers, Jim and Huck, are the poorest, least powerful people in the story and also the most ethical ones carries a message about humanity that Twain was careful to point out.

Syntax

The arrangement of sentences, their length and complexity, also tells us much about characters and themes. The syntax in *The Scarlet Letter* is complex, signaling its nineteenth-century composition. Hawthorne often uses the periodic sentence, holding off the full meaning of the sentence until near the end. And that holding off is part of the plot of the story, for the narrator clearly knows the guilty secret that he keeps readers from knowing for a while and that he keeps the town from knowing for most of the novel.

The syntax helps establish theme. Short bursts of sentences, long flowing sentences, intricately designed sentences—all can give readers ideas about the narrator's position on the story being told and lead us to consider the larger meaning of what we're reading.

A Final Word About Narrative—and About Rhetoric

All the elements of narrative work together to help readers enter the world of the texts they read, to understand that world, and to consider what that world reveals about the larger world outside the text. Writers and readers create together, communicating messages, uncovering connections and differences. Rhetoric works in narrative in many of the same ways as it operates in other genres and for other purposes, highlighting occasion and appropriateness, audiences and speakers, intentions and effects.

Activity

Read the following passage from Tom Stoppard's play *The Real Thing*, where Henry, a playwright, is arguing with his lover, Annie, about writing. Read the passage, and then choose diction, imagery, syntax, metaphor, or symbol to write about. Tell how the element you've chosen might contribute to a reader's view of the characters and provide insight into the theme of the work.

> HENRY: Shut up and listen. This thing here, which looks like a wooden club, is actually several pieces of particular wood cunningly put together in a certain way so that the whole thing is sprung, like a dance floor. It's for hitting cricket balls with. If you get it right, the cricket ball will travel two hundred yards in four seconds, and all you've done is give a knock like knocking the top off a bottle of stout, and it makes a noise like a trout taking a fly. . . . [*He clucks his tongue to make the noise.*] What we're trying to do is to write cricket bats, so that when we throw up an idea and give it a little knock, it might . . . travel. . . .

As this book has attempted to illustrate, rhetoric is in large measure the primary tool we use to communicate with the world around us. Becoming conscious of how rhetoric works for us as speakers, writers, listeners, and readers begins the process of becoming good rhetoricians, effective participants in the lives we live in and out of school. In the speeches, poems, textbooks, cartoons, novels, essays, assignments, and memos we read and write—in fact, in every form of communication between people—rhetoric has its everyday use.

Interchapter

Overview of the Major Points in Chapter 6

- The elements of literature you're familiar with are rhetorical devices, used by writers to draw out and enrich understanding by readers.
- Burke's pentad can help readers discover the significance of literary elements as they relate to other elements in the text.
- Reading literary works is like reading other kinds of writing and like experiencing life itself, with purposes and contexts available for readers to discover.

Activities and Discussion Questions for Chapter 6   Use these questions and comments as guides for your own discussion and writing about these literary works.

Henry David Thoreau, "An Essay on Civil Disobedience" (published 1849)

The text appears on pages 210–225. In your group, discuss the following questions. You might use some of these questions as the basis for a well-organized essay or journal entry.

1. Try to create a plot line for Thoreau's essay. What happens first and next and next? What's the final outcome? How much plot does the story contain? How do you discover conflict in the story?

2. Choosing at least three images or metaphors of your own, write a character description of Thoreau. Do you find him a complex or simple (round or flat) character?

3. Which of Burke's ratios seems most important in this essay? Talk with your group to see how many different ratios your group finds important.

Eavan Boland, "It's a Woman's World" (published 1982)

The text appears on pages 226–227. In your group, discuss the following questions. You might use some of these questions as the basis for a well-organized essay or journal entry.

1. In your group, list some figurative language—metaphor or other imagery—you find most striking. Then talk about how the language underscores conflict in the poem.

2. Select one of Burke's ratios—scene-act or scene-agent would be useful ones—and write an analysis of the poem. Use quotations from the poem to help you. Share your analysis with your group.

3. Discuss the narrator of the poem. Is she omniscient? Limited? How does she see herself in relation to the characters she describes in the poem?

Alice Walker, "Everyday Use" (published 1973)

The text appears on pages 228–237. In your group, discuss the following questions. You might use some of these questions as the basis for a well-organized essay or journal entry.

1. What seems to be the central conflict in Walker's story? Find places in the story that suggest the conflict to you, and discuss those places in the text with your group. Do you find patterns or similarities in your choices?

2. What kind of narrator do you find in the story? Write a paragraph or two of your own from the perspective of another kind of narrator. Then discuss with your group how your response to the story changes with a different narrator.

3. What details of setting seem especially symbolic or important to the story as a whole?

READINGS

Chapters 1 through 6 of this book introduce you to concepts of classical and modern rhetoric. In this section of the book, you'll find three pieces of writing reprinted in their entirety. We expect you to read the three (even if you already know them)—an essay, a poem, and a short story—at the beginning of the course in which you're using this book. We also expect you to come back and reread parts of them as you make your way through the six main chapters of the book. In fact, at the end of each chapter, there's an interchapter waiting for you. Each interchapter will ask you to think about the concepts in the immediately preceding chapter as you focus on the essay, the poem, and the short story in this Readings section.

An Essay

Henry David Thoreau

Henry David Thoreau was born in Concord, Massachusetts, in 1817, and died there in 1862. In between, he lived a life of self-reliance on his own terms rather than society's. Indeed, one of this writer's most famous lines argues, "If a man does not keep pace with his companions, perhaps it is because he hears a different drummer. Let him step to the music which he hears, however measured or far away."

The great theme that permeates the writings of Thoreau is his life in the natural world, his quest to feel within himself the spirit of nature. He wrote his first book, A Week on the Concord *and* Merrimack Rivers, *while living in a self-built hut at Walden Pond, where his goal was to strip away the inessential and to simplify life. There he also kept journals that formed the basis for* Walden, *which would prove to be his masterwork.*

While Thoreau was staying at the pond, the United States was involved in a war with Mexico. Because Henry David Thoreau considered the war unjust, he refused to pay a tax that he thought supported the U.S. government, and he was put in jail for a day. Two years later, he wrote the following essay, setting out his philosophy of passive resistance as a means of protest.

Henry David Thoreau
"On the Duty of Civil Disobedience"

1   I heartily accept the motto,—"That government is best which governs least"; and I should like to see it acted up to more rapidly and systematically. Carried out, it finally amounts to this, which also I believe,—"That government is best which governs not at all"; and when men are prepared for it, that will be the kind of government which they will have. Government is at best but an expedient; but most governments are usually, and all governments are sometimes, inexpedient. The objections which have been brought against a standing army, and they are many and weighty, and deserve to prevail, may also at last be brought against a standing government. The standing army is only an arm of the standing government. The government itself, which is only the mode which the people have chosen to execute their will, is equally liable to be abused and perverted before the people can act through it. Witness the present Mexican war, the work of comparatively a few individuals using the standing government as their tool; for, in the outset, the people would not have consented to this measure.

2   This American government—what is it but a tradition, though a recent one, endeavoring to transmit itself unimpaired to posterity, but each instant losing some of its integrity? It has not the vitality and force of a single living man; for a single man can bend it to his will. It is a sort of wooden gun to the people themselves. But it is not the less necessary for this; for the people must have some complicated machinery or other, and hear its din, to satisfy that idea of government which they have. Governments show thus how successfully men can be imposed on, even impose on themselves, for their own advantage. It is excellent, we must all allow. Yet this government never of itself furthered any enterprise, but by the alacrity with which it got out of its way. It does not keep the country free. It does not settle the West. It does not educate. The character inherent in the American people has done all that has been accomplished; and it would have done somewhat more, if the government had not sometimes got in its way. For government is an expedient by which men would fain succeed in letting one another alone; and, as has been said, when it is most expedient, the governed are most let alone by it. Trade and commerce, if they were not made of India *rubber,* would never manage to bounce over the obstacles which legislators are continually putting in their way—and, if one

were to judge these men wholly by the effects of their actions, and not partly by their intentions, they would deserve to be classed and punished with those mischievous persons who put obstructions on the railroads.

3   But, to speak practically and as a citizen, unlike those who call themselves no-government men, I ask for, not at once no government, but *at once* a better government. Let every man make known what kind of government would command his respect, and that will be one step toward obtaining it.

4   After all, the practical reason why, when the power is once in the hands of the people, a majority are permitted, and for a long period continue, to rule, is not because they are most likely to be in the right, nor because this seems fairest to the minority, but because they are physically the strongest. But a government in which the majority rule in all cases cannot be based on justice, even as far as men understand it. Can there not be a government in which majorities do not virtually decide right and wrong, but conscience?—in which majorities decide only those questions to which the rule of expediency is applicable? Must the citizen ever for a moment, or in the least degree, resign his conscience to the legislator? Why has every man a conscience, then? I think that we should be men first, and subjects afterward. It is not desirable to cultivate a respect for the law, so much as for the right. The only obligation which I have a right to assume is to do at any time what I think right. It is truly enough—said—that a corporation has no conscience; but a corporation of conscientious men is a corporation with a conscience. Law never made men a whit more just; and, by means of their respect for it, even the law disposed are daily made the agents of injustice. A common and natural result of an undue respect for law is, that you may see a file of soldiers, colonel, captain, corporal, privates, powder-monkeys, and all, marching in admirable order over hill and dale to the wars, against their wills, ay, against their common sense and consciences, which makes it very steep marching indeed, and produces a palpitation of the heart. They have no doubt that it is a damnable business in which they are concerned; they are all peaceably inclined. Now, what are they? Men at all? or small movable forts and magazines, at the service of some unscrupulous man in power? Visit the Navy Yard, and behold a marine, such a man as an American government can make, or such as it can make a man with its black arts—a mere shadow and reminiscence of humanity, a man laid out alive and standing, and already, as one may say, buried under arms with funeral accompaniments, though it may be

> "Not a drum was heard, not a funeral note,
> As his corse to the rampart we hurried;
> Not a soldier discharged his farewell shot
> O'er the grave where our hero we buried."

5   The mass of men serve the state thus, not as men mainly, but as machines, with their bodies. They are the standing army, and the militia, jailers, constables, posse comitatus, etc. In most cases there is no free exercise

whatever of the judgment or of the moral sense; but they put themselves on a level with wood and earth and stones; and wooden men can perhaps be manufactured that will serve the purpose as well. Such command no more respect than men of straw or a lump of dirt. They have the same sort of worth only as horses and dogs.—Yet such as these even are commonly esteemed good citizens. Others, as most legislators, politicians, lawyers, ministers, and office-holders, serve the state chiefly with their heads; and, as they rarely make any moral distinctions, they are as likely to serve the devil, without *intending* it, as God. A very few, as heroes, patriots, martyrs, reformers in the great sense, and *men,* serve the state with their consciences also, and so necessarily resist it for the most part—and they are commonly treated as enemies by it. A wise man will only be useful as a man, and will not submit to be "clay," and "stop a hole to keep the wind away," but leave that office to his dust at least:—

> "I am too high-born to be propertied, To be a secondary at control,
> Or useful serving-man and instrument
> To any sovereign state throughout the world."

6   He who gives himself entirely to his fellow-men appears to them useless and selfish; but he who gives himself partially to them is pronounced a benefactor and philanthropist.

7   How does it become a man to behave toward this American government to-day? I answer, that he cannot without disgrace be associated with it. I cannot for an instant recognize that political organization as *my* government which is *the slave's* government also.

8   All men recognize the right of revolution; that is, the right to refuse allegiance to, and to resist, the government, when its tyranny or its inefficiency are great and unendurable. But almost all say that such is not the case now. But such was the case, they think, in the Revolution of '75. If one were to tell me that this was a bad government because it taxed certain foreign commodities brought to its ports, it is most probable that I should not make an ado about it, for I can do without them. All machines have their friction—and possibly this does enough good to counterbalance the evil. At any rate, it is a great evil to make a stir about it. But when the friction comes to have its machine, and oppression and robbery are organized, I say, let us not have such a machine any longer. In other words, when a sixth of the population of a nation which has undertaken to be the refuge of liberty are slaves, and a whole country is unjustly overrun and conquered by a foreign army, and subjected to military law, I think that it is not too soon for honest men to rebel and revolutionize. What makes this duty the more urgent is the fact that the country so overrun is not our own, but ours is the invading army.

9   Paley, a common authority with many on moral questions, in his chapter on the "Duty of Submission to Civil Government," resolves all civil obligation into expediency; and he proceeds to say that "so long as the interest of the

whole society requires it, that is, so long as the established government cannot be resisted or changed without public inconveniency, it is the will of God
that the established government be obeyed, and no longer"—"This principle
being admitted, the justice of every particular case of resistance is reduced to
a computation of the quantity of the danger and grievance on the one side, and
of the probability and expense of redressing it on the other." Of this, he says,
every man shall judge for himself. But Paley appears never to have contemplated those cases to which the rule of expediency does not apply, in which a
people, as well as an individual, must do justice, cost what it may. If I have
unjustly wrested a plank from a drowning man I must restore it to him though
I drown myself. This, according to Paley, would be inconvenient. But he that
would save his life, in such a case, shall lose it. This people must cease to
hold slaves, and to make war on Mexico, though it cost them their existence
as a people.

10   In their practice, nations agree with Paley; but does any one think that
Massachusetts does exactly what is right at the present crisis?

> "A drab of state, a cloth-o'-silver slut,
> To have her train borne up, and her soul trail in the dirt."

11   Practically speaking, the opponents to a reform in Massachusetts are not
a hundred thousand politicians at the South, but a hundred thousand mer-
chants and farmers here, who are more interested in commerce and agriculture than they are in humanity, and are not prepared to do justice to the slave
and to Mexico, *cost what it may.* I quarrel not with far-off foes, but with those
who, near at home, co-operate with, and do the bidding of those far away, and
without whom the latter would be harmless. We are accustomed to say, that
the mass of men are unprepared; but improvement is slow, because the few
are not materially wiser or better than the many. It is not so important that
many should be as good as you, as that there be some absolute goodness.
somewhere; for that will leaven the whole lump. There are thousands who are
in opinion opposed to slavery and to the war, who yet in effect do nothing to
put an end to them; who, esteeming themselves children of Washington and
Franklin, sit down with their hands in their pockets, and say that they know
not what to do, and do nothing; who even postpone the question of freedom to
the question of free-trade, and quietly read the prices-current along with the
latest advices from Mexico, after dinner, and, it may be, fall asleep over them
both. What is the price-current of an honest man and patriot to-day? They hesitate, and they regret, and sometimes they petition; but they do nothing in
earnest and with effect. They will wait, well disposed, for others to remedy
the evil, that they may no longer have it to regret. At most, they give only a
cheap vote, and a feeble countenance and Godspeed, to the right, as it goes by
them. There are nine hundred and ninety-nine patrons of virtue to one virtu-
ous man; but it is easier to deal with the real possessor of a thing than with
the temporary guardian of it.

12   All voting is a sort of gaming, like checkers or backgammon, with a slight moral tinge to it, a playing with right and wrong, with moral questions; and betting naturally accompanies it. The character of the voters is *not* staked. I cast my vote, perchance, as I think right; but I am not vitally concerned that that right should prevail. I am willing to leave it to the majority. Its obligation, therefore, never exceeds that of expediency. Even voting for *the right* is doing nothing for it. It is only expressing to men feebly your desire that it should prevail. A wise man will not leave the right to the mercy of chance, nor wish it to prevail through the power of the majority. There is but little virtue in the action of masses of men. When the majority shall at length vote for the abolition of slavery, it will be because they are indifferent to slavery, or because there is but little slavery left to be abolished by their vote. *They* will then be the only slaves. Only *his* vote can hasten the abolition of slavery who asserts his own freedom by his vote.

13   I hear of a convention to be held at Baltimore, or elsewhere, for the selection of a candidate for the Presidency, made up chiefly of editors, and men who are politicians by profession; but I think, what is it to any independent, intelligent, and respectable man what decision they may come to? Shall we not have the advantage of his wisdom and honesty, nevertheless? Can we not count upon some independent votes? Are there not many individuals in the country who do not attend conventions? But no: I find that the respectable man, so called, has immediately drifted from his position, and despairs of his country, when his country has more reason to despair of him. He forthwith adopts one of the candidates thus selected as the only *available* one, thus proving that he is *himself available* for any purposes of the demagogue. His vote is of no more worth than that of any unprincipled foreigner or hireling native, who may have been bought. Oh for a man who is a *man,* and, as my neighbor says, has a bone in his back which you cannot pass your hand through. Our statistics are at fault: the population has been returned too large. How many *men* are there to a square thousand miles in this country? Hardly one. Does not America offer any inducement for men to settle here? The American has dwindled into an Odd Fellow—one who may be known by the development of his organ of gregariousness, and a manifest lack of intellect and cheerful self-reliance; whose first and chief concern, on coming into the world, is to see that the almshouses are in good repair; and, before yet he has lawfully donned the virile garb, to collect a fund for the support of the widows and orphans that may be; who, in short ventures to live only by the aid of the Mutual Insurance company, which has promised to bury him, decently.

14   It is not a man's duty, as a matter of course, to devote himself to the eradication of any, even the most enormous wrong—he may still properly have other concerns to engage him; but it is his duty, at least, to wash his hands of it, and, if he gives it no thought longer, not to give it practically his support. If I devote myself to other pursuits and contemplations, I must first see, at least, that I do not pursue them sitting upon another man's shoulders. I must get off him first, that he may pursue his contemplations too. See what gross

inconsistency is tolerated. I have heard some of my townsmen say, "I should like to have them order me out to help put down an insurrection of the slaves, or to March to Mexico;—see if I would go"; and yet these very men have each, directly by their allegiance, and so indirectly, at least, by their money, furnished a substitute. The soldier is applauded who refuses to serve in an unjust war by those who do not refuse to sustain the unjust government which makes the war; is applauded by those whose own act and authority he disregards and sets at naught; as if the state were penitent to that degree that it hired one to scourge it while it sinned, but not to that degree that it left off sinning for a moment. Thus, under the name of Order and Civil Government, we are all made at last to pay homage to and support our own meanness. After the first blush of sin comes its indifference; and from immoral it becomes, as it were, unmoral, and not quite unnecessary to that life which we have made.

15   The broadest and most prevalent error requires the most disinterested virtue to sustain it. The slight reproach to which the virtue of patriotism is commonly liable, the noble are most likely to incur. Those who, while they disapprove of the character and measures of a government, yield to it their allegiance and support are undoubtedly its most conscientious supporters, and so frequently the most serious obstacles to reform. Some are petitioning the State to dissolve the Union, to disregard the requisitions of the President. Why do they not dissolve it themselves—the union between themselves and the State—and refuse to pay their quota into its treasury? Do not they stand in the same relation to the State, that the State does to the Union? And have not the same reasons prevented the State from resisting the Union, which have prevented them from resisting the State?

16   How can a man be satisfied to entertain an opinion merely, and enjoy it? *Is* there any enjoyment in it, if his opinion is that he is aggrieved? If you are cheated out of a single dollar by your neighbor, you do not rest satisfied with knowing that you are cheated, or with saying that you are cheated, or even with petitioning him to pay you your due; but you take effectual steps at once to obtain the full amount, and see that you are never cheated again. Action from principle—the perception and the performance of right—changes things and relations; it is essentially revolutionary, and does not consist wholly with anything which was. It not only divides states and churches, it divides families; ay, it divides the *individual,* separating the diabolical in him from the divine.

17   Unjust laws exist; shall we be content to obey them, or shall we endeavor to amend them, and obey them until we have succeeded, or shall we transgress them at once? Men generally, under such a government as this, think that they ought to wait until they have persuaded the majority to alter them. They think that, if they should resist, the remedy would be worse than the evil. But it is the fault of the government itself that the remedy is worse than the evil. It makes it worse. Why is it not more apt to anticipate and provide for reform? Why does it not cherish its wise minority? Why does it cry and resist

before it is hurt? Why does it not encourage its citizens to be on the alert to point out its faults, and *do* better than it would have them? Why does it always crucify Christ, and excommunicate Copernicus and Luther, and pronounce Washington and Franklin rebels?

18   One would think, that a deliberate and practical denial of its authority was the only offence never contemplated by government; else, why has it not assigned its definite, its suitable and proportionate, penalty? If a man who has no property refuses but once to earn nine shillings for the State, he is put in prison for a period unlimited by any law that I know, and determined only by the discretion of those who placed him there; but if he should steal ninety times nine shillings from the State, he is soon permitted to go at large again.

19   If the injustice is part of the necessary friction of the machine of government, let it go, let it go; perchance it will wear smooth—certainly the machine will wear out. If the injustice has a spring, or a pulley, or a rope, or a crank, exclusively for itself, then perhaps you may consider whether the remedy will not be worse than the evil; but if it is of such a nature that it requires you to be the agent of injustice to another, then, I say, break the law. Let your life be a counter friction to stop the machine. What I have to do is to see, at any rate, that I do not lend myself to the wrong which I condemn.

20   As for adopting the ways which the State has provided for remedying the evil, I know not of such ways. They take too much time, and a man's life will be gone. I have other affairs to attend to. I came into this world, not chiefly to make this a good place to live in, but to live in it, be it good or bad. A man has not everything to do, but something; and because he cannot do *everything*, it is not necessary that he should do *something* wrong. It is not my business to be petitioning the Governor or the Legislature any more than it is theirs to petition me; and if they should not hear my petition, what should I do then? But in this case the State has provided no way; its very Constitution is the evil. This may seem to be harsh and stubborn and unconciliatory; but it is to treat with the utmost kindness and consideration the only spirit that can appreciate or deserves it. So is a change for the better, like birth and death which convulse the body.

21   I do not hesitate to say, that those who call themselves Abolitionists should at once effectually withdraw their support, both in person and property, from the government of Massachusetts, and not wait till they constitute a majority of one, before they suffer the right to prevail through them. I think that it is enough if they have God on their side, without waiting for that other one. Moreover, any man more right than his neighbors constitutes a majority of one already.

22   I meet this American government, or its representative, the State government, directly, and face to face, once a year—no more—in the person of its tax-gatherer; this is the only mode in which a man situated as I am necessarily meets it; and it then says distinctly, Recognize me; and the simplest, the most effectual, and, in the present posture of affairs, the indispensablest mode of treating with it on this head, of expressing your little satisfaction

with and love for it, is to deny it then. My civil neighbor, the tax-gatherer, is the very man I have to deal with—for it is, after all, with men and not with parchment that I quarrel—and he has voluntarily chosen to be an agent of the government. How shall he ever know well what he is and does as an officer of the government, or as a man, until he is obliged to consider whether he shall treat me, his neighbor, for whom he has respect, as a neighbor and well-disposed man, or as a maniac and disturber of the peace, and see if he can get over this obstruction to his neighborliness without a ruder and more impetuous thought or speech corresponding with his action? I know this well, that if one thousand, if one hundred, if ten men whom I could name—if ten *honest* men only— ay, if *one* HONEST man, in this State of Massachusetts, *ceasing to hold slaves,* were actually to withdraw from this copartnership, and be locked up in the county jail therefore, it would be the abolition of slavery in America. For it matters not how small the beginning may seem to be: what is once well done is done forever. But we love better to talk about it: that we say is our mission. Reform keeps many scores of newspapers in its service, but not one man. If my esteemed neighbor, the State's ambassador, who will devote his days to the settlement of the question of human rights in the Council Chamber, instead of being threatened with the prisons of Carolina, were to sit down the prisoner of Massachusetts, that State which is so anxious to foist the sin of slavery upon her sister—though at present she can discover only an act of inhospitality to be the ground of a quarrel with her—the Legislature would not wholly waive the subject the following winter.

23   Under a government which imprisons any unjustly, the true place for a just man is also a prison. The proper place to-day, the only place which Massachusetts has provided for her freer and less desponding spirits, is in her prisons, to be put out and locked out of the State by her own act, as they have already put themselves out by their principles. It is there that the fugitive slave, and the Mexican prisoner on parole, and the Indian come to plead the wrongs of his race, should find them; on that separate, but more free and honorable ground, where the State places those who are not *with* her, but *against* her— the only house in a slave State in which a free man can abide with honor. If any think that their influence would be lost there, and their voices no longer afflict the ear of the State, that they would not be as an enemy within its walls, they do not know by how much truth is stronger than error, nor how much more eloquently and effectively he can combat injustice who has experienced a little in his own person. Cast your whole vote, not a strip of paper merely, but your whole influence. A minority is powerless while it conforms to the majority; it is not even a minority then; but it is irresistible when it clogs by its whole weight. If the alternative is to keep all just men in prison, or give up war and slavery, the State will not hesitate which to choose. If a thousand men were not to pay their tax-bills this year, that would not be a violent and bloody measure, as it would be to pay them, and enable the State to commit violence and shed innocent blood. This is, in fact, the definition of a peaceable revolution, if any such is possible. If the tax-gatherer, or any other public officer, asks me, as one has

done, "But what shall I do?" my answer is, "If you really wish to do anything, resign your office." When the subject has refused allegiance, and the officer has resigned his office, then the revolution is accomplished. But even suppose blood should flow. Is there not a sort of blood shed when the conscience is wounded? Through this wound a man's real manhood and immortality flow out, and he bleeds to an everlasting death. I see this blood flowing now.

24   I have contemplated the imprisonment of the offender, rather than the seizure of his goods—though both will serve the same purpose—because they who assert the purest right, and consequently are most dangerous to a corrupt State, commonly have not spent much time in accumulating property. To such the State renders comparatively small service, and a slight tax is wont to appear exorbitant, particularly if they are obliged to earn it by special labor with their hands. If there were one who lived wholly without the use of money, the State itself would hesitate to demand it of him. But the rich man—not to make any invidious comparison—is always sold to the institution which makes him rich. Absolutely speaking, the more money, the less virtue; for money comes between a man and his objects, and obtains them for him; and it was certainly no great virtue to obtain it. It puts to rest many questions which he would otherwise be taxed to answer; while the only new question which it puts is the hard but superfluous one, how to spend it. Thus his moral ground is taken from under his feet. The opportunities of living are diminished in proportion as what are called the "means" are increased. The best thing a man can do for his culture when he is rich is to endeavor to carry out those schemes which he entertained when he was poor. Christ answered the Herodians according to their condition. "Show me the tribute-money," said he;—and one took a penny out of his pocket—if you use money which has the image of Caesar on it, and which he has made current and valuable that is, *if you are men of the State,* and gladly enjoy the advantages of Caesar's government, then pay him back some of his own when he demands it; "Render therefore to Caesar that which is Caesar's, and to God those things which are God's"—leaving them no wiser than before as to which was which; for they did not wish to know.

25   When I converse with the freest of my neighbors, I perceive that, whatever they may say about the magnitude and seriousness of the question, and their regard for the public tranquillity, the long and the short of the matter is, that they cannot spare the protection of the existing government, and they dread the consequences to their property and families of disobedience to it. For my own part I should not like to think that I ever rely on the protection of the State. But, if I deny the authority of the State when it presents its tax-bill, it will soon take and waste all my property, and so harass me and my children without end. This is hard. This makes it impossible for a man to live honestly, and at the same time comfortably in outward respects. It will not be worth the while to accumulate property; that would be sure to go again. You must hire or squat somewhere, and raise but a small crop, and eat that soon. You must live within yourself, and depend upon yourself always tucked up and ready for a

start, and not have many affairs. A man may grow rich in Turkey even, if he will be in all respects a good subject of the Turkish government. Confucius said, "If a state is governed by the principles of reason, poverty and misery are subjects of shame; if a state is not governed by the principles of reason, riches and honors are the subjects of shame." No: until I want the protection of Massachusetts to be extended to me in some distant Southern port, where my liberty is endangered, or until I am bent solely on building up an estate at home by peaceful enterprise, I can afford to refuse allegiance to Massachusetts, and her right to my property and life. It costs me less in every sense to incur the penalty of disobedience to the State than it would to obey. I should feel as if I were worth less in that case.

26   Some years ago, the State met me in behalf of the Church, and commanded me to pay a certain sum toward the support of a clergyman whose preaching my father attended, but never I myself. "Pay," it said, "or be locked up in the jail." I declined to pay. But, unfortunately, another man saw fit to pay it. I did not see why the schoolmaster should be taxed to support the priest, and not the priest the schoolmaster: for I was not the State's schoolmaster, but I supported myself by voluntary subscription. I did not see why the lyceum should not present its tax-bill, and have the State to back its demand, as well as the Church. However, at the request of the selectmen, I condescended to make some such statement as this in writing:—"Know all men by these presents, that I, Henry Thoreau, do not wish to be regarded as a member of any incorporated society which I have not joined." This I gave to the town clerk; and he has it. The State, having thus learned that I did not wish to be regarded as a member of that church, has never made a like demand on me since; though it said that it must adhere to its original presumption that time. If I had known how to name them, I should then have signed off in detail from all the societies which I never signed on to; but I did not know where to find a complete list.

27   I have paid no poll-tax for six years. I was put into a jail once on this account, for one night; and, as I stood considering the walls of solid stone, two or three feet thick, the door of wood and iron, a foot thick, and the iron grating which strained the light, I could not help being struck with the foolishness of that institution which treated me as if I were mere flesh and blood and bones, to be locked up. I wondered that it should have concluded at length that this was the best use it could put me to, and had never thought to avail itself of my services in some way. I saw that, if there was a wall of stone between me and my townsmen, there was a still more difficult one to climb or break through, before they could get to be as free as I was. I did not for a moment feel confined, and the walls seemed a great waste of stone and mortar. I felt as if I alone of all my townsmen had paid my tax. They plainly did not know how to treat me, but behaved like persons who are underbred. In every threat and in every compliment there was a blunder; for they thought that my chief desire was to stand the other side of that stone wall. I could not but smile to see how industriously they locked the door on my meditations,

which followed them out again without let or hindrance, and they were really all that was dangerous. As they could not reach me, they had resolved to punish my body; just as boys, if they cannot come at some person against whom they have a spite, will abuse his dog. I saw that the State was half-witted, that it was timid as a tone woman with her silver spoons, and that it did not know its friends from its foes, and I lost all my remaining respect for it, and pitied it.

28   Thus the State never intentionally confronts a man's sense, intellectual or moral, but only his body, his senses. It is not armed with superior wit or honesty, but with superior physical strength. I was not born to be forced. I will breathe after my own fashion. Let us see who is the strongest. What force has a multitude? They only can force me who obey a higher law than I. They force me to become like themselves. I do not hear of *men being forced* to have this way or that by masses of men. What sort of life were that to live? When I meet a government which says to me, "Your money or your life," why should I be in haste to give it my money? It may be in a great strait, and not know what to do: I cannot help that. It must help itself, do as I do. It is not worth the while to snivel about it. I am not responsible for the successful working of the machinery of society. I am not the son of the engineer. I perceive that, when an acorn and a chestnut fall side by side, the one does not remain inert to make way for the other, but both obey their own laws, and spring and grow and flourish as best they can, till one, perchance, overshadows and destroys the other. If a plant cannot live according to its nature, it dies—and so a man.

29   The night in prison was novel and interesting enough. The prisoners in their shirt-sleeves were enjoying a chat and the evening air in the doorway, when I entered. But the jailer said, "Come, boys, it is time to lock up"; and so they dispersed, and I heard the sound of their steps returning into the hollow apartments. My room-mate was introduced to me by the jailer as "a first-rate fellow and a clever man." When the door was locked, he showed me where to hang my hat, and how he managed matters there. The rooms were whitewashed once a month; and this one, at least, was the whitest, most simply furnished, and probably the neatest apartment in the town. He naturally wanted to know where I came from, and what brought me there; and, when I had told him, I asked him in my turn how he came there, presuming him to be an honest man, of course; and, as the world goes, I believe he was. "Why," said he, "they accuse me of burning a barn; but I never did it." As near as I could discover, he had probably gone to bed in a barn when drunk, and smoked his pipe there; and so a barn was burnt. He had the reputation of being a clever man, had been there some three months waiting for his trial to come on, and would have to wait as much longer, but he was quite domesticated and contented, since he got his board for nothing, and thought that he was well treated.

30   He occupied one window, and I the other; and I saw that if one stayed there long, his principal business would be to look out the window. I had soon read all the tracts that were left there, and examined where former prisoners had broken out, and where a grate had been sawed off, and heard the history of the various occupants of that room; for I found that even here there was a

history and a gossip which never circulated beyond the walls of the jail. Probably this is the only house in the town where verses are composed, which are afterward printed in a circular form, but not published. I was shown quite a long list of verses which were composed by some young men who had been detected in an attempt to escape, who avenged themselves by singing them.

31   I pumped my fellow-prisoner as dry as I could, for fear I should never see him again; but at length he showed me which was my bed, and left me to blow out the lamp.

32   It was like travelling into a far country, such as I had never expected to behold, to lie there for one night. It seemed to me that I never had heard the town-clock strike before, nor the evening sounds of the village—for we slept with the windows open, which were inside the grating. It was to see my native village in the light of the Middle Ages, and our Concord was turned into a Rhine stream, and visions of knights and castles passed before me. They were the voices of old burghers that I heard in the streets. I was an involuntary spectator and auditor of whatever was done and said in the kitchen of the adjacent village inn—a wholly new and rare experience to me. It was a closer view of my native town. I was fairly inside of it. I never had seen its institutions before. This is one of its peculiar institutions; for it is a shire town. I began to comprehend what its inhabitants were about.

33   In the morning, our breakfasts were put through the hole in the door, in small oblong-square tin pans, made to fit, and holding a pint of chocolate, with brown bread, and an iron spoon. When they called for the vessels again, I was green enough to return what bread I had left; but my comrade seized it, and said that I should lay that up for lunch or dinner. Soon after he was let out to work at haying in a neighboring field, whither he went every day, and would not be back till noon; so he bade me good-day, saying that he doubted if he should see me again.

34   When I came out of prison—for some one interfered, and paid that tax—I did not perceive that great changes had taken place on the common, such as he observed who went in a youth and emerged a tottering and gray-headed man; and yet a change had to my eyes come over the scene—the town, and State, and country—greater than any that mere time could effect. I saw yet more distinctly the State in which I lived. I saw to what extent the people among whom I lived could be trusted as good neighbors and friends; that their friendship was for summer weather only; that they did not greatly propose to do right; that they were a distinct race from me by their prejudices and superstitions, as the Chinamen and Malays are; that in their sacrifices to humanity, they ran no risks, not even to their property; that after all they were not so noble but they treated the thief as he had treated them, and hoped, by a certain outward observance and a few prayers, and by walking in a particular straight though useless path from time to time, to save their souls. This may be to judge my neighbors harshly; for I believe that many of them are not aware that they have such an institution as the jail in their village.

35   It was formerly the custom in our village, when a poor debtor came out of jail, for his acquaintances to salute him, looking through their fingers, which were crossed to represent the grating of a jail window, "How do ye do?" My neighbors did not thus salute me, but first looked at me, and then at one another, as if I had returned from a long journey. I was put into jail as I was going to the shoemaker's to get a shoe which was mended. When I was let out the next morning, I proceeded to finish my errand, and, having put on my mended shoe, joined a huckleberry party, who were impatient to put themselves under my conduct; and in half an hour—for the horse was soon tackled—was in the midst of a huckleberry field, on one of our highest hills, two miles off, and then the State was nowhere to be seen.

36   This is the whole history of "My Prisons."

37   I have never declined paying the highway tax, because I am as desirous of being a good neighbor as I am of being a bad subject, and, as for supporting schools, I am doing my part to educate my fellow countrymen now. It is for no particular item in the tax-bill that I refuse to pay it. I simply wish to refuse allegiance to the State, to withdraw and stand aloof from it effectually. I do not care to trace the course of my dollar, if I could, till it buys a man, or a musket to shoot one with,—the dollar is innocent,—but I am concerned to trace the effects of my allegiance. In fact, I quietly declare war with the State, after my fashion, though I will still make what use and get what advantage of her I can, as is usual in such cases.

38   If others pay the tax which is demanded of me, from a sympathy with the State, they do but what they have already done in their own case, or rather they abet injustice to a greater extent than the State requires. If they pay the tax from a mistaken interest in the individual taxed, to save his property, or prevent his going to jail, it is because they have not considered wisely how far they let their private feelings interfere with the public good.

39   This, then, is my position at present. But one cannot be too much on his guard in such a case, lest his action be biased by obstinacy or an undue regard for the opinions of men. Let him see that he does only what belongs to himself and to the hour.

40   I think sometimes, Why, this people mean well; they are only ignorant; they would do better if they knew how: why give your neighbors this pain to treat you as they are not inclined to? But I think, again, This is no reason why I should do as they do, or permit others to suffer much greater pain of a different kind. Again, I sometimes say to myself, When many millions of men, without heat, without ill-will, without personal feeling of any kind, demand of you a few shillings only, without the possibility, such is their constitution, of retracting or altering their present demand, and without the possibility, on your side, of appeal to any other millions, why expose yourself to this overwhelming brute force? You do not resist cold and hunger, the winds and the waves, thus obstinately; you quietly submit to a thousand similar necessities. You do not put your head into the fire. But just in proportion as I regard this as not wholly a brute force, but partly a human force, and consider that I have relations to

those millions as to so many millions of men, and not of mere brute or inanimate things, I see that appeal is possible, first and instantaneously, from them to the Maker of them, and, secondly, from them to themselves. But, if I put my head deliberately into the fire, there is no appeal to fire or to the Maker of fire, and I have only myself to blame. If I could convince myself that I have any right to be satisfied with men as they are, and to treat them accordingly, and not according, in some respects, to my requisitions and expectations of what they and I ought to be, then, like a good Mussulman and fatalist, I should endeavor to be satisfied with things as they are, and say it is the will of God. And, above all, there is this difference between resisting this and a purely brute or natural force, that I can resist this with some effect; but I cannot expect, like Orpheus, to change the nature of the rocks and trees and beasts.

41   I do not wish to quarrel with any man or nation. I do not wish to split hairs, to make fine distinctions, or set myself up as better than my neighbors. I seek rather, I may say, even an excuse for conforming to the laws of the land. I am but too ready to conform to them. Indeed, I have reason to suspect myself on this head; and each year, as the tax-gatherer comes round, I find myself disposed to review the acts and position of the general and State governments, and the spirit of the people, to discover a pretext for conformity.

> "We must affect our country as our parents,
> And if at any time we alienate
> Our love or industry from doing it honor,
> We must respect effects and teach the soul
> Matter of conscience and religion,
> And not desire of rule or benefit."

42   I believe that the State will soon be able to take all my work of this sort out of my hands, and then I shall be no better a patriot than my fellow-countrymen. Seen from a lower point of view, the Constitution, with all its faults, is very good; the law and the courts are very respectable; even this State and this American government are, in many respects, very admirable and rare things, to be thankful for, such as a great many have described them; but seen from a point of view a little higher, they are what I have described them; seen from a higher still, and the highest, who shall say what they are, or that they are worth looking at or thinking of at all?

43   However, the government does not concern me much, and I shall bestow the fewest possible thoughts on it—It is not many moments that I live under a government, even in this world. If a man is thought-free, fancy-free, imagination-free, that which is *not* never for a long time appearing *to be* to him, unwise rulers or reformers cannot fatally interrupt him.

44   I know that most men think differently from myself; but those whose lives are by profession devoted to the study of these or kindred subjects, content me as little as any. Statesmen and legislators, standing so completely within the institution, never distinctly and nakedly behold it. They speak of

moving society, but have no resting-place without it. They may be men of a certain experience and discrimination, and have no doubt invented ingenious and even useful systems, for which we sincerely thank them; but all their wit and usefulness lie within certain not very wide limits. They are wont to forget that the world is not governed by policy and expediency. Webster never goes behind government, and so cannot speak with authority about it. His words are wisdom to those legislators who contemplate no essential reform in the existing government; but for thinkers, and those who legislate for all time, he never once glances at the subject. I know of those whose serene and wise speculations on this theme would soon reveal the limits of his mind's range and hospitality. Yet, compared with the cheap professions of most reformers, and the still cheaper wisdom and eloquence of politicians in general, his are almost the only sensible and valuable words, and we thank Heaven for him. Comparatively, he is always strong, original, and, above all, practical. Still, his quality is not wisdom, but prudence. The lawyer's truth is not truth, but consistency or a consistent expediency. Truth is always in harmony with herself, and is not concerned chiefly to reveal the justice that may consist with wrong-doing. He well deserves to be called, as he has been called, the Defender of the Constitution. There are really no blows to be given by him but defensive ones. He is not a leader, but a follower. His leaders are the men of '87. "I have never made an effort," he says, "and never propose to make an effort; I have never countenanced an effort, and never mean to countenance an effort, to disturb the arrangement as originally made, by which the various States came into the Union." Still thinking of the sanction which the Constitution gives to slavery, he says, "Because it was a part of the original compact—let it stand." Notwithstanding his special acuteness and ability, he is unable to take a fact out of its merely political relations, and behold it as it lies absolutely to be disposed of by the intellect—what, for instance, it behooves a man to do here in America to-day with regard to slavery, but ventures, or *is* driven, to make some such desperate answer as the following, while professing to speak absolutely, and as a private man—from which what new and singular code of social duties might be inferred? "The manner," says he, "in which the governments of those States where slavery exists are to regulate it is for their own consideration, under their responsibility to their constituents, to the general laws of propriety, humanity, and justice, and to God. Associations formed elsewhere, springing from a feeling of humanity, or any other cause, have nothing whatever to do with it. They have never received any encouragement from me, and they never will."

45   They who know of no purer sources of truth, who have traced up its stream no higher, stand, and wisely stand, by the Bible and the Constitution, and drink at it there with reverence and humility; but they who behold where it comes trickling into this lake or that pool, gird up their loins once more, and continue their pilgrimage toward its fountain-head.

46   No man with a genius for legislation has appeared in America. They are rare in the history of the world. There are orators, politicians, and eloquent

men, by the thousand—but the speaker has not yet opened his mouth to speak who is capable of settling the much-vexed questions of the day. We love eloquence for its own sake, and not for any truth which it may utter, or any heroism it may inspire. Our legislators have not yet learned the comparative value of free-trade and of freedom, of union, and of rectitude, to a nation. They have no genius or talent for comparatively humble questions of taxation and finance, commerce and manufacturers and agriculture. If we were left solely to the wordy wit of legislators in Congress for our guidance, uncorrected by the seasonable experience and the effectual complaints of the people, America would not long retain her rank among the nations. For eighteen hundred years, though perchance I have no right to say it, the New Testament has been written; yet where is the legislator who has wisdom and practical talent enough to avail himself of the light which it sheds on the science of legislation?

47   The authority of government, even such as I am willing to submit to—for I will cheerfully obey those who know and can do better than I, and in many things even those who neither know nor can do so well—is still an impure one: to be strictly just, it must have the sanction and consent of the governed. It can have no pure right over my person and property but what I concede to it. The progress from an absolute to a limited monarchy, from a limited monarchy to a democracy, is a progress toward a true respect for the individual. Even the Chinese philosopher was wise enough to regard the individual as the basis of the empire. Is a democracy, such as we know it, the last improvement possible in government? Is it not possible to take a step further towards recognizing and organizing the rights of man? There will never be a really free and enlightened State until the State comes to recognize the individual as a higher and independent power, from which all its own power and authority are derived, and treats him accordingly. I please myself with imagining a State at least which can afford to be just to all men, and to treat the individual with respect as a neighbor; which even would not think it inconsistent with its own repose if a few were to live aloof from it, not meddling with it, nor embraced by it, who fulfilled all the duties of neighbors and fellow-men. A State which bore this kind of fruit, and suffered it to drop off as fast as it ripened, would prepare the way for a still more perfect and glorious State, which also I have imagined, but not yet anywhere seen.

A Poem

Eavan Boland

Eavan Boland was born in Dublin, Ireland, in 1944. Her books of poetry include An Origin Like Water: Collected Poems 1967–1987 *(which includes her earlier volumes* New Territory, The War Horse, In Her Own Image, Night Feed, *and* The Journey*),* Against Love Poems, The Lost Land, In a Time of Violence, *and* Outside History. *Boland also wrote a volume of prose titled* Object Lessons: The Life of the Woman and the Poet in Our Time *and co-edited* The Making of a Poem: A Norton Anthology of Poetic Forms.

The winner of a Lannan Foundation Award in Poetry and an American Ireland Fund Literary Award, Boland currently is director of the creative writing program at Stanford University in California. Her writing deals with Irish culture, politics, and religion. She also writes about relationships between the sexes and women, the subject of this poem.

Eavan Boland
"It's a Woman's World"

Our way of life
has hardly changed
since a wheel first
whetted a knife.

5   Well, maybe flame
burns more greedily
and wheels are steadier
but we're the same

who milestone
10   our lives
with oversights—
living by the lights

of the loaf left
by the cash register,
15   the washing powder
paid for and wrapped,

the wash left wet.
Like most historic peoples

we are defined
by what we forget,

by what we never will be:
star-gazers,
fire-eaters.
It's our alibi

for all time
that as far as history goes
we were never
on the scene of the crime.

So when the king's head
gored its basket—
grim harvest—
we were gristing bread

or getting the recipe
for a good soup
to appetize
our gossip.

And it's still the same:
By night our windows
moth our children
to the flame

of hearth not history.
And still no page
scores the low music
of our outrage.

But appearances
still reassure:
That woman there,
craned to the starry mystery

is merely getting a breath
of evening air,
while this one here—
her mouth

a burning plume—
she's no fire-eater,
just my frosty neighbor
coming home.

A Short Story

Alice Walker

Alice Walker was born to African-American sharecroppers in Eatonton, Georgia, in 1944. From this beginning, she went on to make her mark on American poetry, nonfiction, and fiction. In her writings, Walker explores the victories of black women over the physical and psychic violence they suffer because of racism and sexism.

Walker has won many honors, including a Pulitzer Prize and an American Book Award for The Color Purple. *Among her other heralded works have been* In Search of Our Mothers' Gardens: Womanist Prose; Meridian; The Same River Twice: Honoring the Diffi-cult; The Temple of My Familiar; The Third Life of Grange Copeland; *and* You Can't Keep a Good Woman Down. *"Everyday Use" comes from Walker's 1973 book,* In Love & Trouble: Stories of Black Women. *In addition to writing, Walker has spent her life working for social justice for women and minorities and teaching at the college level.*

Alice Walker
"Everyday Use"

For Your Grandmama

1   I will wait for her in the yard that Maggie and I made so clean and wavy yesterday afternoon. A yard like this is more comfortable than most people know. It is not just a yard. It is like an extended living room. When the hard clay is swept clean as a floor and the fine sand around the edges lined with tiny, irregular grooves anyone can come and sit and look up into the elm tree and wait for the breezes that never come inside the house.

2   Maggie will be nervous until after her sister goes: she will stand hope-lessly in corners homely and ashamed of the burn scars down her arms and legs, eyeing her sister with a mixture of envy and awe. She thinks her sister has held life always in the palm of one hand, that "no" is a word the world never learned to say to her.

3   You've no doubt seen those TV shows where the child who has "made it" is confronted, as a surprise, by her own mother and father, tottering in weakly from backstage. (A pleasant surprise, of course: What would they do if parent and child came on the show only to curse out and insult each other?) On TV mother and child embrace and smile into each other's faces. Sometimes the mother and father weep, the child wraps them in her arms and leans across the table to tell how she would not have made it without their help. I have seen these programs.

4   Sometimes I dream a dream in which Dee and I are suddenly brought together on a TV program of this sort. Out of a dark and soft-seated limousine I am ushered into a bright room filled with many people. There I meet a smiling, gray, sporty man like Johnny Carson who shakes my hand and tells me what a fine girl I have. Then we are on the stage and Dee is embracing me with tears in her eyes. She pins on my dress a large orchid, even though she has told me once that she thinks orchids are tacky flowers.

5   In real life I am a large, big-boned woman with rough, man-working hands. In the winter I wear flannel nightgowns to bed and overalls during the day. I can kill and clean a hog as mercilessly as a man. My fat keeps me hot in zero weather. I can work all day, breaking ice to get water for washing. I can eat pork liver cooked over the open fire minutes after it comes steaming from the hog. One winter I knocked a bull calf straight in the brain between the eyes with a sledge hammer and had the meat hung up to chill before nightfall. But of course all this does not show on television. I am the way my daughter would want me to be: a hundred pounds lighter, my skin like an uncooked barley pancake. My hair glistens in the hot bright lights. Johnny Carson has much to do to keep up with my quick and witty tongue.

6   But that is a mistake. I know even before I wake up. Who ever knew a Johnson with a quick tongue? Who can even imagine me looking a strange white man in the eye? It seems to me I have talked to them always with one foot raised in flight, with my head turned in whichever way is farthest from them. Dee, though. She would always look anyone in the eye. Hesitation was no part of her nature.

7   "How do I look, Mama?" Maggie says, showing just enough of her thin body enveloped in pink skirt and red blouse for me to know she's there, almost hidden by the door.

8   "Come out into the yard," I say.

9   Have you ever seen a lame animal, perhaps a dog run over by some careless person rich enough to own a car, sidle up to someone who is ignorant enough to be kind to him? That is the way my Maggie walks. She has been like this, chin on chest, eyes on ground, feet in shuffle, ever since the fire that burned the other house to the ground.

10   Dee is lighter than Maggie, with nicer hair and a fuller figure. She's a woman now, though sometimes I forget. How long ago was it that the other house burned? Ten, twelve years? Sometimes I can still hear the flames and feel Maggie's arm sticking to me, her hair smoking and her dress falling off her in little black papery flakes. Her eyes seemed stretched open, blazed open by the flames reflected in them. And Dee. I see her standing off under the sweet gum tree she used to dig gum out of; a look of concentration on her face as she watched the last dingy gray board of the house fall in toward the red-hot brick chimney. Why don't you do a dance around the ashes? I'd wanted to ask her. She had hated the house that much.

11   I used to think she hated Maggie, too. But that was before we raised the money, the church and me, to send her to Augusta to school. She used to read to us without pity; forcing words, lies, other folks' habits, whole lives upon us two, sitting trapped and ignorant underneath her voice. She washed us in a river of make-believe, burned us with a lot of knowledge we didn't necessarily need to know. Pressed us to her with the serious way she read, to shove us away at just the moment, like dimwits, we seemed about to understand.

12   Dee wanted nice things. A yellow organdy dress to wear to her graduation from high school; black pumps to match a green suit she'd made from an old suit somebody gave me. She was determined to stare down any disaster in her efforts. Her eyelids would not flicker for minutes at a time. Often I fought off the temptation to shake her. At sixteen she had a style of her own: and knew what style was.

13   I never had an education myself. After second grade the school was closed down. Don't ask me why: in 1927 colored asked fewer questions than they do now. Sometimes Maggie reads to me. She stumbles along good-naturedly but can't see well. She knows she is not bright. Like good looks and money, quickness passed her by. She will marry John Thomas (who has mossy teeth in an earnest face) and then I'll be free to sit here and I guess just sing church songs to myself. Although I never was a good singer. Never could carry a tune. I was always better at a man's job. I used to love to milk till I was hoofed in the side in '49. Cows are soothing and slow and don't bother you, unless you try to milk them the wrong way.

14   I have deliberately turned my back on the house. It is three rooms, just like the one that burned, except the roof is tin; they don't make shingle roofs any more. There are no real windows, just some holes cut in the sides, like the portholes in a ship, but not round and not square, with rawhide holding the shutters up on the outside. This house is in a pasture, too, like the other one. No doubt when Dee sees it she will want to tear it down. She wrote me once that no matter where we "choose" to live, she will manage to come see us. But she will never bring her friends. Maggie and I thought about this and Maggie asked me, "Mama, when did Dee ever *have* any friends?"

15   She had a few. Furtive boys in pink shirts hanging about on washday after school. Nervous girls who never laughed. Impressed with her they worshiped the well-turned phrase, the cute shape, the scalding humor that erupted like bubbles in lye. She read to them.

16   When she was courting Jimmy T she didn't have much time to pay to us, but turned all her faultfinding power on him. He *flew* to marry a cheap gal from a family of ignorant flashy people. She hardly had time to recompose herself.

17   When she comes I will meet—but there they are!

18   Maggie attempts to make a dash for the house, in her shuffling way, but I stay her with my hand. "Come back here," I say. And she stops and tries to dig a well in the sand with her toe.

19   It is hard to see them clearly through the strong sun. But even the first glimpse of leg out of the car tells me it is Dee. Her feet were always neat-looking, as if God himself had shaped them with a certain style. From the other side of the car comes a short, stocky man. Hair is all over his head a foot long and hanging from his chin like a kinky mule tail. I hear Maggie suck in her breath. "Uhnnnh," is what it sounds like. Like when you see the wriggling end of a snake just in front of your foot on the road. "Uhnnnh."

20   Dee next. A dress down to the ground, in this hot weather. A dress so loud it hurts my eyes. There are yellows and oranges enough to throw back the light of the sun. I feel my whole face warming from the heat waves it throws out. Earrings, too, gold and hanging down to her shoulders. Bracelets dangling and making noises when she moves her arm up to shake the folds of the dress out of her armpits. The dress is loose and flows, and as she walks closer, I like it. I hear Maggie go "Uhnnnh" again. It is her sister's hair. It stands straight up like the wool on a sheep. It is black as night and around the edges are two long pigtails that rope about like small lizards disappearing behind her ears.

21   "Wa-su-zo-Tean-o!" she says, coming on in that gliding way the dress makes her move. The short stocky fellow with the hair to his navel is all grinning and he follows up with "Asalamalakim, my mother and sister!" He moves to hug Maggie but she falls back, right up against the back of my chair. I feel her trembling there and when I look up I see the perspiration falling off her chin.

22   "Don't get up," says Dee. Since I am stout it takes something of a push. You can see me trying to move a second or two before I make it. She turns, showing white heels through her sandals, and goes back to the car. Out she peeks next with a Polaroid. She stoops down quickly and lines up picture after picture of me sitting there in front of the house with Maggie cowering behind me. She never takes a shot without making sure the house is included. When a cow comes nibbling around the edge of the yard she snaps it and me and Maggie *and* the house. Then she puts the Polaroid in the back seat of the car, and comes up and kisses me on the forehead.

23   Meanwhile Asalamalakim is going through the motions with Maggie's hand. Maggie's hand is as limp as a fish, and probably as cold, despite the sweat, and she keeps trying to pull it back. It looks like Asalamalakim wants to shake hands but wants to do it fancy. Or maybe he don't know how people shake hands. Anyhow, he soon gives up on Maggie.

24   "Well," I say. "Dee."

25   "No, Mama," she says. "Not 'Dee,' Wangero Leewanika Kemanjo!"

26   "What happened to 'Dee'?" I wanted to know.

27   "She's dead," Wangero said. "I couldn't bear it any longer being named after the people who oppress me."

28   "You know as well as me you was named after your aunt Dicie," I said. Dicie is my sister. She named Dee. We called her "Big Dee" after Dee was born.

29   "But who was *she* named after?" asked Wangero.

30   "I guess after Grandma Dee," I said.

31   "And who was she named after?" asked Wangero.

32   "Her mother," I said, and saw Wangero was getting tired. "That's about as far back as I can trace it," I said. Though, in fact, I probably could have carried it back beyond the Civil War through the branches.

33   "Well," said Asalamalakim, "there you are."

34   "Uhnnnh," I heard Maggie say.

35   "There I was not," I said, "before 'Dicie' cropped up in our family, so why should I try to trace it that far back?"

36   He just stood there grinning, looking down on me like somebody inspecting a Model A car. Every once in a while he and Wangero sent eye signals over my head.

37   "How do you pronounce this name?" I asked.

38   "You don't have to call me by it if you don't want to," said Wangero.

39   "Why shouldn't I?" I asked. "If that's what you want us to call you, we'll call you."

40   "I know it might sound awkward at first," said Wangero.

41   "I'll get used to it," I said. "Ream it out again."

42   Well, soon we got the name out of the way. Asalamalakim had a name twice as long and three times as hard. After I tripped over it two or three times he told me to just call him Hakim-a-barber. I wanted to ask him was he a barber, but I didn't really think he was, so I didn't ask.

43   "You must belong to those beef-cattle peoples down the road," I said. They said "Asalamalakim" when they met you, too, but they didn't shake hands. Always too busy: feeding the cattle, fixing the fences, putting up salt-lick shelters, throwing down hay. When the white folks poisoned some of the herd the men stayed up all night with rifles in their hands. I walked a mile and a half just to see the sight.

44   Hakim-a-barber said, "I accept some of their doctrines, but farming and raising cattle is not my style." (They didn't tell me, and I didn't ask, whether Wangero [Dee] had really gone and married him.)

45   We sat down to eat and right away he said he didn't eat collards and pork was unclean. Wangero, though, went on through the chitlins and corn bread, the greens and everything else. She talked a blue streak over the sweet potatoes. Everything delighted her. Even the fact that we still used the benches her daddy made for the table when we couldn't afford to buy chairs.

46   "Oh, Mama!" she cried. Then turned to Hakim-a-barber. "I never knew how lovely these benches are. You can feel the rump prints," she said, running her hands underneath her and along the bench. Then she gave a sigh and her hand closed over Grandma Dee's butter dish. "That's it!" she said. "I knew there was something I wanted to ask you if I could have." She jumped up from the table and went over in the corner where the churn stood, the milk in its clabber by now. She looked at the churn and looked at it.

47   "This churn top is what I need," she said. "Didn't Uncle Buddy whittle it out of a tree you all used to have?"

48   "Yes," I said.

49   "Uh huh," she said happily. "And I want the dasher, too."

50   "Uncle Buddy whittle that, too?" asked the barber.

51   Dee (Wangero) looked up at me.

52   "Aunt Dee's first husband whittled the dash," said Maggie so low you almost couldn't hear her. "His name was Henry, but they called him Stash."

53   "Maggie's brain is like an elephant's," Wangero said, laughing. "I can use the churn top as a centerpiece for the alcove table," she said, sliding a plate over the churn, "and I'll think of something artistic to do with the dasher."

54   When she finished wrapping the dasher the handle stuck out. I took it for a moment in my hands. You didn't even have to look close to see where hands pushing the dasher up and down to make butter had left a kind of sink in the wood. In fact, there were a lot of small sinks; you could see where thumbs and fingers had sunk into the wood. It was beautiful light yellow wood, from a tree that grew in the yard where Big Dee and Stash had lived.

55   After dinner Dee (Wangero) went to the trunk at the foot of my bed and started rifling through it. Maggie hung back in the kitchen over the dishpan. Out came Wangero with two quilts. They had been pieced by Grandma Dee and then Big Dee and me had hung them on the quilt frames on the front porch and quilted them. One was in the Lone Star pattern. The other was Walk Around the Mountain. In both of them were scraps of dresses Grandma Dee had worn fifty and more years ago. Bits and pieces of Grandpa Jarell's Paisley shirts. And one teeny faded blue piece, about the size of a penny matchbox, that was from Great Grandpa Ezra's uniform that he wore in the Civil War.

56   "Mama," Wangero said sweet as a bird. "Can I have these old quilts?"

57   I heard something fall in the kitchen, and a minute later the kitchen door slammed.

58   "Why don't you take one or two of the others?" I asked. "These old things was just done by me and Big Dee from some tops your grandma pieced before she died."

59   "No," said Wangero. "I don't want those. They are stitched around the borders by machine."

60   "That makes them last better," I said.

61   "That's not the point," said Wangero. "These are all pieces of dresses Grandma used to wear." She did all this stitching by hand. Imagine!"' She held the quilts securely in her arms, stroking them.

62   "Some of the pieces, like those lavender ones, come from old clothes her mother handed down to her," I said, moving up to touch the quilts. Dee (Wangero) moved back just enough so that I couldn't reach the quilts. They already belonged to her.

63   "Imagine!" she breathed again, clutching them closely to her bosom.

64   "The truth is," I said, "I promised to give them quilts to Maggie, for when she marries John Thomas."

65   She gasped like a bee had stung her.

66   "Maggie can't appreciate these quilts!" she said. "She'd probably be backward enough to put them to everyday use."

67   "I reckon she would," I said. "God knows I been saving 'em for long enough with nobody using 'em. I hope she will." I didn't want to bring up how I had offered Dee (Wangero) a quilt when she went away to college. Then she had told me they were old-fashioned, out of style.

68   "But they're *priceless!*" she was saying now, furiously; for she has a temper. "Maggie would put them on the bed and in five years they'd be in rags. Less than that!"

69   "She can always make some more," I said. "Maggie knows how to quilt."

70   Dee (Wangero) looked at me with hatred. "You just will not understand. The point is these quilts, *these* quilts!"

71   "Well," I said, stumped. "What would *you* do with them?"

72   "Hang them," she said. As if that was the only thing you *could* do with quilts.

73   Maggie by now was standing in the door. I could almost hear the sound her feet made as they scraped over each other.

74   "She can have them, Mama," she said, like somebody used to never winning anything, or having anything reserved for her. "I can 'member Grandma Dee without the quilts."

75   I looked at her hard. She had filled her bottom lip with checkerberry snuff and it gave her face a kind of dopey, hangdog look. It was Grandma Dee and Big Dee who taught her how to quilt herself. She stood there with her scarred hands hidden in the folds of her skirt. She looked at her sister with something like fear but she wasn't mad at her. This was Maggie's portion. This was the way she knew God to work.

76   When I looked at her like that something hit me in the top of my head and ran down to the soles of my feet. Just like when I'm in church and the spirit of God touches me and I get happy and shout. I did something I never had done before: hugged Maggie to me, then dragged her on into the room, snatched the quilts out of Miss Wangero's hands and dumped them into Maggie's lap. Maggie just sat there on my bed with her mouth open.

77   "Take one or two of the others," I said to Dee.

78   But she turned without a word and went out to Hakim-a-barber.

79   "You just don't understand," she said, as Maggie and I came out to the car.

80   "What don't I understand?" I wanted to know.

81   "Your heritage," she said. And then she turned to Maggie, kissed her, and said, "You ought to try to make something of yourself, too, Maggie. It's really a new day for us. But from the way you and Mama still live you'd never know it."

82   She put on some sunglasses that hid everything above the tip of her nose and her chin.

83   Maggie smiled; maybe at the sunglasses. But a real smile, not scared. After we watched the car dust settle I asked Maggie to bring me a dip of snuff. And then the two of us sat there just enjoying, until it was time to go in the house and go to bed.

Glossary of Rhetorical Terms

act: In a dramatistic pentad created by a speaker or writer in order to invent material, the words the speaker or writer uses to describe what happened or happens in a particular situation.

aesthetic reading: Reading to experience the world of the text.

agency: In a dramatistic pentad created by a speaker or writer in order to invent material, the words the speaker or writer uses to describe the means by which something happened or happens in a particular situation.

agent: In a dramatistic pentad created by a speaker or writer in order to invent material, the words the speaker or writer uses to describe the person or persons involved in taking action in a particular situation.

aim: The goal a writer or speaker hopes to achieve with the text—for example, to clarify difficult material, to inform, to convince, to persuade. Also called intention and purpose.

allegory: An extended metaphor of consonant sounds at the beginning or in the middle of two or more adjacent words.

alliteration: The repetition of consonant sounds at the beginning or in the middle of two or more adjacent words.

allusion: A reference in a written or spoken text to another text or to some particular body of knowledge.

anadiplosis (a-nuh-duh-PLOH-suhs): The repetition of the last word of one clause at the beginning of the following clause.

anaphora (un-NA-fuh-ruh): The repetition of a group of words at the beginning of successive clauses.

anecdote: A brief narrative offered in a text to capture the audience's attention or to support a generalization or claim.

Anglo-Saxon diction: Word choice characterized by simple, often one- or two-syllable nouns, adjectives, and adverbs.

antagonist: The character who opposes the interests of the protagonist.

antecedent-consequence relationship: The relationship expressed by "if . . . then" reasoning—for example, "If the Cubs sign Greg Maddux, then they will win the National League pennant."

anticipated objection: The technique a writer or speaker uses in an argumentative text to address and answer objections, even though the audience has not had the opportunity to voice these objections.

antimetabole (an-ti-me-TA-boh-lee): The repetition of words in successive clauses in reverse grammatical order—for example, "You can take the boy out of the country, but you can't take the country out of the boy."

antithesis: The juxtaposition of contrasting words or ides, often in parallel structure—for example, "Place your virtues on a pedestal; put your vices under a rock."

antihimeria (an-ti-the-MEER-e-a): The substitution of one part of speech for another—for example, "The poet says we 'milestone our lives.'"

apologist: A person or character who makes a case for some controversial, even contentious, position.

apology: A elaborate statement justifying some controversial, even contentious, position.

apostrophe: Type of soliloquy where nature is addresses as though human.

appeal: One of three strategies for persuading audiences—logos, appeal to reason; pathos, appeals to emotion; and ethos, appeals to ethics.

appeal to authority: In a text, the reference to words, action, or beliefs of a person in authority as a means of supporting a claim, generalization, or conclusion.

appeal to emotion: See *PATHOS*.

appositive: A noun or noun phrase that follows another noun immediately or defines or amplifies its meaning.

argument: A carefully constructed, well-supported representation of how a writer sees an issue, problem, or subject.

argument by analysis: An argument developed by breaking the subject matter into its component parts.

Aristotelian triangle: A diagram showing the relations of writer or speaker, audience (reader or listener), and text in a rhetorical situation.

arrangement: In a spoken or written text, the placement of ideas for effect.

assonance: The repetition of vowel sounds in the stressed syllables of two or more adjacent words.

assumption: An opinion, a perspective, or a belief that a writer or speaker thinks the audience holds.

asyndeton (uh-SIN-duh-ton): The omission of conjunctions between related clauses—for example, "I came, I saw, I conquered."

attitude: In an adapted dramatisitic pentad created by a speaker or writer in order to invent materials, the manner in which an action is carried out.

audience: The person or persons who listen to a spoken text or read a written one and are capable of responding to it.

basic topic: One of the four perspectives that Aristotle explained could be used to generate material about any subject matter: greater or less, possible and impossible, past fact, and future fact.

begging of the question: The situation that results when a writer or speaker constructs an argument on an assumption that the audience does not accept.

brainstorming: Within the planning act of the writing process, a technique used by a writer or speaker to generate many ideas, some of which he or she will later eliminate.

canon: One of the traditional elements of rhetorical composition—invention, arrangement, style, memory, or delivery.

casuistry: A mental exercise to discover possibilities for analysis of communication.

causal relationship (cause-and-effect relationship): The relationship expressing, "If X is the cause, then Y is the effect," or, "If Y is the effect, then X caused it"—for example, "If the state builds larger highways, then traffic congestion will just get worse because more people will move to the newly accessible regions," or, "If students plagiarize their papers, it must be because the Internet offers them such a wide array of materials from which to copy."

character: A personage in a narrative.

claim: The ultimate conclusion, generalization, or point that a syllogism or enthymeme expresses. The point, backed up by support, of an argument.

climax: The arrangement of words, phrases, or clauses in order of increasing number or importance.

climbing the ladder: A term referring to the scheme of climax.

cloze test: A test of reading ability that requires a person to fill in missing words in a text.

common topic: One of the perspectives, derived from Aristotle's topics, used to generate material. The six common topics are definition, division, comparison, relation, circumstances, and testimony.

complex sentence: A sentence with one independent clause and one or more dependent clauses.

compound-complex sentence: A sentence with two or more independent clauses and one or more dependent clauses.

compound sentence: A sentence with two or more independent clauses.

compound subject: The construction in which two or more nouns, noun phrases, or noun clauses constitute the grammatical subject of a clause.

conclusion (of syllogism): The ultimate point or generalization that a syllogism expresses.

confirmation: In ancient Roman oratory, the part of a speech in which the speaker or writer would offer proof or demonstration of the central idea.

conflict: The struggle of characters with themselves, with others, or with the world around them.

connotation: The implied meaning of a word, in contrast to its directly expressed "dictionary meaning."

consulting: Seeking help for one's writing from a reader.

context: The convergence of time, place, audience, and motivating factors in which a piece of writing or a speech is situated.

contraction: The combination of two words into one by eliminating one or more sounds and indicating the omission with an apostrophe—for example, "don't" for "do not."

contradiction: One of the types of rhetorical invention included under the common topic of relationships. Contradiction urges the speaker or writer to invent an example or a proof that is counter to the main idea or argument.

contraries: See CONTRADICTION.

data (as evidence): Facts, statistics, and examples that a speaker or writer offers in support of a claim, generalization, or conclusion.

deductive reasoning: Reasoning that begins with a general principle and concludes with a specific instance that demonstrates the general principle.

delivery: The presentation and format of a composition.

denotation: The "dictionary definition" of a word, in contrast to its connotation, or implied meaning.

descriptive writing: Writing that relies on sensory images to characterize a person or place.

dialect: The describable patterns of language—grammar and vocabulary—used by a particular cultural or ethnic population.

dialogue: Conversation between and among characters.

diction: Word choice, which is viewed on scales of formality/informality, concreteness/abstraction, Latinate derivation/Anglo-Saxon derivation, and denotative value/connotative value.

double entendre: The double (or multiple) meanings of a group of words that the speaker or writer has purposely left ambiguous.

drafting: The process by which writers get something written on paper or in a computer file so that they can develop their ideas and begin moving toward an end, a start-to-finish product; the raw material for what will become the final product.

dramatic monologue: A type of poem, popular primarily in the nineteenth century, in which the speaker is delivering a monologue to an assumed group of listeners.

dramatic narration: A narrative in which the reader or viewer does not have access to the unspoken thoughts of any character.

dramatistic pentad: The invention strategy, developed by Kenneth Burke, that invites a speaker or writer to create identities for the act, agent, agency, scene, and purpose in a situation. An adaptation of the pentad also calls for the speaker or writer to identify attitude in the situation.

dynamic character: One who changes during the course of the narrative.

editing: The final observation, before delivery, by a writer or speaker of a composition to evaluate appropriateness and to locate missteps in the work.

effect: The emotional or psychological impact a text has on a reader or listener.

efferent reading: Reading to garner information from a text.

ellipsis: The omission of words, the meaning of which is provided by the overall context of a passage.

enthymeme (EN-thuh-meem): Logical reasoning with one premise left unstated.

epistrophe (e-PIS-truh-fee): The repetition of a group of words at the end of successive clauses—for example, "They saw no evil, they spoke no evil, and they heard no evil."

epithet: A word or phrase adding a characteristic to a person's name—for example, "Richard the Lion-Hearted."

ethos: The appeal of a text to the credibility and character of the speaker, writer, or narrator.

euphemism: An indirect expression of unpleasant information in such a way as to lessen its impact—for example, saying a person's position was eliminated rather than saying the person was fired.

evidence: The facts, statistics, anecdotes, and examples that a speaker or writer offers in support if a claim, generalization, or conclusion.

exaggeration: An overstatement; see HYPERBOLE.

example: An anecdote or a narrative offered in support of a generalization, claim, or point.

exordium: In ancient Roman oratory, the introduction of a speech; literally, the "web" meant to draw the audience into the speech.

extended analogy: An extended passage arguing that if two things are similar in one or two ways, they are probably similar in other ways as well.

extended example: An example that is carried through several sentences or paragraphs.

fable: A narrative in which fictional characters, often animals, take actions that have ethical or moral significance.

figurative language: Language dominated by the use of schemes and tropes.

figures of rhetoric: Schemes—that is, variations from typical word or sentence formation—and tropes, which are variations from typical patterns of thought.

flashback: A part of the plot that moves back in time and then returns to the present.

flashforward: A part of the plot that jumps ahead in time and returns to the present.

flat character: A figure readily identifiable by memorable traits but not fully developed.

format: The structural elements—such as font and font size, cover page, page numbering, title and heads, bulleted and numbered lists, footnotes, end notes, and Works Cited/Reference pages—that constitute the presentation of a written text.

freewriting: Intuitive writing strategy for generating ideas by writing without stopping.

functional part: A part of a text classified according to its function—for example, introduction, example, or counterargument.

generalization: A point that a speaker or writer generates on the basis of considering a number of particular examples.

genre: A piece of writing classified by type—for example, letter, narrative, eulogy, or editorial.

heuristic: A systematic strategy or method for solving problems.

house analogy: In ancient Roman oratory, the method that speakers used to memorize their speeches, connecting the introduction to the porch of a house, the narration and partition to the front foyer, the confirmation and refutation to rooms connected to the foyer, and the conclusion to the back door.

hyperbole: An exaggeration for effect.

image: A passage of text that evokes sensation or emotional intensity.

imagery: Language that evokes particular sensations or emotionally rich experiences in a reader.

implied metaphor: A metaphor embedded in a sentence rather than expressed directly as a sentence. For example, "His voice cascaded through the hallways" contains an implied metaphor; "His voice was a cascade of emotion" contains a direct metaphor.

inductive reasoning: Reasoning that begins by citing a number of specific instances or examples and then shows how collectively they constitute a general principle.

inference: A conclusion that a reader or listener reaches by means of his or her own thinking rather than by being told directly by a text.

intention: The goal a writer or speaker hopes to achieve with the text—for example, to clarify difficult material, to inform, to convince, or to persuade. Also called aim and purpose.

invention: The art of generating material for a text; the first of the five traditional canons of rhetoric.

investigating: Activities that writers use, during the writing process, to locate ideas and information.

irony: Writing or speaking that implies the contrary of what is actually written or spoken.

jargon: The specialized vocabulary of a particular group

journal: A text in which writers produce informal compositions that help them "think on paper" about topics and writing projects.

journaling: The process of writing in a journal.

konnoi topoi: People's topics; ordinary patterns of reasoning; also called basic topics.

Latinate diction: Vocabulary characterized by the choice of elaborate, often complicated words derived from Latin roots.

limited narration: A narrative in which the reader or viewer has access to the unspoken thoughts of one character or partial thinking of more than one character.

litotes (LIE-toh-*tees*): Understatement—for example, "Her performance ran the gamut of emotion from A to B."

logic: The art of reasoning.

logos: The appeal of a text based on the logical structure of its argument or central ideas.

loose sentence: A sentence that adds modifying elements after the subject, verb, and complement.

memory: Access to information and collective knowledge for use in composition.

metaphor: An implied comparison that does not use the word *like* or *as*—for example, "His voice was a cascade of emotion"; the most important of all the tropes.

metonymy (muh-TAH-nuh-mee): An entity referred to by one of its attributes or associations—for example, "The admissions office claims applications have risen."

mnemonic device: A systematic aid to memory.

mood: The feeling that a text is intended to produce in the audience.

narration: In ancient Roman oratory, the part of a speech in which the speaker provided background information on the topic.

narrative: An anecdote or a story offered in support of a generalization, claim, or point. Also, a function in texts accomplished when the speaker or writer tells a story.

narrative intrusion: A comment that is made directly to the reader by breaking into the forward plot movement.

omniscient narration: A narrative in which the reader or viewer has access to the unspoken thoughts of all the characters.

onomatopoeia: A literary device in which the sound of a word is related to its meaning—for example, "buzz" and "moan."

oxymoron: Juxtaposed words with seemingly contradictory meanings—for example, "jumbo shrimp."

pace: The speed with which a plot moves from one event to another.

paradox: A statement that seems untrue on the surface but is true nevertheless.

parallelism: A set of similarly structured words, phrases, or clauses that appears in a sentence or paragraph.

parenthesis: An insertion of material that interrupts the typical flow of a sentence.

partition: In ancient Roman oratory, the part of a speech where the speaker would divide the main topic into parts.

pathos: The appeal of a text to the emotions or interests of the audience.

peer review: A system calling for writers to read or listen to one another's work and suggest ways to improve it.

pentad: Kenneth Burke's system for analyzing motives and actions in communication. The five points of the pentad are act, agent, agency, scene, and purpose.

people's topics: The English translation of *konnoi topoi,* the four topics that Aristotle explained could be used to generate material about any subject matter; also called basic topics.

periodic sentence: A sentence with modifying elements included before the verb and/or complement.

periphrasis (puh-KI-frah-suhs): The substitution of an attributive word or phrase for a proper name, or the use of a proper name to suggest a personality characteristic. For example, "Pete Rose—better known as 'Charlie Hustle'—admitted his gambling problem" or "That young pop singer thinks she's a real Madonna, doesn't she?"

peroration: In ancient Roman oratory, the part of the speech in which the speaker would draw together the entire argument and include material designed to compel the audience to think or act in a way consonant with the central argument.

persona: The character that a writer or speaker conveys to the audience; the plural is personae.

personae: Plural of persona.

personification: The giving of human characteristics to inanimate objects.

persuasion: The changing of people's minds or actions by language.

petitio principi: Begging of the question; disagreeing with premises or reasoning.

planning: Determining appropriateness of information for audience and for purpose.

plot: Arrangement of events in a story.

plot devices: Elements of plot that operate to cause or resolve conflicts and to provide information.

poem: Louise Rosenblatt's term for the interpretive moment when reader and text connect.

point of view: The perspective or source of a piece of writing. A first-person point of view has a narrator or speaker who refers to himself or herself as "I." A third-person point of view lacks such as "I" in its perspective. See also DRAMATIC NARRATION, LIMITED NARRATION, OMNISCIENT NARRATION.

premise, major: The first premise in a syllogism. The major premise states an irrefutable generalization.

premise, minor: The second premise in a syllogism. The minor premise offers a particular instance of generalization stated in the major premise.

protagonist: The major character in a piece of literature; the figure in the narrative whose interests the reader is most concerned about and sympathetic toward.

pun: A play on words. Types of puns include *anataclasis*, words that sound alike but behave different meanings ("The spoiled turkey meat was fowl most foul"); *paranomasia*, words alike in sound but different in meaning ("When Sybil's two boyfriends started fighting, her friends referred to it as 'The Sybil War,' or 'The War Between the Dates'"); and *syllepsis*, a word used differently in relation to two other words it governs or modifies ("Bright lights attract flies and celebrity watchers").

purpose: The goal a writer or speaker hopes to achieve with the text—for example, to clarify difficult material, to inform, to convince, and/or to persuade. Also called aim and intention. In a dramatistic pentad created by a speaker or writer in order to invent material, the words the speaker or writer uses to describe the reason something happened or happens in a particular situation.

ratio: Combination of two or more elements in a dramatistic pentad in order to invent material.

reader's repertoire: The collection of predictions and revisions a person employs when reading a text.

reading: The construction of meaning, purpose, and effect in a text.

reading journal: A log in which readers can trace developing reactions to what they are reading.

recursive: Referring to the moving back and forth from invention to revision in the process of writing.

refutation: In ancient Roman oratory, the part of a speech in which the speaker would anticipate objections to the points being raised and counter them.

reliable narrator: A believable, trustworthy commentator on events and characters in a story.

repertoire: A set of assumptions, skills, facts, and experience that a reader brings to a text to make meaning.

repetition: In a text, repeated use of sounds, words, phrases, or clauses to emphasize meaning or achieve effect.

revising: Returning to a draft to rethink, reread, and rework ideas and sentences.

rhetor: The speaker who uses elements of rhetoric effectively in oral or written text.

rhetoric: The art of analyzing all the choices involving language that a writer, speaker, reader, or listener might make in a situation so that the text becomes meaningful, purposeful, and effective; the specific features of texts, written or spoken, that cause them to be meaningful, purposeful, and effective for readers or listeners in a situation.

rhetorical choices: The particular choices a writer or speaker makes to achieve meaning, purpose, or effect.

rhetorical intention: Involvement and investment in and ownership of a piece of writing.

rhetorical question: A question posed by the speaker or writer not to seek an answer but instead to affirm or deny a point simply by asking a question about it.

rhetorical situation: The convergence in a situation of exigency (the need to write), audience, and purpose.

rhetorical triangle: A diagram showing the relations of writer or speaker, reader or listener, and text in a rhetorical situation.

romance language: A language that is derived from Latin.

round character: A figure with complexity in action and personality.

sarcasm: The use of mockery or bitter irony.

scene: In a dramatistic pentad created by a speaker or writer in order to invent material, the words the speaker or writer uses to describe where and when something happened or happens in a particular situation.

scenic narration: Narration in which an event or a moment of a plot is stretched out for dramatic effect.

scheme: An artful variation from typical formation and arrangement of words or sentences.

setting: The context—including time and place—of a narrative.

sharing: See PEER REVIEW.

simile: A type of comparison that uses the word *like* or *as.*

simple sentence: A sentence with one independent clause and no dependent clause.

situation: See RHETORICAL SITUATION.

six-part oration: In classical rhetoric, a speech consisting of exordium, narration, partition, confirmation, refutation, and peroration.

slang: Informal language, often considered inappropriate for formal occasions and text.

soliloquy: Dialogue in which a character speaks aloud to himself or herself.

speaker: The person delivering a speech, or the character assumed to be speaking a poem.

stance: A writer's or speaker's apparent attitude toward the audience.

static character: A figure who remains the same from the beginning to the end of a narrative.

stock settings: Stereotypical time and place settings that let readers know a text's genre immediately.

style: The choices that writers or speakers make in language for effect.

subject: One of the points on the Aristotelian or rhetorical triangle; the subject matter a writer or speaker is writing or speaking about.

subordinate clause: A group of words that includes a subject and verb but that cannot stand on its own as a sentence; also called dependent clause.

summary narration: Narration in which a brief statement of events moves the plot quickly.

support: In a text, the material offered to make concrete or to back up a generalization, conclusion, or claim.

syllogism (SIH-luh-jih-zəm): Logical reasoning from inarguable premises.

symbol: In a text, an element that stands for more than itself and, therefore, helps to convey a theme of the text.

synecdoche (suh-NEK-duh-kee): A part of something used to refer to the whole—for example, "50 head of cattle" referring to 50 complete animals.

syntax: The order of words in a sentence.

tautology: A group of words that merely repeats the meaning already conveyed.

theme: The message conveyed by a literary work.

thesis: The main idea in a text, often the main generalization, conclusion, or claim.

thesis statement: A single sentence that states a text's thesis, usually somewhere near the beginning.

tone: The writer's or speaker's attitude toward the subject matter.

topic: A place where writers go to discover methods for proof and strategies for presentation of ideas.

trope: An artful variation from expected modes of expression of thoughts and ideas.

understatement: Deliberate playing down of a situation in order to make a point—for example, "As the principal dancer, Joe Smith displayed only two flaws: his arms and his legs."

unity: The sense that a text is, appropriately, about only one subject and achieves one major purpose or effect.

unreliable narrator: An untrustworthy or naïve commentator on events and characters in a story.

verisimilitude: The quality of a text that reflects the truth of actual experience.

voice: The textual features, such as diction and sentence structure, that convey a writer's or speaker's persona.

writing process: The acts a writer goes through, often recursively, to complete a piece of writing: inventing, investigating, planning, drafting, consulting, revising, and editing. The book also uses the plural—writing processes—because no two writers have exactly the same set of acts in exactly the same order.

zeugma: A trope in which one word, usually a noun or the main verb, governs two other words not related in meaning ("He maintained a business and his innocence").

Credits

Text Credits

Page 8. Reprinted by courtesy of *Sports Illustrated* "Smelling Like a Rose" by Frank Deford, August 5, 2002. Copyright © 2002. Time Inc. All rights reserved.

Page 14."How About One Study at a Time?" from *Washington Merry Go Round.* Published by United Media. Permission of United Feature Syndicate, Inc.

Page 22. Editorial from *The Daily Illini,* student newspaper. University of Illinois at Urbana-Champaign. Used by permission of Illini Media Co.

Page 26. Spring 2000 Solicitation Letter from Franklin College, original letter to Rachel Howell from Steve Richards, Dean Admissions and Financial Aid. Reprinted by permission of Franklin College.

Page 26. Spring 2000 Solicitation letter from Arizona State University, original letter to Rachel Howell. Reprinted by permission of Timothy J. Desch and Arizona State University Tempe, AZ.

Page 41. "Corporate Sponsorship of Our Schools" by Joel Caris. Published in *The Scrivener.* Reprinted by permission of Joel Caris.

Page 49. Julia Morse, "The ABCs of Home Schooling." Time.com, June 29, 2001. Reprinted by permission of Time.com.

Page 65. Reprinted by permission of the publisher from "On Being the Object of Property" in *The Alchemy of Race and Rights: Diary of a Law Professor* by Patricia J. Williams, pages 223–224, Cambridge, Mass.: Harvard University Press. Copyright © 1991 by the President and Fellows of Harvard College.

Page 95. Sandra Cisneros, "My Name" from *The House on Mango Street.* Reprinted by permission of Random House.

Page 111. "Family Ancestry and Justice: Our Inescapable History" from Greensboro, NC, News and Record. Reprinted by permission of *Greensboro News and Record.*

Page 112. "Remembering Dr. King Using Our History," from Greensboro, NC, News and Record. Reprinted by permission of *Greensboro News and Record.*

Page 124. Partial paragraph from page 5 of *Chaos: Making a New Science* by James Gleick. Reprinted by permission of William Morris & Co., Inc.

Page 127. Excerpt from Chapter 1 of *Wonderful Life: Burgess Shale and the Nature of History* by Stephen Jay Gould. Reprinted by permission by W.W. Norton.

Page 133. Excerpts from Toni Morrison's 1993 Nobel Prize acceptance speech. Reprinted by permission of University of Pittsburgh Press.

Page 135. Copyright © 1987 by Amy Tan. First appeared in *Seventeen* magazine. Reprinted by permission of the author and the Sandra Dijkstra Literary Agency.

Page 135. Beginning of William Zinsser, "College Pressures," as reprinted in *The Norton Reader,* 5th ed., New York: 1980. From *Blair & Ketchum's Country Journal,* April 1979. Copyright © by William Zinsser.

Page 139. From *Yellow Woman and a Beauty of the Spirit* by Leslie Marmon Silko. Copyright © 1996 by Leslie Marmon Silko. Reprinted with the permission of Simon & Schuster Adult Publishing Group.

Page 143. Naomi Shihab Nye, *One Moment On Top of the Earth.* Reprinted with the permission of University of South Carolina Press.

Page 150. Reprinted by permission of the publisher from *One Writer's Beginnings* by Eudora Welty, pages 11–12. Cambridge Mass: Harvard University Press. Copyright © 1983, 1984, by Eudora Welty.

Page 156. Excerpt from released SAT exam: *AP Advanced Placement Program: A Student Guide to the AP English Courses and Examinations.* Language & Composition. Literature & Composition. The College Board 2000, 2001. Reprinted with the permission of Education Testing Service, Princeton. The College Board.

Page 158. Passage from Beryl Markham, *West with the Night.* Copyright © 1935. Reprinted by permission of Farrar, Straus and Giroux. North Point Press.

Page 162. *Voice and No Voice* by Peter Elbow. Reprinted by permission of Oxford University Press.

Page 163. *Chaos* by James Gleick. Reprinted by permission of William Morris & Co., Inc.

Page 165. Passage from *West With the Wind* by Beryl Markham. Copyright © 1935. Reprinted by permission of Farrar, Straus and Giroux.

Page 166. Passage from *West With the Wind* by Beryl Markham. Copyright © 1935. Reprinted by permission of Farrar, Straus and Giroux.

Page 168. Passage from *West With the Wind* by Beryl Markham. Copyright © 1935. Reprinted by permission of Farrar, Straus and Giroux.

Page 181. Wayne Booth, "The Rhetoric of Fiction." Two of Booth's quotations from the *E.V. Rieu Translation of the Odyssey.* Published by Penguin in 1959. Used by permission of Penguin Group.

Page 185. From *The Shipping News* by E. Annie Proulx. Copyright © 1993 by E. Annie Proulx. Reprinted with the permission of Scribner, an imprint of Simon & Schuster Adult Publishing Group.

Page 190. *The Real Thing* by Tom Stoppard. Reprinted by permission of Faber and Faber.

Page 196. Excerpt from *A Dolls' House,* Act One by Henrik Ibsen. Used by permission of New York University Press.

Page 199. Excerpt from *All the King's Men.* Copyright ©1946 and renewed 1974 by Robert Penn Warren. Reprinted by permission of Harcourt, Inc.

Page 199. From *The Woman Warrior* by Maxine Hong Kingston. Copyright © 1975, 1976, by Maxine Hong Kingston. Used by permission of Alfred A. Knopf, a division of Random House, Inc.

Page 201. From *The Lime Twig* by John Hawkes. Copyright © 1961 by John Hawkes. Reprinted by permission of New Directions Publishing Corp.

Page 204. "Rosa" a poem by Rita Dove, from *On the Bus with Rosa Parks: Poems.* New York: Reprinted by permission of W.W. Norton.

Page 206. Excerpt from "The Real Thing" by Tom Stoppard, page 52. Used by permission of Faber & Faber.

Page 226. "It's a Woman's World," from *An Origin like Water: Collected Poems* by Eavan Boland. Copyright © 1982. Reprinted by permission of W.W. Norton.

Page 228. "Everyday Use" from *In Love & Trouble: Stories of Black Women.* Copyright © 1973 and renewed 2001 by Alice Walker. Reprinted by permission of Harcourt, Inc.

Illustration Credits

Page 1. Copyright © *The New Yorker Collection,* 1976 George Booth from Cartoonbank.com. All Rights Reserved.

Page 33. Copyright © *The New Yorker Collection,* 1992 Robert Weber from Cartoonbank.com. All Rights Reserved.

Index